SAUCY JACK

JACK

THE ELUSIVE RIPPER

Ian Allan
PUBLISHING

First published 2009

ISBN 978 0 7110 3410 5

Published by Ian Allan Publishing

an imprint of Ian Allan Publishing Ltd, Hersham, Surrey KT12 4RG. Printed by CPI Mackays, Chatham, Kent ME5 8TD.

Visit the Ian Allan Publishing website at **www.ianallanpublishing.com**

Contents

Foreword

Avert not your eyes from the sight of blood, reader,
for the trails of blood are everywhere.
In this, the second volume of *The Devil's History Book*, we are in
search of that elusive figure whose name has become synonymous
with bloodshed.
Whose cultural notoriety is such that only other cultural legends
– such as Superman, or Jesus Christ – have been ascribed names that
are perhaps more instantly recognisable than his.
For these are the scarlet historical trails that meet in the legend of
Jack the Ripper,
the most infamous man in the history of Western culture to
effectively have no face, and to possess not one defined identity,
but dozens...

Acknowledgements

The composition period of this book was both aided and inspired by *Jack the Ripper and the East End* – a unique and historic exhibition which ran at the Museum of London in Docklands from May to November 2008.

As attendees of the conferences which accompanied the exhibition, the authors' approach to the subject was stimulated, challenged and occasionally reinforced by the following lecturers (in order of appearance): Professor Clive Bloom; Alexandra Warwick; Martin Willis; Sir Christopher Frayling; Julia Hofbrand (exhibition curator); Donald Rumbelow. We have therefore quoted selectively (but accurately!) from the above lecturers at relevant junctures in this book, and hope that they feel our context does them justice.

Further thanks are due to the Whitechapel Society – particularly Frogg Moody and William Beadle, who graciously granted their time and shared their enthusiasm. The authors began this volume of *Devil's Histories* with our general interest in historic murder cases as a starting point; the diverse range of viewpoints surrounding the Whitechapel Murders of 1888 has subsequently persuaded us that 'ripperology' is a subject one could easily devote a lifetime to.

In criminological terms, the contributions to this book by Jon Ogan have been invaluable. As an investigative psychologist and a 'ripperologist' of some renown, his specialised knowledge and insights are expressed in an everyman manner accessible to all. We are similarly indebted to Professor Laurence Alison, Jon's colleague at the University of Liverpool's School of Psychology. Both Laurence and Jon have allowed us a glimpse at how criminological professionals might regard the Ripper crimes today, with Prof. Alison making particular reference to the contemporary case of Robert Napper.

Paul Woods would like to thank Bobby Wayman and his family for speaking with us. As the former licensee of the Ten Bells/Jack the Ripper pub, Bobby occupies a unique niche in modern East End lore; his generosity in providing unique visual materials is very much appreciated.

And finally – thanks once again to Jay Slater and Nick Grant for inviting the Devil over the threshold . . .

Introduction

A long scalpel slices through the London fog with surgical precision.

Now there can be no mistaking her isolation, her vulnerability. The voluptuous young woman pouts, this time not as a come-on but in terror, as her lips quiver visibly. As she backs up against a street light, seeing barely more than a few inches in front of her face, the gent who she'd promised a good time – and who in return had offered a good time to her – has become a cold-eyed monster, a Mr Hyde with surgeon's bag and top-hat.

Her generous cleavage rises and falls as she hyperventilates. The glint of the scalpel comes ever nearer her throat but she cannot scream. She can only obey the coldness of his watchful eye as he presides over this, his experiment in terror.

Her ear-splitting scream will only come as the blade cuts across her oesophagus, disconnecting her mouth from her vocal cords. The discordant shriek is as alarming as it is impossible . . .

***

Cut!

So runs the classic gothic-horror version of the Ripper murders. Sanitised in the sense that its victims have to appear pulchritudinous, playing its main trope in the form of a charismatic but deadly upper-class character with an obscure and obscene agenda, it's a familiar scenario to most of us who have grown up in the shadow of the mass media.

It was also apparent at the very beginning of this book that such popular myths would have to be both embraced and debunked, if we were to set off in pursuit of that predatory chimera we've all learned to call 'Jack the Ripper'.

But to put the synthetic allure of the silver screen and pulp fiction into its rightful context, we have to spend more time trawling around the gutter. Let's try our opening scenario again . . .

***

It's August Bank Holiday, and Martha and Pearly Poll are out carousing. Martha – who's now in her fortieth year – looks no older than her age but carries every minute of it on her goodtime girl's shoulders. Martha, who's left her bloke Bill back at their lodgings, is no better than she ought to be and she knows it.

But she's not going to let the cares and worries of age creep up on her like that. For tonight, all she's worried about is the here and now. Instead of worrying yourself into the grave because you haven't got a pot to piss in, what's the harm in a little bit of what you fancy, a bit of slap and tickle here and there?

That's our Martha's philosophy, such as it is. Now, here in the shoulder-to-shoulder bonhomie of the Two Brewers, with the thronging punters all drunk and lively, our two girls are going to have themselves a good time with a couple of good sorts they've picked up.

They're proper men too, a couple of guardsmen going by their uniforms. After a few more drinks up the road in Whitechapel High Street, her and Poll take their leave of each other and go off with their separate gentlemen friends. Life can be short and life is dreary, so Martha has only half a bad conscience about sharing this bloke's bed for the night. If such a luxurious amenity as a bed is on offer, that is . . .

But Martha's got no illusions – can't afford 'em. If one up against the wall is what it's gotta be, then that's what it's gotta be. They can always slip back down the road for another quick one afterwards, at the pubs that show no signs of closing. That's our Martha – game for anything, always up for it.

But in the post-midnight gloom, at the far end of George Yard Buildings, poor Martha will get more than what she bargained for. She will find that the pleasures of the flesh and the desecration of the human form can merge into each other quickly, on the turn of a coin . . .

***

There are some who might argue that Martha Tabram doesn't belong in these pages. That her murder, supposedly by an unidentified serviceman, excludes her from the official 'canon' of victims of the Whitechapel murderer. Others will more vehemently suggest that the surgeon who examined her, one Dr Killeen, has thrown an artificial veil over events by suggesting that she was hacked and punctured by a soldier's bayonet, thus separating her from the later 'civilian' murders.

For now, let's just allow the facts to speak for themselves, before we go wading into the enticing pools of rumour, myth and fantasy: thirty-nine rapid stab wounds to the body; most targeted at the breasts, the abdomen and the genitalia. Later researchers will point out how the difference in the wounds even suggests different bladed weapons, with a possibly ambidextrous killer carving her this way and that with each one.

And before we intoxicate ourselves with the gothic archetypes of pop culture, it's as well to bear mind that criminologists say a serial killer's MO – his *modus operandi* – never arrives fully formed. It's subject to a degree of experimentation at first.

Let's also remember that – whether or not all the women died by the same hand – Martha's death, on that early morning of 7 August 1888, will in a matter of days be seen to herald a wave of extreme violence in London's East End, seemingly sexual in nature and psychotic in origin.

It's from this point that so many fascinatingly diverse and foreboding offshoots sprout like bloody flowers from gaps in the broken concrete. In searching for our perpetrator, for the oft-invoked Jack the Ripper, we follow the numerous grim homicidal trails that permeate every aspect of our culture.

I

Gored by Gaslight

By 1888, the 51st year of Victoria Regina, the good people of England had long ago had their glut of horrors. Before Dickens shone his compassionately romantic torchlight on the poor of the workhouse and the exploited of Blake's 'dark, satanic mills', real-life tragedies were played out that passed by word of mouth into everyday lore, their details repeated or embellished by the romancers who wrote cheap chapbooks or authors of stage melodramas.

The first to attain squalid immortality was an atrocity committed almost eight years before Victoria's birth, on the Ratcliffe Highway – running from the eastern edge of the City of London to the old East End dockland area of Wapping. Known today simply as the Highway, London E1, it runs parallel both to the Docklands Light Railway and the Limehouse Link Tunnel. Then, before the advent of either stream-driven engines or motor transport, it was a pedestrian thoroughfare for local tradesmen and workers, commercial travellers and horse-drawn carts.

It was also the scene of a series of murders that made England collectively gasp in horror. On Saturday 7 December 1811, a servant girl working for the family of hosier Timothy Marr returned to her employer's house around midnight, to discover a scene for which no Sunday school admonitions about the terrors of hell had prepared her.

Marr, his wife Cecilia, their 13-year-old apprentice boy, John Goen, and even their helpless little babe in arms were all found in the same state of bloody disrepair; their throats slashed from ear to ear, their skulls smashed in by bludgeoning mallet blows. The motive was apparently robbery, but then no instance could be found of anything missing. (It was believed that the girl's return had scared the killer off.)

Fixated as we are on the crimes of the man we call 'Jack the Ripper', it should be noted that the Ratcliffe Highway murders foreshadowed the sheer gratuitousness of modern crime. Extremely violent homicide was committed without mercy or compunction, on the off-chance of a little material gain that was not forthcoming.

So it was to be again on 18 December, when a lodger at the Kings Arms pub at Gravel Lane, close to the highway, was awoken by a woman's screams. He found a stranger "in creaking shoes" standing over the bodies of his landlord John Williamson, wife Catherine and maid Bridget Harrington. Making his escape, the lodger alerted a local nightwatchman who returned to bear witness to the atrocities: the publican's head had been beaten in with a crowbar, his limbs slashed; both of the women had suffered similar wounds to their head and their throats were cut wide open to the bone, so that they were almost decapitated. As Stephen King suggests of the killing of the old man in Stevenson's *Dr Jekyll and Mr Hyde*, the scene could not have been more redolent of the modern nightmare if 'Helter Skelter' and 'Piggies' were daubed in blood on the walls. Only the couple's young granddaughter had somehow escaped the carnage.

With the local constabulary roused, the immediate suspect was a seaman due to a sailor's maul found at the scene. When it was confirmed that the owner of the apparel was at sea, an arrest was made of his roommate and fellow sailor, a near-namesake of the murdered publican called John Williams. For the seaman had also returned to the inn where he was staying covered in blood – caused, he claimed, by a drunken brawl.

Williams was held in gaol to await trial, but was hanged from a cell-rail on 28 December. It may be a fair assumption that his jailers had given him a 'leg up', unless they'd have preferred to see him swing publicly at Tyburn.

As a suicide, in keeping with the superstition of the day, Williams was not to be accorded a Christian burial. Taken by cart to the crossroads that now marks the crossing of Cannon Street and Cable Street, where the City of London touches the East End, his body was staked through the heart to prevent his restless soul from wandering. At the far end of the century Bram Stoker would publish his gothic romance *Dracula*, evoking the bloody folklore of Eastern Europe with a repressed eroticism; eight decades earlier, but a world away from the rationalism of the Enlightenment, the wretched Williams was treated with the same supernatural caution as Stoker's vampire count.

Something about the case caught the public imagination – not least due to a chronicler of the times, Thomas de Quincey, author of the autobiographical *Confessions of an English Opium Eater*. Quincey mythologised Williams' appearance as "slenderly built, rather thin but wiry, tolerably muscular, and clear of all superfluous flesh" – making him sound more like the junkie aesthete that he himself was, rather than the stocky, mutton-chop-sideburned corpse depicted in the contemporary illustration 'View of the Body of John Williams'.

The circumstantial evidence against Williams was considered damning at the time, but there was nothing approaching modern standards of forensic proof. A posthumous inquest found him to be the sole murderer in both cases, hardly consistent with two sets of unidentified footprints found at the Ratcliffe Highway scene and the testimony of a neighbour who heard several men running away. It may well have been that Williams was silenced pre-trial to save the constabulary the trouble of tracing an entire gang of 'ruffians', prior to the establishment of London's Metropolitan Police.

In any case, the image of the solitary homicidal maniac took grip of the public imagination, inspiring neighbourhood fear and penny-dreadful fiction alike. In terms of what may have motivated the young sailor to behave so extremely in a case of mundane robbery, the sexually-active Williams was reputed to have told a barmaid, "I am unhappy, and can't remain easy." This has been taken as a reference to the debilitating effects of syphilis; conjecture that it also inspired his rage and violence is echoed by some who attribute similar motive to the elusive Ripper.

In 1886, it would be reported that workmen laying a gas pipe had disinterred the staked skeleton of Williams, the Ratcliffe Highway murderer, two years before the Whitechapel murders were visited upon the East End.

Other murder cases that grabbed the pre-Victorian imagination were more mundane, if still essentially vicious. In September 1823, a gambling sportsman named John Thurtell had, with his passive accomplice Joseph Hunt, ambushed an acquaintance named William Weare. All were en route from London in a pair of two-wheeled horse carriages to visit the home of a fourth member of the gaming community at Elstree, in the county of Hertfordshire. Convinced Weare had cheated him out of a large sum of money at billiards, Thurtell took no prisoners. Alighting on arrival, he jumped Weare, firing a pistol point-blank in his face which merely grazed his cheek. As Weare ran off, begging for his life, Thurtell fell upon him and cut his throat with a penknife; the arterial blood apparently spurted into the killer's mouth. As he finished him by touching his pistol to Weare's forehead and firing direct into his brain, the barrel filled with blood and cerebral tissue.

Both Thurtell and Hunt were tried for murder, but Hunt saved himself by turning King's Evidence and was transported to Australia. Thurtell, despite a reputedly eloquent plea for mitigation in his own defence, was hanged in January 1824. In a rare instance that British *sub judice* laws would not tolerate today, the trial was delayed by the presentation of a play on the murder of William Weare at the Surrey Theatre.

From our vantage point it's hard to see what was compelling about the Thurtell case. But it's been suggested by pop-philosopher/criminologist Colin Wilson that the answer lies in England's class distinctions of the time. As the Industrial Revolution created an 'embourgeoisement' effect which allowed the middle classes to grow and prosper, the prospect of murder in a leafy environ like Elstree seemed somehow dramatic. Meanwhile, crime in the impoverished inner cities continued to grow, particularly among the poor of London's East End.

Rigid class distinctions may also have prolonged public interest in the case of William Corder, whilst repertory theatre and the music hall certainly mythologised it. Corder was an unworldly farmer's son in the village of Polstead, Suffolk, who took up with a local girl named Maria Marten when she was very much on the rebound. Maria, a mole catcher's daughter, had borne an illegitimate child by one lover, given birth to another by Corder's brother, which died in infancy, and was being paid off by another man at the then reasonable sum (in 1827) of £20 per year.

Returning from London after being sent away in disgrace for stealing his father's pigs, William took up with Maria after his brother Thomas died in a drowning accident. True to form, after nights spent making love in the red barn on his father's farm, Maria became pregnant. Again, the child was sickly and died. This time, however, the wanton Maria talked her man into making an honest woman of her. Corder agreed to marriage, instructing her to meet him at the barn on the evening of 18 May. At this point she suddenly disappeared; Corder explained that she had taken lodgings in the town of Ipswich. Faced with local suspicion, he advertised for a wife and found a respectable woman wealthy enough to support him. He headed back to the capital for her to set him up as the headmaster of a school in Ealing, then a village in Middlesex, to the west of London.

Back in Polstead, Maria's mother had a dream in which she saw William Corder shoot her daughter in the red barn. At her family's insistence the barn was dug up and, inevitably, the girl's body discovered. Corder was arrested and publicly hanged that same August, outside the gaol of the cathedral town of Bury St Edmunds.

The disproportionate interest in the case seems to have arisen, again, from its scandalous shattering of gentility. It was also immortalised as an enduring stage melodrama, *Maria Marten, or The Murder in the Red Barn*, in which the murdered girl was depicted as a wounded innocent and her mother's dream (which seemed to arise from local rumour and natural fears) presented as a psychic vision.

(The play remained popular well into the early 20th century, when Corder was played on stage and screen by aptly-named theatrical ham Tod Slaughter. Corder may have been 28 when he hanged, but the middle-aged and portly Slaughter added him to his list of popular villains – including penny-dreadful archetypes Sweeney Todd and Spring-Heeled Jack, though he never played Jack the Ripper, strangely.)

Within a year of the murder in the red barn, however, British murder took on a suitably more murky tone.

***

"Burke's the murderer, Hare's the thief,
And Knox the boy who buys the beef."

19th-century Edinburgh rhyme.

Throughout the British Isles, anatomists and medical experimenters were subject to the laws of the day that restricted bodily dissection. Live operations on the poor by supposedly philanthropic surgeons could be witnessed by students in operating theatres that literally *were* theatres, i.e. arenas of public performance. But the practice of bodily dissection was virtually taboo; religious and moral conventions still regarded the body of a deceased person as sacrosanct, and the handiwork of God was not to be undone by the probing curiosity of man.

So it was that the fundamentals of human physiology became subject to the laws of supply and demand, and prohibition ensured that the black market thrived. The practice must have flourished close to all centres of medical learning, at least to a degree. But in Scotland, the medical researchers of Edinburgh – based at the aptly-named Surgeon's Square – soon established a discernible trade for 'resurrectionists' who retrieved freshly-buried corpses from the ground before decomposition could do its worst.

Into this predatory pool waded William Burke and William Hare, two travelling Irishmen whose former criminal proclivities are not known. What is known about Burke's previous life suggests an adaptability born from doing whatever was necessary to survive, including mending old shoes. Still, both men took to their new trade with gusto.

The opportunity first presented itself when a man known as 'Old

Donald' died at the boarding house where they both lived. For stealing his corpse and taking it to an experimental anatomist called Dr Knox, they received the sum of £7. It was more than they'd ever made in honest labour and seems to have converted them instantly. Burke and Hare joined the ranks of those Robert Louis Stevenson referred to as the 'bodysnatchers' – though it seems a misnomer in their case, as there's little evidence of them snatching dead bodies rather than procuring them by more direct means.

Another boarder, known as 'Joe the Mumper', was smothered with his pillow; they got a door-to-door hawker named Abigail Simpson drunk, Hare smothering her while Burke held onto her legs; two prostitutes were murdered in the same way, and a student of Knox recognised that he'd formerly patronised one of the dead women.

Hare later murdered the retarded daughter of one of the women; Burke strangled an Irish beggarwoman and broke her mute grandson's back across his knee. Knox is believed to have recognised a local idiot known as 'Daft Jamie', whose body they procured for him, but still held his tongue. These are only the known victims, the case not being fully documented. Their downfall came when other tenants discovered the corpse of a beggarwoman named Docherty that they'd asphyxiated. At Edinburgh's High Court, Hare escaped the consequences by turning King's Evidence; he was set free whilst Burke was sentenced to death. (Dr Knox was never even called as a witness.)

Burke was hanged before a large crowd on 28 January 1829. Little is known of Hare's later years, though he is believed to have turned up in London as a blind beggar. (According to legend, he was supposedly blinded by fellow workers who discovered his past whilst working at a lime kiln in the Midlands. In the films about Burke and Hare, his blinding is attributed to the vengeful people of Edinburgh.)

Burke and Hare are occasionally referenced in studies of 'serial killers' as one of the earliest known multiple-murder partnerships; despite the necrophiliac aspects of their case, however, the term has little application. They were simply rats who learned to survive and prosper in the open sewer of their society. Their killings were not committed for gratification but for easy money, which was soon spent on their prostitute common-law wives and booze.

By a macabre irony, Burke may have been one of the few people to legitimately turn up on the dissection table at the time. In the year 2008, at a conference on the Ripper murders held 120 years after the events, university lecturer Alexandra Warwick would make the following observation:

"Before the passage of the Anatomy Act in 1832, the bodies of executed criminals provided the major source of material for the practice of human dissection, and kept up much earlier ideas about the possibility of seeing physical signs of evil inside the body once it was opened up. After the Anatomy Act, the destitute dead from the workhouses replaced the criminal on the anatomy student's table. With the criminal's body's interior no longer accessible, during the nineteenth century it became the criminal's exterior that was thought to betray signs of deviance. As scientists like Lombroso and Galton and others argued, the marks of criminality were readable on the face and the body of the individual."

Francis Galton was a cousin of Charles Darwin, inspired by his relative's epochal 1859 work *The Origin of Species* to apply the idea of hereditary characteristics throughout human society, thus originating the hugely disputed science of eugenics. He in turn inspired the Italian criminologist Cesare Lombroso, who came to prominence around the time of the Whitechapel murders. Though ostensibly liberal in terms of believing in rehabilitation and opposing capital punishment, Lombroso's concept of congenital criminality is long out of favour. The criminal, he argued, could be identified from his or her facial characteristics, beginning a cycle of criminologists and phrenologists photographing what they believed to be the less-evolved head shapes. It's perhaps ironic that the signature crimes of their age would be committed by a man who has never been successfully identified in any form.

In the Victorian era, murder for the sake of sexual gratification was also noted for the first time, existing quietly and almost unnoticed in dark little corners.

One sunny weekend in July 1867, in the countryside close to the town of Alton, Hampshire, a young man named Frederick Baker approached three young children. He gave them a half-penny each and persuaded little eight-year-old Fanny Adams to go for a walk with him. By the time the other children told her mother where Fanny had gone it was too late. Baker would be described in popular journal the *Illustrated Police News* – of which we will certainly hear more – as subject to attacks of "acute mania". It was probably one such attack that led him to murder the child, disarticulate her body and distribute it over a wide rural area. The journal was coy about any overt sexual motive, but when Baker wrote in his diary, "Killed a young girl today. It was fine and hot," we can only conjecture as to whether he was referring to the weather at the time of his appalling crime.

Baker would appear again in print in 1886, as a case study in Richard von Krafft-Ebing's *Psychopathia Sexualis* – a pioneering psychosexual study that introduced the terms 'sadism' (which certainly seems to apply to Baker) and 'masochism', alongside a head-spinning plethora of case studies that dispel any illusion of the nineteenth century as an era devoid of deviance. As for poor Fanny, the destruction of her body would lead to her name becoming a byword for nothingness, 'sweet Fanny Adams' – devolving via the etymology of slang to 'sweet FA', or 'sweet fuck-all'.

"Which is what the sailors said when they were offered awful cans of meat," says investigative psychologist and crime historian Jon Ogan. "They said it was 'Sweet Fanny Adams', or what was left of her, because they couldn't find all her body parts." As he notes of the now archetypical perpetrator, "The crime was committed by a mild-mannered solicitor – 'not the type of person to have done that, such a quiet chap, etc, etc'."

If the crime confounded much of Victorian England as to the killer's motive, then it's a sad fact that it was its extremity, rather than the sexual abuse of a child, which was the extraordinary factor. As social historian Judith Wolfowitz said of the 1880s in 'Shadow of the Ripper', a documentary produced for BBC2's *Timewatch* in the 'centenary year' of 1988, "For at least twenty years there had been agitation around the issue of prostitution, first coming from middle-class moral reformers and feminist agitators who were concerned about the state regulation of prostitution, and then heightened and elaborated in a newspaper exposé of child prostitution by [newspaper editor] W. T. Stead – in which Stead documented how poor daughters of the people were snared and trapped in locked rooms, and drugged and subjected to defloweration and flogging for the sexual delectation of an upper-class gentleman."

Stead's landmark 1885 exposé of child prostitution in London, 'The Maiden Tribute of Babylon', was published in his paper, the *Pall Mall Gazette*. It would be instrumental in raising the age of sexual consent from twelve to sixteen, in that same year. According to art historians, it was also the inspiration for a painting by George Frederick Watts entitled *The Minotaur* – depicting the bull-headed monster of Greek myth, who every seven years demanded a tribute of seven virgins be brought to the Labyrinth in which he dwelled, for him to feast on their unspoiled flesh.

In 2008, 120 years after the historic spate of crimes committed in Whitechapel, the Museum of London in Docklands presented what was, almost incredibly, the first seriously authoritative exhibition on the subject: *Jack the Ripper and the East End*. Included amongst the more tangential material was Watts' painting. As curator Julia Hoffbrand described it, "the Minotaur is meant to symbolise male lust and this kind of appetite for young, innocent boys and girls, and the Minotaur is goring one of these innocent creatures."

***

There is little unspoiled flesh going spare in Whitechapel, this sweaty late summer of 1888. All the girls here live by the motto of 'As needs must when the Devil drives,' and Old Nick has got the whip hand over the horses. Polly knows that.

The last few years since she parted from her Bill have passed in a bit of a fog. Even now, on this nice clear Thursday night, she's got a bit of a head from the gin. Not drunk enough to feel right, not quite sober enough to look after anyone but her own self, but she's steady enough on her pins.

Never quite steady enough to look after anyone, that's what the gentleman magistrate said. A pox on him! If the law don't care to provide Mrs Mary Ann Nichols, estranged wife of that holier-than-thou tosspot Mr Bill Nichols, with maintenance from his day's work, then Mary Ann Nichols don't give two cusses for the law. "Living off immoral earnings," that's what they said. "Unfit to fulfil her duties as a mother since," when was it? These last eight years? Ten? Twelve? Ever since Bill took up with his fancy bit, her that attended when she birthed young Liza, and Polly took to the streets.

What right has he got to judge me, when he's living out of wedlock with 'er and I'm still bearing his name?

It hurts, her two girls and the two youngest boys being with Bill and his fancy, and her Edward being back at home with his granddad. "I hope you are all right and the boy has work," she'd finished off the letter the last time she wrote to Father. "So goodbye now for the present. Yours truly, 'Polly'." Always Polly, hardly ever Mary, to those who once cared about her.

She'd told her father about the nice family she was working for in Walworth, tee-totalling, God-fearing people. She didn't write back to tell him when the fancy had come over her for a drink and she'd pocketed a few brass farthings. Didn't tell him she was out on her ear again.

But that's life, innit? Your feet ache. Your teeth ache – those you've got left anyway. A few drops takes it all away before it all comes back again, rearing up like some rotten stray mongrel to bite you. But what's the use?

What's the use in worrying yourself to death about what's gone? Lambeth Workhouse. Roughing it in the street at Trafalgar. Workhouses out in the sticks, and now here, Whitechapel. The past is done and let tomorrow take care of itself. Tonight she's going to get herself another drink, then a bloke and a bed.

For the last few nights she's been dossing at a place where they let men and women share a room together. But they won't have her back to 'Flowery Dean' tonight, not when she's got the drink on her and no coins to pay for it.

Well after midnight she leaves the Frying Pan at Brick Lane and goes back to Thrawl Street, where she shared a room with three women and a bed with a girl called Ellen all last week. But the night manager says he can't be having it, not unless she's got the fourpence to pay.

"I'll soon get my doss money," Polly tells him, all jolly and half-cut, "look what a fine bonnet I've got now."

***

Polly Nichols was to be the first in the so-called 'canon' – almost sainted victims, assumed to be the handiwork of a man with no face and, as of yet, no name. She was distinguished from others who'd face a similar miserable end by the very exclusion of those others. Not that it would have mattered to Polly. Nor to any other woman, down on her uppers and her luck, who'd chance a kneetrembler with a stranger to pay for another night's lodging. The Devil was driving, and times were as hard as the cobblestones.

As Julia Hoffbrand, curator of *Jack the Ripper and the East End*, later explained at her lecture: "The Descriptive Map of Poverty was produced as a result of a landmark social survey that was actually taking place at the time, in the few years prior to the murders and during the murders, and published in 1889. Charles Booth, a wealthy philanthropist, got together a team of investigators who went round London and interviewed householders, street by street, about their income, collated the information and then drew it up, correlated them all and mapped the results onto a map. The colour coding went from beige in the wealthiest areas down to black, which were absolutely the poorest, 'the vicious and semi-criminal'.

"Of course, when you look at the names of those streets and those areas, they are Dorset Street, Flower and Dean Street, Thrawl Street, all the streets where the women were lodging. We also borrowed for the exhibition one of the notebooks that the investigators completed in 1886, when they were doing their investigations. The column they've allocated to Flower and Dean Street on the map is already black, so it's already been placed in the lowest category. And then they've written some comments saying that most of the houses are divided and sublet into small furnished rooms, 'latterly used mostly by prostitutes'."

***

It's gone half past two in the morning, and Polly meets Ellen from the Flowery Dean dosshouse at the corner of Osborn and Whitechapel High Streets. Her bonny new bonnet has done its work. "I've earned my doss money thrice over," Polly slurs, almost boasting, "and I've drunk it all away." Piddled down the drain grill like droplets of gin-soaked rain. Ellen asks if she's coming back to the White House, as they call it, but Polly needs to go through the whole song-and-dance again to get her doss money.

Not that it matters much to her anymore. At 42 years of age, it's the only settled routine she's found in a good while: Drink. Solicit. Doss. Drink. Solicit. Doss. Except it doesn't run quite as smoothly as that, with the times for drinking now outnumbering the times for sleep. And for every penny spent on gin, there's another gentleman required to replace it.

Polly is not too insensible to know that she's already living in Hell, though she'd drink herself beyond all knowledge if she could. But she gives a smile, which shows off the great gaping coal cellar of her missing front teeth, and she puts on a brave front. She bids Ellen ta-ta, full of Dutch courage and the knowledge that another gentleman will be along soon enough.

A proper gentleman, perhaps? Or just a bloke?

This one's just a bloke really, so it seems to her. Nice enough, solid, not too different from any of the others. He doesn't have much to say as they wander off up the High Street toward Buck's Row. But he's pleasant enough and she's pleased enough that he's found her. Inside she knows that her life depends on blokes like him.

But she normally knows what a bloke wants, or at least what his type wants. Not this one though! As he gets ready to take her up against the wall, he's treating her more roughly than she's accustomed to. He grabs and fumbles here and there, but the hand that drew up her skirt keeps darting around.

She's about to tell him to have a care, when she just about makes out what she thinks he's drawn from his pocket. The nearest gaslight is a little way away, but from the way he holds his hand toward her and the small flat pointed silhouette in front of her eyes, Polly suddenly knows she's come a-cropper.

She'd scream if she could. She'd call to every copper and every busybody who ever bothered her and implore them to come prove their worth to her. But Polly can't speak, for his vicious fingers have got her jaw from chin to lip clasped tight between 'em. Polly wants to cry out, but she can make no sound. Polly would like to weep, but there are not enough tears for this in all of Heaven and Earth...

Now Polly's on the cobbles. She can't murmur, because a cold sharpness has run its way across her windpipe and disconnected her from her herself. No voice. No breath. If she were still breathing she'd be drowning in her own blood, suffocating in her own substance.

It's not much more than an hour since she and Ellen bade each other bye-bye when they find Polly Nichols. Lying there with her throat cut and her skirt raised all unseemly, there's no mistake as to what state she's in. Some local lads alert the rozzers, and they too rouse some slaughterers from the local knacker's yard. They see their pitiful sights every day, but not ever anything like this – not a human being in such an abject state, so badly done by and looking like a crumpled old woman before her time.

In death, Polly suddenly becomes of more account than when she was last seen walking the streets, for the most part alive and more than a little drunk. A few of the boys raise her from the ground and lift her off to the local workhouse infirmary, early in the morning of 31 August 1888. She's visited by a doctor there, who had never given her any of his attention in life, and he notes down all the wrongs that he can see have been inflicted on her poor body.

Then she's left in the workhouse mortuary for days. Like a saintly sinner lying in state, part of a canon she would never know of nor would have wanted to be part of.

When Bill Nichols finally turns up to look at what's become of her, all suited and booted, he's still playing the wounded party. But when he's taken inside he finds some humility. For they tell him the wicked devil who has done this to his once pretty Polly was trying to do still more. He stuck his filthy left hand below and drew his knife down toward her bowels, cutting sharp and deep in a jagged line from her belly. Like he was trying to draw the very stuff of life out of her, but ran suddenly out of time or lost the will.

As Bill takes deep breaths and finds his own voice again, he tells Polly in a loud whisper, "Seeing you as you are now, I forgive you for what you have done to me."

***

When they laid Polly Nichols out on the mortuary slab, just a few miles' walking distance toward the west, at Marylebone, murderers were among Madame Tussaud's main attractions. In the Chambers of Horrors they displayed crude waxwork effigies of the body of William Burke and the head of Jonathan Thurtell, the Elstree murderer. Callous men who committed bloody acts to fill their pockets, or to compensate their wounded pride. But the natural morbid curiosity of the public had never fastened itself onto anything like the first (or the *first recognised*) of the Whitechapel murders.

In the popular press coverage that quickly followed, the Nichols killing produced a chilly *frisson* familiar to readers of modern crime reportage. For as horrified as the metropolitan middle classes may have been by the detailed reports (sans photographs at the time), there may also have been a comforting *Schadenfreude*. The people that they were reading about were, after all, the denizens of what the more conservative papers were already calling 'the Abyss'. The East End was seen by some not only as a geographical pocket of deprivation but also as a pit of immorality, and the area's worst unfortunates were therefore also the architects of their own misfortune.

For now at least, the bourgeois news reader could be reassured by the suggestion that such things took place in a world socially distant (if geographically proximate) to their own. But as we will see, there was also a mounting sense of drama to the reportage that would fix the Whitechapel murders in criminal history forever.

It's more pertinent to ask, perhaps, why the urban poor of the city, many of them used to harsh lives and random outbursts of drunken violence, paid such attention to the murder of one woman. In marital and common-law relationships aggravated by poverty and stuck in the vicious relief-elation-depression circle of heavy boozing, it could be taken as given that partners would lash out at each other, sometimes resulting in murder by the physically dominant male. Nor had the malaise of violence against women in general elicited much concern from the authorities.

But in this aspect, as in a number of others, the Whitechapel murderer would be perceived in a different historical light. As Alexandra Warwick explains, "he is regarded as the inaugurator of his particular form of modern identity" – that is, as the first serial killer – "even though he was certainly not the first. He was also not the only person killing women in the East End in 1888, which is one of the reasons why the number of his victims has ranged from the more usually accepted five to as many as 12 or even 20. There were at least six other murders of women in Whitechapel that year, some committed by partners of the women but others unsolved."

So did the miasma of violence that choked the East End help to cloak the killer? Did it contribute to his actions, or even perhaps conceal other crimes? We know of Martha Tabram and her bitter end, occurring just 24 days before that of 'Pretty Polly', on the cusp of the East End and the City.

But what of Emma Smith, who had also been viciously attacked in Whitechapel earlier in the year, on Easter Monday. An impoverished 45-year-old widow who often sold herself to stay alive, like so many others, she was making her way home after midnight when set upon by three youths in their late teens, according to the account the critically injured woman gave to the police. Knocked to the ground, robbed and gang-raped, a blunt-ended stick was inserted deep into her vagina. She died in the London Hospital as a result, of peritonitis, just over two days later.

If police records are accurate, this one act alone belies the idea of Victorian England as a moralistic society free from the random, nihilistic violence that blights the nation in modern times. In its viciousness and its misogyny, it foreshadows the violent youth culture which would be colourfully depicted in the novel and film *A Clockwork Orange*, over 75 years later.

Quite distinct from the classic narrative account of the Whitechapel murders, after the murder of Polly Nichols, Emma Smith was briefly depicted by the press as a likely victim of the same assailant – as, indeed, was Martha Tabram. Martin Willis of Glamorgan University, co-author with Alexandra Warwick of *Jack the Ripper: Media, Culture, History*, described this process at his Museum of London lecture:

"The circumstances of these crimes were quite different, but there was sufficient similarity between them for a story to begin to emerge. All three women were impoverished prostitutes and their deaths occurred in the same squalid area of London – although concretely to connect these crimes was to present them as the deeds of the same assailant. Now that's not inconsistent with the more general warnings [of the time] about social degradation and so on, and the *Morning Advertiser* combined its description of savagery in the East End with speculations about the killers. Two different narratives are therefore available to press reporters covering these murders. The first attributes the murders to a gang of 'ruffians' enforcing a protection racket."

In more recent times, the self-styled historians of the Whitechapel murders ('ripperologists') firstly attributed the rape and violation of Emma to the Old Nichol Gang, hailing from the 'the Nichol', the slum buildings around Old Nichol Street at the top of Brick Lane. Their first published mention appeared in *The Identity of Jack the Ripper* by Donald McCormick – a 1959 work which had a huge influence, though today much of its detail remains unsubstantiated and heavily disputed. There is even doubt that the Old Nichol Gang existed, but no such questions attached to the wounded Emma's statement that she was attacked by a gang of youths.

"The second narrative is the existence of a single killer," continues Willis. "Now it's the *Star*, one of the papers at the forefront of the New Journalism, founded that year, which took this line and led with the story, a constructed narrative of an individual. The *Star* matches the story with speculation about the circumstances of the crimes. 'All this leads to the conclusion,' said the *Star*, 'that the police have now thought that there is a maniac haunting Whitechapel and that the three women were all victims of a murderous frenzy.'

"Over the next few days the idea of this 'maniac' gains ground. *Pall Mall Gazette* lends its weight to the story, and the *Times* and *Daily News* drop their support for the 'gang of ruffians'. Two days later this was added to, and within a week the idea of a lone killer was circulating more widely and was being covered in greater depth than the alternative narrative of a criminal gang . . . So the press of the early Whitechapel murders was of course the beginning of a greater sensation [to be] immortalised: Jack the Ripper, in the autumn of 1888."

***

As the shadowy figure of the Whitechapel murderer begins to form – he is not yet 'the Ripper', for the soubriquet has not yet been coined for him – elements of the 'lone monster' hypothesis persist from the 1811 Ratcliffe Highway atrocities, along with the ghosts of Victorian fictional characters who supply a readymade archetype. So were all of these three women killed by the same man? Both Martha Tabram and Emma Smith are now excluded from 'the canon', due to the posthumously published opinions of Sir Melville Macnaghten, a late Victorian Commissioner of Scotland Yard who didn't join the force until 1889.

A hundred years after that date, criminologist and noted ripperologist Jon Ogan penned an article for the specialist magazine *Ripperana*, entitled 'Martha Tabram – The Forgotten Ripper Victim'. In sequel, he answered a series of questions as to his belief in Martha as the first victim: "I would suspect that [Macnaghten's] final summing up and listing of the now 'infamous five' victims came down to his 'gut instinct' based upon the seeming reluctance of Pearly Poll to identify a soldier . . .

"It appears via the note in the Home Office file that there was an early assumption of the character of the wounds equals bayonet, which in turn equals the soldier is the guilty party. But the note seems to flag up the belief that a bayonet was first suspected and a subsequent opinion prevailed that the wounds [produced by two separate blades] were quite unmistakable . . . The irony is that perhaps of all the Whitechapel Murder files held in the Public Records Office, Tabram's is the thickest."

Emma Smith, it seems, can be more safely discounted on the basis of the ubiquity of sexual violence and her own dying word that she was a gang-rape victim. But the curator of the Ripper exhibition in Docklands adopted a more egalitarian approach to the victims, citing and concentrating on "eleven women murdered between April 1888 and February 1891. All of them, except possibly one, were prostitutes, all of them, according to witness evidence at the inquests, were addicted to alcohol, and all of them were on the streets on the nights on which they were murdered, because they were out there to earn fourpence for a bed for the night in one of the common lodging houses in which they were living."

(Interestingly, Colin Wilson cites an article in a 1920s magazine linked with the surrealist movement, by Maurice Heine, which makes an off-the-cuff reference to the Ripper's "eleventh victim" – even proffering an apparently suspect photo of said victim. The magazine was entitled *Minotaur*, and the article imagined a dialogue between the Whitechapel murderer and the Marquis de Sade, progenitor of the term 'sadism'. As the Whitechapel murder coverage hit fever pitch, W. T. Stead would evoke Sade in a more moralistic framework, contributing to the early Ripper archetype of the decadent aristocrat.)

But if all of these individual tragedies are thrown in together, then we have to consider Rose Mylett, for example, as a likely victim of the same killer. Poor Rose died in late 1888, strangled in the docklands of Poplar, close to Limehouse – very much a district of the East End, but it would take a manic pace to arrive quickly from Whitechapel by foot. She was seen arguing with a sailor early on the evening of her death.

Instead, for our purposes, let us try to follow the faceless man who meted out death to Polly, and possibly to Martha, to try to determine if he was then in the process of escalating from one level of violence to the next, and to track his footsteps through our culture.

II

Penny Dreadfuls and Tuppenny Bloods

"The Whitechapel murders – especially the very menacing and spectral figure of Jack the Ripper – had an immediate and lasting impact on many forms of popular culture. Now this isn't always directly apparent. Jack the Ripper does not always appear solidly and [is] often very frighteningly re-imagined by the artists, filmmakers and actors. But many of the imagined locations of Jack the Ripper stress his slipperiness, his ghostly presence-cum-absence, his immateriality, the very shadowy figure in the doorway, the clicking footsteps, the swirl of the black cloak . . ." – from 'Detecting Jack in Popular Fiction and Performance', a lecture by Martin Willis, 13 September 2008.

It's strangely unremarkable that we associate an unidentified violent criminal not with any kind of police composite portrait, but with a set of fictional accoutrements. 'The Ripper', as the soubriquet would soon be coined, summons up not a single facial characteristic but suggests instead a set of dark, dapper apparel. The dangerous aristocrat. The murderous toff. Selective eyewitness accounts would later add credence to such a description, but just as many – if not more – would contradict the idea of the Whitechapel murderer as anything but an anonymous man of the crowd.

Yet still the deadly, devil-may-care villain persists, providing pop culture with a recognisable identity where none truly exists. In a perverse way, the archetype of the Ripper may have pre-existed the crimes themselves. For in the Victorian era, the literary serials and chapbooks – made respectable by Dickens and, later, proto-detective fiction authors Wilkie Collins and Arthur Conan Doyle – also had a more salacious counterpart. It was in the 'penny dreadfuls' and 'tuppenny bloods', and the scarcely more respectable *Illustrated Police News* – not, as its title might suggest, a propaganda sheet for the Metropolitan Police, but a prototype crime comic – that the charismatic do-badder came to be celebrated.

And even before the penny dreadfuls, there were the strange actualities and half-rumours that inspired much of the cheap magazines' content. Chief among these was a strange series of offences committed almost exactly 100 years before the Whitechapel murders, and several decades before London had a unified professional police force.

One day in central London during 1788, a woman named Maria Smyth was accosted in Fleet Street (shortly to become the 'street of shame', the hub of the British newspaper industry). The bizarre nature of the attack upon her was seemingly replicated many times over, attracting the attention of the pre-tabloid press.

Miss Smyth was cursed at in the street by "a thin, vulgar looking man with very ugly legs". His apparent misogyny tipped over from verbal abuse to violence, as he struck out against her hip. Shocked, she stole away from her assailant, soon realising that she was bleeding from a cut to her upper leg. From 1788-90, the attack on Maria Smyth provided an apparent blueprint for other subsequent offences. So many reports came in of women receiving superficial knife wounds – both to the legs and other regions – that public and press began to attribute them to an anonymous figure known, rather melodramatically, as 'the London Monster'.

Up to 60 accounts of similar attacks followed over that two-year period. In fact, so many different descriptions of the Monster's style of dress and hairstyle were given that some deduced the maniac must have been a master of disguise. When a man named Rhynwick Williams was finally tried for the attacks, in 1790, he presented a slightly down-at-heel version of the bewigged dandy of the day, and it was suggested that he may have disguised his identity by regularly switching his hairpiece.

The strong possibility that the offences were committed by a range of different cutpurses and ne'er-do-wells seemed to cut no ice (or indeed no flesh). Williams received a notably lenient six-year sentence for attempted murder, though it was doubtless served under the harsh punitive terms of the day. The fact that he'd been turned in on the basis of a £100 reward – then a considerable sum – for the Monster's capture may have been a triumph of expediency over commonsense. Or perhaps the defendant, a manufacturer of artificial flowers, may have been responsible for one particular series of attacks in which young women were invited to sniff a bouquet of flowers and then slashed across the face.

Seen in a contemporary light, many crimes attributed to the Monster have the air of current-day bag slashings, where carelessness on the part of the thief may result in injury to the victim. But the sense of compulsive fetishism pervades some of the accounts, perhaps bringing the Monster closer to the modern-day sexual stalker. In a striking echo, over the period spanning December 2005 to November 2006, shoe fetishist Abd-el-Gowad carried out a series of eight robberies on London women in order to relieve them of their footwear; on reconstituting themselves after the shock of what seemed to be a violent mugging, el-Gowad's victims would find themselves unharmed but with one bare foot, their assailant taking one of their shoes back to his flat in order to masturbate. On arrest and charge, a contrite el-Gowad confessed, "It was only when I read the statements of my victims I felt like a monster."

Abd-el-Gowad received a compassionate 12-month suspended sentence from an enlightened judge. He is fortunate (or perhaps just sufficiently humane) not to have slipped into the same spiral followed by fellow shoe-fetishist Jerry Brudos, in late-1960s Oregon, USA. Spiralling down from stealing shoes or underwear, and manipulating women into posing for fetish photos, the pudgy electrician escalated to rape and four counts of murder. He used the bodies of some of his victims for necrophile fetish sessions, dressing them up in his favourite shoes, panties and bras. Sentenced to life without parole, the authorities recognised his exemplary behaviour as a prisoner by letting him keep women's mail-order catalogues in his cell.

If the London Monster can be said to have committed at least some of the crimes attributed to him out of sexual compulsion, then there may be a similar lineage of escalation between him and the Ripper – 100 years hence – to that which exists in reverse between el-Gowad and Brudos. For *picquerism*, the fetishised penetration of the (invariably female) body with a knife, is a controversial yet widely subscribed-to theory propagated by modern criminal psychologists. It is the province of the 'serial killer' – that dramatic yet nebulous catch-all term which connects men like Brudos back to the elusive and unidentified Ripper.

But before we climb further down into the basement of compulsive homicide, let's examine the fictional archetypes that came readymade for our faceless killer.

***

"In all the annals of crime, no blacker-hearted villain than Sweeney Todd ever existed. He met his doom on Tuesday morning last at 8 o'clock . . . To the last Todd remained defiant; he refused all spiritual aid and consolation and died with a curse on his lips. His body was cut down, and buried in quicklime within the prison walls. Todd was born in Stepney in London, October 26th, 1756 . . . being accused . . . of a petty theft he was condemned to serve a sentence of five years hard labour. He protested in vain his innocence. Upon his release his nature became so hardened and embittered that he swore a perpetual vengeance against the human race." – attributed to the *Newgate Calendar* of 29 January 1802, in the theatrical programme for the play *Todd*, September 1924.

It's a measure of the role that Sweeney Todd plays in mythical London that the above could be taken as fact. In actual fact, researchers have confirmed that no copies of the *Newgate Calendar* were published for the entire year of 1802, whilst Todd's execution was attributed to public hangman Jack Ketch, who died over a century earlier in 1686. (His namesake who inherited the title of 'Ketch', John Price, was himself hanged for the murder, maiming and attempted rape of an old woman in 1718. One can only assume he enjoyed the cruelty inherent in his work.)

The story of the polite but misanthropic demon barber – who 'polished off' his gentleman customers by cutting their throats and dispatching them down the hatch to Mrs Lovett, the pie-maker next door – had its origin traced by author Michael Kilgarrif in *The Golden Age of Melodrama*. According to Kilgarrif, the pre-Grand Guignol scenario is first found in a short French story in a collection entitled *Les Rues de Paris*, translating as 'Horrible Affair in the Rue de la Harpe', which again purported to be true.

The most crucial elements are all there – the murderous barber; his thieving activities; the outrageous device of luring unwary pie eaters into cannibalism. What is most remarkable is that this staple of stage melodramas and penny dreadfuls entered folklore to the extent where many assumed the story was true. (Many such people might also have assumed Jack the Ripper to be a fictional character.)

In fact the first British appearance of Sweeney Todd was in the very early Victorian era, roughly contemporary to the French story; a bloodthirsty 'romance' novel called *The String of Pearls*, published in about 1840, was followed in 1842 by a popular music-hall adaptation at the Britannia Theatre in Hoxton. (The author of the book was anonymous, though it's now thought likely to have been penny-dreadful writer Thomas Peckett Prest.) The anglicised name of the miscreant may have come, it has been suggested, from the 1830s trade directories listing one 'S. Todd, pearl stringer' in Clerkenwell. This neighbourhood is not far from Fleet Street, where the fictional Sweeney conducted his trade – and where, coincidentally or otherwise, the London Monster is believed to have made his first attack with a knife or razor.

The novel and play coincided with the growing popularity of penny dreadfuls, whilst the absence of effective copyright laws ensured that variations on the story of the demon barber began to proliferate. In the numerous proto-pulp magazine versions, illustrations or etchings of Sweeney show a vicious character – perhaps to undermine any sympathy the reader felt for his predicament – becoming ever more brutal in appearance, to the point where he resembles Neanderthal Man.

Sweeney Todd's cannibalism-by-proxy was endlessly regurgitated. His last penny-dreadful appearance was in *Boys' Standard* magazine five years before the Whitechapel murders, in a particularly gory variation entitled 'The Link Boys Of Old London'. He would be portrayed on stage and screen multiple times by old theatrical ham Tod Slaughter, who also popularly incarnated William Corder – murderer of Maria Marten – and William Burke. Performing as Sweeney in 1947, for the British troops in post-war Germany, Slaughter made the extraordinary remark that the story had its origins in that same country.

In his book *Penny Dreadfuls*, former British comic-book writer Michael Anglo conjectures that the actor was making reference to the gruesome spate of cannibalistic murderers in Germany. But these men – Haarmann, the 'Butcher of Hanover'; Grossman, the 'Bread and Butter Brides' killer; Denke, who murdered and pickled the tenants of his boarding house – were all active during the Weimar Republic period after World War 1, when many were starving and would gratefully buy 'halbfleisch' – 'horsemeat' or, more accurately, human flesh – on the black market, with no questions asked.

The Germans' crimes actually occurred almost a century after Sweeney Todd crept into the public consciousness. By then the penny dreadfuls had created an interesting symbiotic relationship with historical reality. Just as they helped perpetuate the myth of a fictional character like Sweeney, they also drew from London folklore and rumour.

In his *fin de siecle* historical work, *London in the Nineteenth Century*, popular author Sir Walter Besant made the intriguing observation that, in the earliest days of Victoria's reign, London was "haunted by Spring-Heeled Jack who especially selected women for attack". It's all the more startling a claim when we consider that 'Jack' appears to have been an early urban myth, who found his way into folklore via popular fiction.

It was in late 1837 that the stories first started to surface. Early the next year, a young woman resident between the Essex villages of Old Ford and Bow – not far from the Ratcliffe Highway, both since long assimilated into the East End – complained of a frightening encounter with a mysterious cloaked figure. According to her police statement, the demonic figure "vomited blue and white flames and his eyes were balls of white fire"; other accounts describe a horned super-being variously claimed to possess bat-like wings and a reptilian tail. In London's more modest quarters it seemed that the Devil himself was abroad.

Sightings of Spring-Heeled Jack soon became all the rage. Claims that a gargoyle-like creature was seen leaping from the spire of Bow Church or climbing the walls of the Tower of London are said to have led the Mayor to fund patrols of special constables. Soon he was making his supernatural presence felt way beyond the East End, with appearances in the counties of Surrey, Sussex and Essex, and in the Midlands. The last known example of such mass hysteria was a sighting in the army town of Aldershot in 1878. Some believed this attributable to a military gymnastics instructor dressing up for a prank, and doubtless other pranksters played their roles in the panics surrounding this mythical figure.

It was a phenomenon that exemplifies the mass inclination to believe in paranormal visitations, finding its antecedents in the 18th-century belief in succubi – impish night visitors who drained the sleeper of his or her vital energies – and its echoes in modern-day accounts of abduction by UFO.

The sexual undertones of these strange secular beliefs also find parallel in the accounts of women who claimed that they'd encountered Jack. At least at first, the purpose of his manifestations seemed to be to bear them away to some unknown fate, but this was before he turned up in the penny dreadfuls as a kind of demonic avenger. Depicted by the magazine artists as a hybrid of Mephistopheles and the pagan god Pan, Jack was now an instrument of retribution against various aristocratic Victorian villains. However, this most adaptable of urban legends was still engaged in a long process of metamorphosis.

By 1867, the 40-part 'dreadful' *Spring-Heeled Jack* portrayed him as an altogether more human figure. In some of the cover illustrations that survive, the moustachioed Jack resembles a more conventional Victorian villain – think perhaps Sir Percival Glyde in Wilkie Collins' *The Woman in White* – but with the ability to leap away into the night with a damsel in distress in his arms. (Inside the covers, Jack's extraordinary powers were explained away as assisted by such ingeniously unlikely devices as spring contraptions in his boots.)

There was always something morally ambiguous about Spring-Heeled Jack. It seems that the women he bore off into the night never came to any real harm, but, even so, by the time that the as-yet unnamed Whitechapel murderer erupted onto the streets, the idea of a mysterious sexual predator named Jack, with an ability to disappear into the shadows, was already imbedded in the popular consciousness.

At the lectures corresponding with the 2008 *Jack the Ripper and the East End* exhibition, one female member of the audience described her own personal conception of the Whitechapel murderer: "People believed in ghosts and the supernatural, so why shouldn't they actually see him as a supernatural force?" she asked lecturer Martin Willis. Perhaps more startlingly, she went on to elaborate, "I'm an atheist, but to me he's a spiritual figure as much as God is, or any other."

Willis's colleague Clive Bloom was broadly in sympathy with the idea of the killer as a supernatural archetype, rather than merely a seedy sex criminal. In fact, in the frenzied weeks and months that followed the first canonical murder of 31 August 1888, Bloom claims that the elements many associate with the idea of the Ripper – the genteel upper-class malevolence, the aristocratic dress sense – were already being fabricated from scraps of legend and pop culture.

"Jack had to be an aristocrat, a reprise of the penny-dreadful villains of the 1840s who hovered over half-fainting virgins," opines Bloom. "His ubiquitous cloak envelops his victim like the cloak of Dracula and the Ripper becomes a type of vampire, but this time a vampire who throws a particular shadow . . . Thomas Peckett Prest's *Varney, the Vampire* is the ultimate origin of the aristocratic Jack the Ripper idea."

In fact, this rambling and overripe, anonymously-published serial (collected in an 800-plus-page edition subtitled *The Feast of Blood*) is now more often attributed to James Malcolm Rymer than to *Sweeney Todd* author Prest. In any case, the essential elements remain the same: Sir Francis Varney (apparently named after a real 18th-century nobleman) embodies the cruder elements of the aristocratic vampire archetype; his manic appearance and long, undisciplined hair give him the demeanour of a libertine or 'rake' from the previous century; as a disreputable member of the titled gentry, he is the missing link between John Polidori's Lord Ruthven in 'The Vampyre' and Bram Stoker's more sophisticated Count Dracula.

If the lineage between such gothic horror characters and the Whitechapel murderer requires a spring-heeled leap of the imagination, it can't be denied that the East End killings formed a cultural backdrop to late Victorian expressions of the gothic imagination. Contemporary to the murders, the American actor Richard Mansfield was giving a reputedly histrionic tour de force in the double role of *Dr Jekyll and Mr Hyde*, at the Lyceum Theatre in the Strand. Despite some breathless rave reviews in the press of the day, Mansfield came under attack by moralists who believed it unacceptable for him to be hamming it up as Stevenson's Janus-faced polarisation of good and evil whilst poor women were getting ripped in the East End.

Mansfield tried to redeem himself with a benefit performance on behalf of the Suffragan Bishop of London, in aid of reformed prostitutes, but it was to no avail. Whether connected to the moral outcry or not, audiences were falling off and the malevolent Mr Hyde was forced to leave the stage whilst the Whitechapel murderer still stalked the boards in real life. Privy to all this was the Lyceum's business manager, the Irishman Abraham ('Bram') Stoker. He had yet to write his masterpiece, *Dracula*, but its twin elements of repressed sexuality and bloodshed were doubtless already forming in his mind. It may or may not be coincidence that the popular image of his timeless aristocratic vampire is that of a cloaked sexual predator.

Dr Jekyll and Mr Hyde had, in fact, opened to quite a fanfare, just days before the slaughter of Polly Nichols in Whitechapel. As the *Pall Mall Gazette* wrote: "Scratch John Bull and you will find an ancient Briton who revels in blood, who loves to dig deep in murder." The Victorian public would soon find that this morbidly lustful archetype played an even more significant role in reality than in the rarefied world of the gothic imagination.

The Jekyll-and-Hyde archetype survived the era of the Whitechapel murders to become the analogy that greets virtually every case of serial murder. Its suggestion of a schizoid personality was infamously applied to John Wayne Gacy – the Chicagoan building contractor and charity worker who became known as the 'Killer Clown'. The polarised aspects of Gacy's personality allowed him to dress as a clown at parties for underprivileged children, whilst raping, torturing and killing 33 young men or boys at his suburban house.

On his arrest in the late 1970s, Gacy was quick to place the blame for his transgressions on Jack Hanley, a corrupt police officer. It soon became clear that this particular construction named 'Jack' was a repository for those aspects of himself which Gacy felt unable to face directly. At his trial Gacy's defence attorney, Sam Amirante, quoted directly from Stevenson's *The Strange Case of Dr Jekyll and Mr Hyde*: "If I am the chief of sinners, I am the chief of sufferers, also. Both sides of me were in dead earnest."

Dr Helen Morrison, editor of *The Handbook of Forensic Psychiatry*, described the constructed personality of Jack as "the policeman, the investigator, the big man . . . He was a protector against . . . inner disorganisation . . . He was a safety mechanism." What he was *not*, in her opinion, was a distinct personality that functioned independently of its host.

The prosecution picked this point up and ran with it. In the words of their psychiatric witness, Dr Robert Reifman, "it became very clear that most of the murders were committed with no witness and that the only information we have about the murders is information given us by John Gacy, and the information was considerable. So, therefore, the idea that Jack Hanley was a person who functioned in this way without Mr Gacy's knowledge was not true."

Sentenced to death in 1980, Gacy spent 14 years on Death Row until he faced lethal injection in 1994. The distance from his crimes allowed the multiple murderer to withdraw into his personal retreat of wounded innocence. ". . . I did not kill or murder anyone," he wrote to Jason Moss, an ostensible serial-killer groupie using contact with offenders as the path to a career with the FBI. "They say I confessed, but have no confession when asked in court. I have had three hours of truth serums, showing that I had no knowledge . . . I was sold out by my own attorneys for book rights. That's what I have been appealing all of these years."

At the same time, Gacy wanted it both ways. With a twisted sense of celebrity he painted kitschy portraits to order, finding their way (along with his correspondence) into a self-sanctioned book entitled *They Call Him Mr Gacy*. Alongside such all-American images as Disney's Snow White, the man who protested his innocence was happy to provide grainy little paintings of Ed Gein, Charles Manson and himself – the latter in the persona of Pogo the Clown. (Rumours among collectors that the sexual deviant mixed his own faeces and semen into the paint were never substantiated.)

But the absurd apogee of the Jekyll-Hyde syndrome is Kenneth Bianchi, one of the two 'Hillside Stranglers' sentenced to life imprisonment in the late 1970s and early 1980s. Arrested for two sexually-motivated strangulations in Washington State, his apparent connections with a sadistic series of torture-murders in Los Angeles during late 1977-early 1978 led the State of California to apply for his extradition. In return for a plea bargain to evade the death penalty, he was also to testify against his cousin, Angelo Buono, a fellow sadist and brutal pimp. (By a macabre coincidence, Buono appears to be a distant relative of Victor Buono, the character actor who took the title role in 1964 B-movie *The Strangler*.)

Everyone who knew Bianchi – including his girlfriend, the mother of his child – expressed disbelief that such a mild-mannered, white-bread character could be involved in such extreme crimes. It was in the prelude to extradition that an apparent explanation for his behaviour was found. Under voluntary hypnosis, Bianchi suddenly took on the persona of 'Steve' – an aggressive, foul-mouthed sadist who expressed malign intent against Ken, the opposite side of his personality, and against the female of the species in general. Talking in sneering, guttural tones, the schizoid persona of Steve was captured on camera for investigators and later found his way into a documentary film.

Bianchi could not be moved back to California if he was psychologically unfit to give evidence. He was either the living exemplar of a psychological phenomenon or else he was putting on a bravura performance. The latter likelihood was suggested by Dr Martin Orne, who noted how Bianchi had studied psychology in the hope of becoming a psychoanalyst. Belief in authentic instances of multiple-personality disorder among traumatised people was then voguish, due to the success of *Sybil*, a book and TV movie about psychiatric patient Sybil Mason, who had fragmented into 16 distinct personae.

It later became clear that Bianchi had watched the film whilst on remand in Washington State. When asked for his surname, 'Steve' proffered Walker – Thomas Steven Walker being the name of a psychology student whose credentials Bianchi was found to have stolen. When the defendant immediately played up to the examining psychiatrist's suggestion that he might be playing host to more than two personalities, theatrically overacting at the suggestion of an imaginary presence in the room, there was little room for doubt.

Much of the outmoded belief in serial killers as schizoids seems to stem from Tony Curtis' powerfully low-key performance in the title role of *The Boston Strangler*, adapted from Gerold Frank's case study. As convicted serial rapist and mental patient Albert De Salvo, ex-matinee idol Curtis was surprisingly plausible as a handyman tricking his way into the apartments of women ranging from an 85-year-old to a girl in her late teens, all of whom he raped and strangled. (The fact that the victims fell into two such distinct age groups has led many – including the present writer – to doubt whether they all died by the same hand. De Salvo was never actually convicted of murder and was later stabbed to death in prison.)

In one of the film's final scenes, beneath the glaring artificial light of an interrogation cell, De Salvo has flashes of recall about his crimes that seem to be the intrusive memories of another person. It's a highly persuasive depiction of how the mind compartmentalises itself, shutting out negative stimuli which might prevent the individual's normal daily functions. But, as a portrayal of the classic 'split personality', it's also a little simplistic.

Self-righteous commentators have railed against suggestions that the sex murderer can tell us anything about wider human behaviour; it can't be denied, however, that we all compartmentalise ourselves to some degree. The ebb and flow of our daily lives and the varying personalities we have to deal with means that we shut out different aspects of ourselves, according to the differing needs of the moment. So it is with the sex murderer, and thus the idea that he may not be cognisant of his own most extreme acts starts to seem rather naïve.

***

It was the birth of another popular fictional character, in the months immediately pre-dating the Whitechapel murders, that has come to be closely (but inadvertently) associated with the faceless felon we now know as 'the Ripper'.

At his Museum of London lecture, Martin Willis drew attention to the following passage from *A Study in Scarlet*: "'[Sherlock Holmes] appears to have a passion for direct and exact knowledge that may be pushed to excess,' Stamford [the character who introduces Holmes to sidekick/foil Dr Watson] continues.

"'When it comes to beating the subjects in the dissecting rooms with a stick, it certainly takes a rather bizarre shape.'

"'Beating the subjects?' asks Watson.

"'Yes! To verify how far bruises may be produced after death. I saw him at it with my own eyes. And yet you say he's not a medical student?'

"'No. Heaven knows what the objects of his studies are.'"

According to Willis, "When Conan Doyle returns to detective fiction with *The Sign of Four* (1889), several months after the Whitechapel murders, two years since he had written *A Study in Scarlet*, Sherlock Holmes' characterisation has been slightly altered . . . Holmes isn't cold-blooded and violent in *The Sign of Four*, but cool and nonchalant, what J. B. Priestley has identified as a completely different Holmes, an intellectual aesthete. So the amoral Holmes, who a few years ago had been hammering away at corpses with his stick and wandering into the lowest portions of London, is no longer mysterious, maniacal. I think Doyle's alterations of the character of Sherlock Holmes are an attempt to recalibrate, in the aftermath of the Whitechapel murders, what Doyle would have seen as a misalliance of his detective with a very notorious and recent set of criminal acts. And this making safe of Sherlock Holmes was one of the several ways in which Conan Doyle's detective fiction recoils, I feel, from the reality of the Whitechapel murders and the procedure of crime after 1888."

Indeed, the longstanding association of the decadent-yet-disciplined detective with 'the Ripper' exists despite the fact that Conan Doyle never actually wrote a story about the Whitechapel murders. (This would be remedied by his successors and imitators in the Holmes canon – see Chapter Four.) Given the almost simultaneous debuts in print of these two archetypal figures, it's perhaps only natural that some later readers of the Holmes stories in *Strand* magazine saw him as the only fitting nemesis for the still-uncaught killer. This is not to say they were indulging in some latter-day soap-opera fan's conflation of entertainment with reality, but that Conan Doyle had fashioned a powerful figure who encapsulated the furthest reaches of human intellect with the as yet-untested potential of the new forensic science. (Fingerprinting, in particular, was being studied by Sir Francis Galton in the year of the Whitechapel murders, but would not become a part of Scotland Yard's methodology until the early 20th century.)

Much of this is due to the author's imaginative sleight of hand. Conan Doyle had the luxury of being able to devise a compelling mystery and work backwards to contrive a novel solution, for detective fiction – as well as forensic detective work – was then both new and novel. Holmes is a man of genius, but the odds are loaded in his favour by an author who, it's fair to say, would himself have floundered in the dogged reality of detective work as opposed to the fanciful fiction.

In later years Conan Doyle would attach himself to the highly-popular spiritualist movement; ignoring (without actually challenging) the Christian orthodoxy of the dead's dispersal to either paradise or eternal torment, spiritualism fulfilled the emotional needs of those who found themselves bereaved – as with Conan Doyle, who lost a son after he was wounded at the Battle of the Somme – and desperate to speak again with their loved one. He also famously spoke in favour of the veracity of the 'Cottingley fairies', the famous photographic hoax colluded in by two schoolgirls.

For all his credulousness, however, Conan Doyle's earliest incarnation of Holmes introduced the idea that the psychology of the criminal and the detective may be closely intertwined. This had already been demonstrated in real life by the formation of the Surete – the elite detective branch of the Parisian police department – in 1810, before London even possessed a unified police force. The head of the Surete, Eugene-Francois Vidocq, was the absolute epitome of the poacher-turned-gamekeeper. A former smuggler and thief who broke out of jail and escaped from the galleys to which French criminals were often deported for hard labour, at the time he was 'turned' by the Paris prefecture he was part of a gang of coiners (or forgers). Despite his numerous acts of treachery whilst working as a double agent, his ability to straddle both sides of the criminal fence reputedly ensured he kept cordial relations with many of the men he sent to prison, or even to the guillotine.

The well-worn phrase, "It takes a thief to catch a thief," has its origins with Vidocq. It has passed through popular folklore, painting many fictional lawmen in colourful shades of moral ambiguity. It would reach its heyday in the 1980s and 1990s, when the relatively new discipline of psychological profiling was applied to unsolved murder cases. According to both former FBI investigator Robert Ressler – said to have first coined the term 'serial killer' – and fiction writer Thomas Harris – a former reporter who consulted Ressler at length in the composition of his first crime novel – the profiler was an adeptly intuitive individual, able to make Holmes-ian deductions about the criminal's psyche from a reading of the crime scene.

The fictional epitome of this figure is Will Graham, the retired federal agent at the centre of Harris's early 1980s novel, *Red Dragon*. Tormented by the uncomfortable proximity to the serial killer's mind he reaches during an investigation, he is outdone only by his opposite number – Dr Hannibal Lecter, the cultured sophisticate whose numerous transgressions include cannibalism, and whose amoral objectiveness offers a better insight into his fellow murderers' minds than anything the feds can provide.

As a fictional creation, Lecter is almost beautiful to behold. His acts of extreme violence – often hinted at, only intermittently seen in the four novels in which he features – are not wanton opportunism but expressions of his satanic genius, in the manner of Milton's antiheroic Satan in the epic poem *Paradise Lost*. His intellectual and aesthetic superiority almost palpable, the charismatic amoralist never once loses our sympathy via details of gratuitous acts against women or children.

In short, he's perhaps the unlikeliest serial killer of all time, his attitude and lifestyle detached by light years from the urine-stinking back-alleys of Whitechapel where our perception of serial murder begins. And yet, some claim, this same place was also where modern forensic psychology first came into its own . . .

When Metropolitan Police surgeon Dr Thomas Bond was called in to perform the post-mortem on the last of the Whitechapel murderer's 'canonical' victims, he cast a critical eye over the events of the previous few months, stretching back to the lonesome end of Polly Nichols in Bucks Row. Working mainly from a personal analysis of the notes, he asserted confidently, "All five murders were committed by the same hand." His ad hoc profile went on to include the observations or claims that "the women must have been lying down when first murdered and in every case the throat was first cut." (This is at odds with modern forensic examinations of the case notes, which have led to a latter-day belief that the Ripper did in fact kill by strangling – before beginning his post-mortem mutilations.)

Dr Bond continued to embellish his medical observations with an imaginative (if ungrammatical) portrait of the perpetrator: "In each case the mutilation was inflicted by a person who had no scientific nor anatomical knowledge. In my opinion he does not even possess the technical knowledge of a butcher or horse slaughterer or any person accustomed to cut up dead animals." By this stage the doctor's opinion was already controversial, as the killer's escalating intrusions into his victims' physiology had provoked a host of speculation about whether he may have been a butcher, or a kosher slaughterman from the East End's Jewish refugee community. It had also provided the imaginative archetype of 'Dr Jack', stalking the streets with his little black leather medical bag, which, as we shall see, has persisted through the decades.

"The murderer must have been a man of physical strength and of great coolness and daring," continued Bond, almost admiringly. "There is no evidence that he had an accomplice. He must in my opinion be a man subject to periodic attacks of Homicidal and erotic mania. The character of the mutilations indicate that the man may be in a condition sexually, that may be called satyriasis. It is of course possible that the Homicidal impulse may have developed from a revengeful or brooding condition of the mind, or that Religious Mania may have been the original disease, but I do not think either hypothesis is likely. The murderer in external appearance is quite likely to be a quiet inoffensive-looking man probably middle-aged and neatly and respectably dressed. I think he must be in the habit of wearing a cloak or overcoat or he could hardly have escaped notice in the streets if the blood on his hands or clothes were visible."

Dr Bond's imaginative conclusions here seem particularly modern. There's a touch of Sherlock Holmes – or, more latterly, *Cracker* – in his deductions as to the killer's apparel, inadvertently reinforcing the image of the Ripper as a caped penny-dreadful or gothic-horror character. Most pertinent is his consideration and dismissal of the various theories doing the rounds at the time – the 'Avenger', the religious zealot – in favour of the idea of a sex murderer. As prominent forensic psychologist/ geographical profiler David Canter opines in his study *Criminal Shadows*, "There is no information to suggest that Dr Bond was drawing on anything except his professional experience, yet the possibilities he proposes would probably be accepted as thoughtful and intelligent by police forces today. Indeed, when FBI agents acknowledged the 'Jack the Ripper' centenary by drawing up their own account of the offender they produced a description virtually indistinguishable from Bond's.

"An experienced Victorian detective might have proposed something very similar." As indeed might have a certain fictional Victorian detective.

But it seems that the doctor may have inexpertly overstepped the lines between his own medical field and the infant discipline of forensic psychology, or 'alienism', as it was then called. Why should it be assumed that the killer was in the grip of satyriasis – a condition named after the Pan-like goat creatures of legend, which leads the sufferer into compulsive sexual activity but leaves him insatiable – when the doctor's own examinations indicated no evidence of rape?

As our study moves on and our pages darken further, we will consider the idea of the Ripper as a sex killer. But, as a police surgeon with contemporary access to the case notes, it tells us that Bond had *seen it before* – that he knew Eros and Thanatos, sex and death, often walked hand in hand.

"Assuming the murderer to be such a person as I have just described he would probably be solitary and eccentric in his habits," concluded the doctor, "also he is most likely to be a man without regular occupation, but with some small income or pension. He is possibly living among respectable persons who have some knowledge of his character and habits and who may have grounds for suspicion that he is not quite right in his mind at times."

Isolated but respectable. Middle-aged and lower middle-class. In his impossible-to-prove assertions, Dr Bond could be a twentieth-century scriptwriter of low-budget US films – painting a shorthand portrait of that 'nice quiet man' Ed Gein, or his fictional offspring Norman Bates, who "wouldn't hurt a fly".

"It is difficult to assess how accurate his conclusions were as we are no nearer to identifying the culprit," observes investigative psychologist Jon Ogan of Bond. "They are deductive, rather than psychological in nature. We cannot be too harsh on the good doctor as psychology was in its infancy. However, we can push the boundaries a bit further back in relation to experts giving their opinions on JtR, as there were a number of suggestions opined by doctors – superintendents of 'lunatic' asylums – who wrote to *The Lancet* earlier in the series [of murders]."

Currently completing a thesis on the murder of senior citizens, Ogan is a contributor to *The Journal of Investigative Psychology and Offender Profiling* and has presented to an investigative psychology conference on the identification of child sex offenders. He has also gleaned from his own research into Victorian criminology and alienists that there may be little that is entirely new to forensic psychology. "While I was researching my thesis, examining the classification of violence," he tells us, "I came across Isaac Ray who, in 1839 (yes, that's 1839 – not a typo), offers two basic types of murderer."

The psychologist goes on to quote from his thesis: "Ray delineates two types: one, a homicidal monomaniac murderer, and two, a criminal murderer that could be categorised from their relevant crime scene activity. The distinction between the two typologies was drawn from the methods used by the perpetrator and their motive. Ray notes that the monomaniac kills spontaneously with high levels of violence. Conversely, the criminal murderer will only use what violence is necessary to kill. Moreover, the homicide occurs concurrent to some other crime such as robbery. The levels of cognitive actions displayed by the offender are also crucial to Ray's categorisation of offenders. He maintains that the criminal murderer attempts to plan the crime to avoid capture, whilst the monomaniacs will not attempt to conceal their actions. Ultimately, according to Ray, this type of offender is likely to surrender to the police."

In other words, the American alienist Isaac Ray identified the Ripper's criminal type almost 50 years before the Whitechapel murders occurred. His description of the transgressor's gratuitous levels of violence, in fulfilment of some internally private agenda, throws into question the wisdom that the Whitechapel murderer was among the first of his kind – a new type of criminal representing the alienation of the industrial age.

"This is important, because Jack the Ripper is seen as 'ours'," remarks lecturer Alexandra Warwick of the historical factor, "as belonging to the kind of times and the kind of conditions that we recognise, and therefore motivated and influenced by conditions similar to those that we experience: principally, the dangerous isolation of the individual in the faceless urban mass, where the anonymity of the modern person is the condition of the production of both victims and perpetrators."

But the Ripper remains a blank screen onto which we retrospectively project our own notions and hypotheses. Whilst the killer can be said to fit Ray's template for the monomaniac murderer (killing for its own sake, with extreme levels of violence), there is no suggestion that a credible suspect ever handed himself into the police. This is where forensic psychology remains at the level of educated guesswork rather than an exact science – as its more realistic practitioners will admit.

On the hundredth anniversary of the Whitechapel murders, Murray Cox, a psychotherapist at the UK's Broadmoor hospital for the criminally insane, told Professor Christopher Frayling in his BBC documentary on the subject: "Unless one knows an individual at depth for a prolonged time, knowing his fantasies, his dreams, understanding his own world from the inside, we're really left with conjecture, inference and merely guessing." These words were spoken a mere couple of years before offender profiling was hypothesised by the mass media as a magical solution to violent crime, and they have proven prophetic. No super-being or supernatural monster, the anonymous repeat-homicide offender will only stand out from the crowd in those brief, lethal moments in which he chooses to act.

***

"'Mass man', the metropolitan crowd, fascinated Edgar Allan Poe, who wrote a short story which traces the perambulations of a nameless and faceless individual, whose very nature delineates him as a symbol of the vicious," denoted Clive Bloom at his Docklands lecture. "It is no accident that the story is called 'The Man of the Crowd'. Poe's character is a man hiding a wicked secret, never to be discovered. He hides it within the crowd itself, all individuality is lost."

Poe, the 19th-century American poet of melancholia and obsession, was a contemporary of the alienist Isaac Ray and spent five years of his childhood being schooled at Stoke Newington – then a Middlesex village three miles outside the City of London, now a long-established neighbourhood of the urban borough of Hackney. London's environs then were not so far-reaching, yet the geographically-inexact pursuit of a seedy old stranger in this 1840 story shows that Poe was at least familiar with them.

As he sleeplessly follows the old man's seemingly directionless pacing toward the edge of the city, the anonymous narrator chances upon the place that conservative commentators later describe as 'the Abyss':

"It was the most noisome quarter of London, where everything wore the worst impress of the most deplorable poverty, and of the most desperate crime. By the dim light of an accidental lamp, tall, antique, worm-eaten, wooden tenements were seen tottering to their fall, in directions so many and capricious that scarce the semblance of a passage was discernible between them. The paving stones lay at random, displaced from their beds by the rankly-growing grass. Horrible filth festered in the dammed-up gutters. The whole atmosphere teemed with desolation. Yet, as we proceeded, the sounds of human life revived by sure degree, and at length large bands of the most abandoned of a London populace were seen reeling to and fro . . . Suddenly a corner was turned, a blaze of light burst upon our sight, and we stood before one of the huge suburban temples of Intemperance – one of the palaces of the fiend, Gin."

Just as Poe perceives the alcoholic squalor of the East End almost 50 years before the Whitechapel murderer would do his worst (and before his fellow American author Jack London would write *The People of the Abyss*), so Professor Bloom, from his modern vantage point, perceives the foreshadow of what will follow in 'The Man of the Crowd':

"The Ripper is part of the crowd, but not of it. The throng that fills the boulevards of the West End, or its bookshops and cafés, that walks its pampered pets, that may be at the races or at the department stores, dressed in the height of fashion, is not the East End crowd."

As if in confirmation, Poe concludes his breathless sketch of a story thus: "'This old man,' I said at length, 'is the type and the genius of deep crime. He refuses to be alone. *He is the man of the crowd*. It will be in vain to follow; for I shall learn no more of him, nor of his deeds."

In sharp contrast to the charismatic villains and fictional fiends Bloom also cites as the Whitechapel murderer's antecedents, this figure is but one pulsing vein of malevolence in a diseased communal body. But when he haemorrhages out again from the crowd, the entire Western world will begin to take notice.

III

Constructing Jack

Some call it the 'worst street in London', the place where the peelers won't patrol unless they can walk down there four-handed. One of the main thoroughfares off Commercial Street, a mere spit from Spitalfields market, Dorset Street has been renamed 'Dosset Street' by some of the wittier locals.

It's at one of its flea-ridden dosshouses that Annie has been spending the last three or four months, or thereabouts. Crossingham's Lodging House, at number 35, is a refuge for those who need basic bed and shelter for the night, and are not too particular about sharing it. But even the lowly of the manor and the denizens of the streets require that fourpence for their basic creature comfort.

When Tim Donovan, the deputy manager of Crossingham's, lets Annie into the kitchen, it's so that she can take her medicinal pills with some water. She's suffering from some unnamed malady that she complained about to the workhouse infirmary, but when he sees her fumble and scoop the pills up from the floor, it seems to him that she's drunk as a sot.

That was shortly before the hour of midnight. Now, two hours later, not long after a half past one, she's back and scoffing a tater in the kitchen. Now she seems soused right up to the gills.

"I haven't got it," she tells Tim when he asks for her doss money. "I am weak an' ill an' have been in the infirmary." He's seen it too many times with the girls round here. Not a one of 'em knows what's good for her, and Dark Annie's no exception.

But he tries to have some faith in human nature when she tells him, "Don't let the bed. I'll be back soon." He holds his tongue, giving her neither scorn nor pity. He knows she means it, as she shuffles off into the night, and that she will be back soon – if she doesn't piss her bed money up the wall first. It is only in the aftermath of the night's events, with the eyes of the press upon Spitalfields, that Donovan will become conscious of his own callousness in turning a desperate woman back onto the streets.

***

Some may think Annie Chapman has pickled herself in gin, like so many of the girls round here. Right up to the end of her life and beyond they'll be saying it was the drink that was upon her. But poor old Annie knows different.

It's not that a sup from the cup doesn't help, or that she's never been found disorderly in her own cups. But Annie knows that her aches and pains, her dizziness and unsteadiness, are there of their own account. The Salvation Army can bang their tambourine and blow their horn, but if they try to tell her God is watching over her then they know where they can stick their trumpets!

It's pain and pain alone that dogs Annie every step of the way. That will only cease when all else ceases.

The bruising around her bosoms doesn't help much, nor the black eye that's just gone down. Not much more than a couple of years short of her 50th, her skin coarsened and bloated, her breath short and rasping, Annie can still fight like a little hellion. She's had a scrap with Liza, another of the girls at Crossingham's, just this last week. Annie says it was because she told Harry the Hawker, another lodger, that Liza had nicked a two-bob bit from him and replaced it with a ha'penny; Liza says Annie threw the ha'penny in her face, on account of her asking for the return of the soap Annie had borrowed for a man friend.

It's all the same difference. Money and blokes. Blokes and money. You never know how much you need 'em till you've got neither. And it's in your time of need that they always let you down. But as she works her way down the sidestreets that punctuate Spitalfields, she's hoping for one who's not too choosy nor too sober to scorn a woman who's down on her luck and long in the tooth.

It takes some time. Annie plonks herself down for a while in one of the pubs that never seem to close, eager to get the weight off her pins and to wait for some kindly soul to buy her a glass or two, if it ever happens.

By the time she's walking unsteadily on her way again the night has passed, and it's gone five in the morning. Now she's soliciting for the following night's lodging money, on this early morning of Saturday 8 September – if the money doesn't burn a hole in her pocket sometime between now and midnight.

"Will you?" he asks her as she totters slowly up the fenced-off backyards of Hanbury Street. At last, here's one who'll do the business while it's still dark before the dawn.

The squat little woman looks up at him and murmurs, "Yes," in a breath. What price pride in such a world, where the well-to-do reap the benefits of empire whilst the poor can barely rattle the cage of their own existence? There's no one else to save poor old Annie. Even her own family keep their distance now, for fear of the destitute woman coming round 'on the ear'ole'.

There is only him now, standing silent in the pre-dawn darkness, about to take her up against the backyard fence.

Annie Chapman, who has lost one beloved daughter, whose son has been crippled by illness, whose husband had rejected her before his own death from drink, no longer has any expectations of life treating her gently. This is no exception, just a small transaction to allow her to stumble her way through another day. A quick, blind poke for a few pennies.

But she did not expect this.

***

"No!"

One short cry. Never did such a plea fall on such deaf ears.

She's a plump one, this girl. It takes a moment for his fingers to lock onto the short expanse of throat beneath her double chin. But when he does there's no getting out of it for her. The handkerchief he suddenly strings around her in a tightly-wrenching knot takes her by surprise. Her eyes widen in terror, as the veins in her eyeballs start to pop and bleed. As her airway tightens and the full length of her swelling, purple tongue forces itself into her gagging mouth, her benefactor, her man of the moment, her deliverer, breathes just a little heavier. He eases off the strangling grip of his left hand to reach for his blade.

She drops suddenly, bumping down against the wooden fence like a graceless sack of spuds. Lying supine, the trollop can no longer cry out as the knife makes an almost full circular navigation of her upper throat. The deep gash judders its way from left to right, from front to back, the last point of the jagged incision almost meeting up with the first.

His left hand holds steady as the blade fights its way beneath the skin through flesh, gristle and muscle. What might have been a death rattle is submerged beneath her suffocation. Her silly old head wobbles as he moves her, connected by a stubborn strand of upper backbone to her dying body.

She is finished. But now it will begin. Here in the pitch-darkness of this side street not even a stray, starving mongrel has been disturbed. Now he will get what he paid for.

Up! And the long blade slashes at redundant, corrupt flesh which has already long borne the pallor of death. Downward . . . he opens her from breastbone to belly, reaching through her torn cunny, exploring the womanly byways he has hitherto only visited at brevity. Upward . . . he reaches to the wet, glistening, organic jewels of her debased body, squirming and twitching in his hand.

Open . . . with one further invasion the mystery of womanhood is possessed by him. The fleshly birthing chamber of all mankind, concealed by prim propriety and the lightly bearded pudenda, is within his grasp.

For a moment the exhilaration is intoxicating, what he possesses beyond the purchase of any other man. He pants, flushed by excitement, almost overwhelmed.

The moment cannot last forever. Even in this quiet backstreet, the sounds of the workaday world are stirring, as those inhabitants of the East End fortunate enough to be in employment start to make their way to 14 and 16-hour shifts.

Escape must be his. There will be time enough for this later. Time enough to recall. Time enough to relive . . .

***

When they find Dark Annie lying flat out on her back, square alongside the fence of 29 Hanbury Street, her frayed old dress has been pulled up to her knees, showing off her red-and-white stripy stockings. Her throat has been carved right through to the upper vertebral column, and her head is barely hanging on. There's something strewn across her lifeless shoulder, maybe a string of heirloom pearls that she never had the heart to pawn.

It takes just a moment to realise that it comes from within the woman herself. For Annie has been disembowelled, her intestines draped over her like a visceral necklace. If what happened just a week ago, just up the road, to Polly Nichols can be seen as some kind of prologue, then this destruction of the female form has taken things unimaginably further.

By the time she lays there upon the slab in the mortuary, bruised, swollen and gape-mouthed, the scant possessions found in the itinerant woman's pockets are all bagged up and accounted for – including two solitary brass farthings. Payment, perhaps, for services so professionally rendered. Doss money now superfluous to requirements.

The Metropolitan Police's surgeon, Dr Bagster Phillips, remarks upon how well-preserved Annie's upper front teeth are, though the bottom row are long since rotted away and gone. (Or perhaps removed, for unknown purposes, by her unknown assailant.) But for all her state of disrepair, the doctor can barely conceal his begrudging admiration for the deeds of a man who, it must be assumed, held no professional surgical status:

The head almost decapitated. The intestines and upper bowel removed in their entirety. The upper part of the vagina, the back portion of the bladder and the entire uterus removed – all the gynaecological organs absent from the scene of the crime, unlike the exposed guts. When asked by the coroner for his opinion as to the difficulty of such an undertaking, at a secondary inquest held out of the public eye, Dr Bagster Phillips describes himself royally in the third person:

"He thought he himself could not have performed all the injuries he described, even without a struggle, under a quarter of an hour. If he had done it in a deliberate way such as would fall to the duties of a surgeon it probably would have taken him the best part of an hour."

Such a generous appraisal of the felon's deed will begin a controversy that never ends. Is the individual who bears no known identifying marks – save, perhaps, the mark of Cain – a butcher, a surgeon, or merely a sadist?

The doctor also remarks upon poor old Annie's general state. How her consumptive lungs are congested and discoloured; how the membranes of her poor old brain are severely distorted and diseased. Even in death, the rot hasn't stopped yet for Annie Chapman. And yet, he notes, there are few signs of intoxication or recent consumption of alcohol. Perhaps the manager at Crossingham's was merely gazing upon the frailty of the human form when he thought he was regarding yet another inebriate woman.

He notes the abrasive marks on her ring finger and the absence of any adornment, suggesting that the two brass rings recalled by the staff at Crossingham's may have been stolen by her killer. (Or maybe, some have suggested, by avaricious mortuary staff.)

The good doctor is of the opinion that, if Annie hadn't been subjected to all of her final indignities, then she was destined for the boneyard soon in any case. If her murderous benefactor hadn't delivered her from her world of pain, then the very source of that pain would have done for her.

Maybe. But that can never be put to the test now, can it?

There are those who said soon after and those that still say today – so many years and so many other innocent cries and screams away from Annie and all her pains – that a life such as Annie's was barely worth living. That he who did for her did her a service. That the Whitechapel killer, if we can assume that the same man who gutted Annie Chapman also snuffed out Polly Nichols, was engaged in some kind of sanitary function, cleaning the streets of worn-out, diseased and unwanted women.

People can say what they like, just as they always have and always will. But none of them ever gave a silent, wide-eyed plea for mercy into hard, unblinking eyes that gave back no response. Never felt the desperate will to live firing up their tired soul and worn-out body, only for it to be cruelly denied.

If he that did for her did her any favours at all, it was only in choking and ripping the life out of her windpipe before he could truly do his worst.

***

By the time of Annie Chapman's death, the unknown murderer of Polly Nichols had already been granted a nickname by press and public: 'Leather Apron'. The fact that a leather apron was also found in the yard of 29 Hanbury Street, where Annie was killed, was now enough to cement that connection in the public consciousness, and to infer that the Whitechapel murderer and the Spitalfields murderer were one. (Although both were directly accessible via the East End thoroughfare of Commercial Street, they were regarded as two distinct neighbourhoods – Spitalfields touching the very edge of the City, London's financial hub, whilst Whitechapel was closer to the modest environs of Stepney.)

The fact that the apron in the Hanbury Street yard belonged to the warehouseman who was first to discover Annie did little to alleviate the tension. 'Leather Apron' had already been identified – by Tim Donovan of Crossingham's, among others – as a local man who extorted money from prostitutes by menacing. ('Blackmailing', as it was then termed.) He had also been named as a part of the initial police enquiry.

Jack Pizer owns the unfortunate distinction of being both the first 'Jack' and the first Jew to be suspected of being the Whitechapel murderer. Fitting the description of a dark, moustachioed bully who wore the then-fashionable deerstalker hat (not just the apparel of fictional sophisticate Sherlock Holmes, but also of a hard-up boot finisher like Pizer), he found himself the subject of the mob's attention.

When the discovery of the warehouseman's apron correlated the killing with Pizer in the public mind, indiscriminate street attacks on Jews were justified by the sentiment, "No Englishman would commit such murders." Pizer, an East Ender of Polish-Jewish descent, with a record of criminal assault (on a fellow cobbler), complained that the mob had given chase to him the week before Annie died, after the first mention of 'Leather Apron' appeared in the *Daily Telegraph*.

Arrested in connection with the murders of Polly Nichols and Annie Chapman on 10 September, it would be another month before his appearance at the inquest into Annie's death officially cleared him. According to contemporary records, the deciding factor was confirmation of Pizer's staying at a lodging house in Holloway on the night of 30/31 August, several miles away from the East End. The fact that he cannot have been guilty of Polly's murder was thus instrumental in clearing him for that of Annie – for the first time, it became clear that the legal authorities regarded both atrocities as the work of the same hand.

***

On 1 May 2009, *The Times* (perhaps rather belatedly) revealed that "'Jack the Ripper' was invented by journalists". Its source for the revelation was ripperologist Dr Andrew Cook, whose optimistically-titled book, *Jack the Ripper: Case Closed*, draws upon the evidence of Percy Clark, assistant police surgeon for the Whitechapel Division at the time of the murders, to establish his thesis that the Ripper was a media construct, concealing how the murders ascribed to him were the work of several different killers. The story itself suggests several things: for one, Jack the Ripper remains a bountiful source of copy for editors on quiet news days, providing headlines well over a century after the event; for another, such revelatory reports have a habit of turning out to be old news, reheated for consumption when contemporary crime provides lean pickings.

The idea that the Ripper crimes were not actually serial murders is nothing new and has been explored in several variants over the years. The belief that the letters that gave Jack his 'trade name' were hoaxes – and that therefore the very concept of 'Ripper crimes' is a misnomer – can also be traced way back. In 1910, the memoirs of Sir Robert Anderson, CID Assistant Commissioner at the time of the crimes, were serialised in *Blackwood's* magazine; Anderson insists that the crucial letter was "the creation of an enterprising London journalist", whose identity he claims to know but declines to reveal. Sir Melville Macnaghten, a high-ranking CID officer in the years following the murders, published his memoirs in 1914; he also thought he "could discern the stained forefinger of the journalist" behind the hoax, and hinted that he could identify the perpetrator.

While these retired law enforcement officers may have been wise after the event, police files from the time illustrate that the official view of the Metropolitan Police was that the most infamous letter allegedly sent by the perpetrator was a fake. For the Central News Agency had claimed to receive, on 27 September, a letter addressed simply to 'The Boss, Central News Office, London City', dated 25 September 1888, and written in red ink. Running to two pages, it read:

Dear Boss,

I keep on hearing the police have caught me but they wont fix me just yet. I have laughed when they look so clever and talk about being on the right track. That joke about Leather Apron gave me real fits. I am down on whores and I shant quit ripping them till I do get buckled. Grand work the last job was. I gave

*the lady no time to squeal. How can they catch me now. I love
my work and want to start again. You will soon hear of me with
my funny little games. I saved some of the proper red stuff in a
ginger beer bottle over the last job to write with but it went
thick like glue and I cant use it. Red ink is fit enough I hope ha.
ha. The next job I do I shall clip the lady s ears off and send to
the police officers just for jolly wouldnt you. Keep this letter back
till I do a bit more work, then give it out straight. My knife's so
nice and sharp I want to get to work right away if I get a
chance. Good Luck.*

*Yours truly
Jack the Ripper*

Dont mind me giving the trade name

An afterthought was added at right angle to the main letter:

*PS Wasnt good enough to post this before I got all the red ink off
my hands curse it No luck yet. They say I'm a doctor now. ha ha*

By 29 September, the letter had found its way to the police, with a covering
letter from the Central News Agency noting that they had regarded it as a
joke. The note was unsigned, but some experts have since suggested that the
handwriting is that of Central News journalist Tom Bulling. This was the
first time that the name 'Jack the Ripper' was ever used.

In the absence of any firm reliable identification, an ersatz identity was
being created for the killer. One woman had seen Annie Chapman
walking with a man in a modest dark coat, with a deerstalker hat and a
dark complexion – possibly a Jew (though also probably not Jack Pizer,
who had already faced the fury of the mob). A fellow prostitute – of whom
there were many among the unemployed and desperate of the East End
– told of a man who had asked her to accompany him for a kneetrembler
in the Hanbury Street backyard, between two and three hours before
Annie met her death there. She had declined, later describing him as quite
shabbily dressed: short dark jacket, dark vest and trousers; black scarf and
felt hat; late thirties, dark beard and moustache, speaking with a foreign
accent. (Again, foreign immigrants to the East End of the time were
largely assumed to be Jewish, due to the influx of refugees fleeing
pogroms in Russia and Eastern Europe.)

But, whoever the Whitechapel murderer may have been, 'the Ripper' was being constructed into an archetype of his time. Whilst the murders of both Polly and Dark Annie had taken place on clear evenings, both would later be attributed to near-mythical figures stalking a fog-swathed London Town.

The later dissemination of the 'Dear Boss' letter was a controversial move, undertaken with the hope of flushing out the hoaxer who was wasting police time – and then presumably making an example of him in court – rather than with much hope of catching the killer. The press of the day too appear to have been overwhelmingly of the opinion that the letters were malicious frauds – *The Star* described them as a "discredited rumour" written by a "practical joker" – and some editors took the moral high ground by condemning rival newspapers for publicising them. The journalist who subjected the alleged Ripper letters and the crimes themselves to the most withering analysis was George R. Sims. In his 1888 'Dagonet' columns for *The Referee*, Sims – also a prolific author and playwright – anticipated the revelations of Dr Andrew Cook by some 120 years. Although he did put a foot wrong on the odd occasion:

"The Whitechapel murders, which have come to the relief of newspaper editors in search of a sensation, are not the kind of murders which pay best," Sims suggested in his first coverage of the crimes on 9 September. "The element of romance is altogether lacking, and they are crimes of the coarsest and most vulgar brutality – not the sort of murders that can be discussed in the drawing-room and the nursery with any amount of pleasure." Of course, as his copious future commentary on the Ripper would illustrate, he had much underestimated the interest those crimes would inspire. Some other elements of his analysis are unlikely to meet with much approval among modern ripperologists, such as his endorsement of contemporary theories that criminality could be identified in the physical – particularly facial – features of a suspect. But Sims also offers invaluable insights on the Ripper crimes and on the role of the press in reporting them.

"The fact that the self-postcard-proclaimed assassin sent his imitation blood-besmeared communication to the Central News people opens up a wide field for theory," writes Sims. "How many among you, my dear readers, would have hit upon the idea of 'the Central News' as a receptacle for your confidence? You might have sent your joke to the *Telegraph*, the *Times*, any morning or any evening paper, but I will lay long odds that it would never have occurred to communicate with a Press agency. Curious, is it not, that this maniac makes his communication to an agency which serves the entire Press? It is an idea which might occur to a Pressman perhaps; and even then it would probably only occur to someone connected with the editorial department of a newspaper, someone who knew what the Central News was, and the place it filled in the business of news supply. This proceeding on Jack's part betrays an inner knowledge of the newspaper world which is certainly surprising. Everything therefore points to the fact that the jokist is professionally connected with the Press. And if he is telling the truth and not fooling us, then we are brought face to face with the fact that the Whitechapel murders have been committed by a practical journalist – perhaps by a real live editor! Which is absurd, and at that I think I will leave it."

Sims is making a very good point. Press agencies were a natural consequence of news becoming a commercial commodity. Competition was cutthroat between the Central News Agency and its rival, the Press Association, where accuracy was sometimes sacrificed on the altar of profit. Might someone at the Central News Agency have gone so far as to fabricate a letter from the killer, christening him with a catchy 'trade name' in a quest for a saleable scoop?

"Central News developed something of a reputation for underhand practices and supplying stories of dubious veracity, particularly in its overseas operation, and in 1895 *The Times* printed a highly critical article accusing Central News of embellishments in its reports," notes Paul Begg in his excellent study, *Jack the Ripper: The Definitive History*.

In 1913, George Sims received a letter from John George Littlechild, who had been a detective chief inspector at Special Branch in 1888, which appears to confirm his suspicions that the name 'Jack the Ripper' was concocted by a Central News journalist as a hoax. Littlechild's letter gets some of the names wrong (Tom Bulling becomes Tom Bullen), but the substance of his account chimes with that which appears in *Life and Death at the Old Bailey*, the memoirs of J. Thurston Hopkins who worked in Fleet Street in the early 1900s:

"It was perhaps a fortunate thing that the handwriting of this famous letter was not identified, for it would have led to the arrest of a harmless Fleet Street journalist," writes Hopkins in a chapter dedicated to the Ripper crimes. "This poor fellow had a breakdown and became a whimsical figure in Fleet Street, only befriended by the staff of newspapers and printing works. He would creep about the dark courts waving his hands furiously in the air, would utter stentorian 'Ha, ha, ha's,' and then, meeting some pal, would button-hole him and pour into his ear all the 'inner-story' of the East End murders. Many old Fleet Streeters had very shrewd suspicions that this irresponsible fellow wrote the famous Jack the Ripper letter, and even Sir Melville L. Macnaghten, Chief of the Criminal Investigation Department, had his eye on him."

Subsequent researchers have combined the accounts of Hopkins, Littlechild, Anderson and Macnaghten, concluding that the 'Dear Boss' letters were actually written by Bulling (who did indeed have a nervous breakdown after the crimes), probably at the behest of his boss, John Moore. This almost certainly makes 'Jack the Ripper' a fictional character – in name at least. The victims remain as stark reminders that the atrocities were real, but it poses some difficult questions about the role of the press in this and subsequent criminal investigations.

Whilst always purporting to be assisting enquiries, there can be little doubt that some modern crime reporting has hampered or even compromised certain cases. Precious police time has been wasted sifting through endless crackpot correspondence, much of it inspired by the sensationalist reporting of the Ripper case by publications. Even supposing the 'Dear Boss' correspondence was genuine, the British press had turned a corner in the autumn of 1888, with uncomfortable implications for the relationship between media, public and law enforcement authorities ever since.

"Lest I should be accused of doing myself that which I blame in others, let me come to my point, which is that we are in very grave danger of an epidemic of butchery," opined Sims in his column of 16 September 1888, criticising the blanket coverage of the Ripper crimes. "The minute details given by the papers of the hideous mutilation of the last Whitechapel victim only repel a certain class – a very much larger class is fascinated by them. The public mind becomes familiarised with the details of outrage, and is literally saturated with blood. We shall begin to expect too much from our murderers by-and-by, and an ordinary crime will pass without recognition. On the whole, there is good reason to look upon the Whitechapel horrors as national misfortunes, coming as they do in the middle of the silly season, when the papers are glad to fill up with anything – blood for choice. Better a whole year of the Failure of Marriage than a week of the Success of Murder and Mutilation."

"West End newspapers had turned those killings into a major media event," observed Professor Christopher Frayling in his 1988 *Timewatch* documentary, 'Shadow of the Ripper'. "In this they were led by papers like the *Pall Mall Gazette*, whose Liberal editor, W. T. Stead, was experimenting with a new, eye-catching style, in contrast to the compact, dull style of traditional newspapers. It was known at the time as the 'New

Journalism', and in the 1890s it was to be known as the 'tabloid style'. The year which produced the name 'Jack the Ripper' produced another new phrase in the English language: 'leader writer'."

The Ripper crimes occurred at a pivotal point in the development of the British press, and it's fair to say that they were instrumental in fuelling the success of the New Journalism. Papers prospered or collapsed based upon their coverage of the crimes. (*The Daily Mail* was nearly stillborn when its predecessor, *Answers to Correspondents*, almost folded; its founder, Alfred Harmsworth, blamed this on rival coverage of the Ripper.) It's perhaps equally true that without the New Journalism, 'Jack the Ripper' would not have existed.

The Victorian era saw an explosive growth in the newspaper business. Between 1846 and 1880, the number of different daily and evening papers published in the UK soared over tenfold, from 14 to 158. During the 1880s the number of newsagents in London doubled. It was also the era in which newspapers first truly became a business. Previously, they had been densely laid-out publications, full of political speeches frequently reported in full, aimed squarely at the nation's professional classes and elite. They were designed to inform, not to educate, let alone entertain.

An increasingly crowded marketplace – combined with the tide of free-market capitalism sweeping through the empire – encouraged innovative new approaches to content and design that made the press more luridly accessible. Critics have seen it as an early example of 'dumbing down'; others point to it as evidence of the vital role the media plays in the spread of democracy, as editors like Stead employed sensationalist reportage as a weapon of social justice, whereby the failings of the establishment could be exposed to the public gaze.

According to Frayling, the Ripper murders were "just another fearful crime, until the West End newspapers began to relate the story to a whole series of moral and social issues of the day. In this they were led along by W. T. Stead, who'd recently taken over the London paper *The Pall Mall Gazette*, a liberal Whig from the North of England with a nonconformist conscience and strong ideas about reform. One all-important clue as to why Stead himself was so interested in this particular story lay in the waxworks at Madame Tussaud's. Among the new additions to the Chamber of Horrors in 1888 was a young immigrant to the East End called Israel Lipski. Now Lipski, the year before, had been indicted for poisoning his mistress, an event which occurred just one street away from the site of one of the future Whitechapel murders. W. T. Stead, through his *Pall Mall Gazette*, in a lonely and very angry campaign, was determined to establish Lipski's innocence – by, among other things, suggesting that police had set him up. The campaign was rather proudly and for the first time called 'trial by journalism'. But in the end Lipski was hanged, and Stead was determined to hound the police force on every possible occasion, and in particular to hound the Commissioner of the Metropolitan Police, Sir Charles Warren. For in the same year as the Lipski case, it had been Warren who ordered his mounted police to charge a group of unarmed working-class activists in Trafalgar Square. And Stead's campaign against Warren, for using such military tactics against civilian targets, had become in the nature of a personal vendetta."

The term 'New Journalism' appears to have been coined in 1887 by one of Stead's rivals. "We have had opportunities of observing a New Journalism which a clever and energetic man has lately invented," wrote Matthew Arnold of Stead's style. "It has much to recommend it; it is full of ability, novelty, variety, sensation, sympathy, generous instincts; its one great fault is that it is featherbrained." Support for this cynical view came from Frank Harris, when looking back on his tenure as editor of the *Evening News* between 1883-94. (Harris is now best remembered for his swaggering, sexually explicit memoir, *My Life and Loves*.)

"I edited the *Evening News* first as a scholar and man of the world of 28," Harris told a friend, "nobody wanted my opinions but as I went downwards and began to edit as I felt at 20, then at 18, then at 16, I was more successful; but when I got to my tastes at 14 years of age I found instantaneous response. Kissing and fighting were the only things I cared for at 13 or 14 and these are the things the British public desires and enjoys today . . . when I got one or other or both of these interests into every column, the circulation of the paper increased steadily." That increase took the circulation of the *Evening News* from seven to 70,000 under his editorship, his policing of 'kissing and fighting' extending to near-blanket coverage of the Ripper crimes.

"Bloodshed always has an immense fascination for ordinary mortals," observed George Sims on 7 October. "Murders and battles are the things to hurl the circulation of a newspaper sky high, and the Whitechapel lady-killer's essays in lightning surgery have become as a boon and a blessing to men of the Press, who were weary of concocting in the office letters on various subjects of domestic interest, and trying to make them look like genuine outside contributions."

***

"Loads of things have been written about people saying that they were Jack the Ripper," forensic psychologist Laurence Alison tells the authors. "But I think particularly with the Kelly murder [see Chapter Eight], these people probably would have claimed responsibility at some time or another. I think with the actual murderer himself though, it's not going to happen. The only case I've heard of in recent history that's very similar is the Zodiac Killer in the States, who did write letters to the press. But it's incredibly rare. The idea of someone writing on a wall, or leaving your name on a watch [see Chapter Thirteen], or in some other quasi-clandestine, cryptic little way, doesn't happen."

Northern California's 'Zodiac' is still officially unidentified, despite the obsessive investigation and theorising of former *San Francisco Chronicle* cartoonist Robert Graysmith (as seen in David Fincher's recent film of the case). Known to have committed five shooting murders of necking couples in cars, and to have seriously wounded two other luckless lovers, his crimes now play as a macabre antecedent of New York's 'Son of Sam' killings in the late 1970s. Theorists and profilers alike have conjectured about Zodiac as a lonely, sexually-repressed nebbish, expressing his resentment about human relationships all too loud and clear.

But the killer himself developed a relationship with the media that added layers of mythology to his seemingly petulant displays of murderousness. In the early August of 1969, this sub-literate letter was sent to Graysmith's paper, the *Chronicle*:

Dear Editor
This is the murderer of the
2 teenagers last Christmass
at Lake Herman & the girl
on the 4th of July near
the golf course in Vallejo
To prove I killed them I
shall state some facts which
only I & the police know.
Christmass
1 Brand name of ammo
   Super X
2 10 shots were fired
3 the boy was on his back
   with his feet to the car

4 the girl was on her right
    side feet to the west
4th July
1 girl was wearing patterned
    slacks
2 The boy was also shot in
    the knee.
3 Brand name of ammo was
    western
(Over)

As with those that followed, this first letter was supplemented by a
cipher comprising astrological symbols, Morse code, the Greek alphabet
and other pieces of restricted code. (The sign of the Zodiac – a cross
drawn within a circle and overlapping its perimeter – was the killer's self-
proclaimed symbol, resembling crudely-drawn gun sights.) Besides
threats to take more victims, the probably virginal Zodiac supplemented
his kill-spree with an almost poignant element of fantasy:
" . . . it is almost better than getting your rocks off with a girl the best
part of it is when I die I will be reborn in paradise and all I have killed will
become my slaves . . ."
As the Zodiac killings appear to fall off, the letter writer still
maintained his relations with the media. In 1971, a letter to the *Los
Angeles Times* claimed a total of 17 victims; in 1974, a missive to the San
Francisco Police Department boasted of 37. If these figures reflect reality
in any way, it's possible that the Zodiac's subsequent crimes were met by
the kind of media indifference that he initially warned the SF press would
cause him to kill more: relegation to the back pages.
When we suggest to Laurence Alison that the Zodiac's campaign was
inspired by the 'Dear Boss' letter that made Jack the Ripper a media
entity, he agrees that it's highly likely. "And that's what was feeding his
notoriety, so that is part of it. If you're going to say that you've done it,
be upfront about it – it's a dramatic piece of theatrics. But I think it's
unusual, as a kind of driving motivation."

***

"I'm Jack." The softly-spoken north-eastern accent pauses, presumably
for dramatic effect. "I see you are still having no luck catching me. I have
the greatest respect for you, George, but Lord, you are no nearer catching

me than four years ago when I started. I reckon your boys are letting you down, George. You can't be much good, can ya?

"The only time they came near catching me was a few months back in Chapeltown [red-light district of Leeds] when I was disturbed. Even then it was a uniform copper not a detective.

"I warned you in March that I would strike again, sorry it wasn't Bradford, I did promise you that but I couldn't get there. I'm not quite sure when I'll strike again, but it will be definitely some time this year, maybe September or October, even sooner if I have the chance. I'm not sure where, maybe Manchester. I like it there. There's plenty of them knocking about. They never learn, do they, George? I bet you've warned them, but they never listen.

"At the rate I'm going I should be in the *Book of Records*. I think it's up to eleven now, isn't it? Well, I'll keep on going for a while yet. I can't see myself being nicked just yet. Even if you do get near I'll probably top myself first.

"Well, it's been nice chatting with you, George. Yours, Jack the Ripper.

"No good looking for fingerprints. You should know by now it's as clean as a whistle. See you soon. Bye, hopes you like the catchy tune at the end."

The sinister tones ended on a note of forced sardonic laughter, to the tune of a piece of Californian pop-pap called 'Thank You for Being a Friend'. So spoke the so-called 'Yorkshire Ripper', in a cassette tape recorded in 1979. It was a lengthier sequel to two brief letters received by the West Yorkshire police and one by the *Daily Mirror* over the previous 18 months. The taunts were aimed at the addressee, Assistant Chief Constable George Oldfield, the policeman assigned in charge of his capture.

As Britain's most infamous serial killer of the 1970s, the as-yet unidentified Ripper produced a frisson of fear among the general public that some found irresistible. One of the authors' wives, then a 14-year-old Essex girl, admits to her and her friends getting cheap thrills from dialling the Yorkshire police number in order to listen to the 'I'm Jack' tape.

In the northwest itself women lived in fear; the victims – prostitutes at first, but later seemingly just any vulnerable female – had been bludgeoned to death with a variety of implements, before vicious post-mortem wounding that earned the killer his 'Ripper' soubriquet from the press. (For a discussion as to whether the Whitechapel Ripper's atrocities truly fit the definition of 'sex crimes', see Chapter Twelve.) And it seemed to be a media label which the perpetrator embraced; look at the way in which he signed off the tape – just a word short of 'Yours truly, Jack the Ripper', from the 'Dear Boss' letter of 1888.

The north-eastern tones of the 'Ripper' certainly convinced George Oldfield to switch the team's focus to hunting for an offender from the city of Sunderland, on the River Wear, after consultation with linguists. It was a decision that was to cost two further lives and allow serious injuries to be inflicted on two more surviving victims.

By the time lorry driver Peter Sutcliffe stood trial for the Ripper crimes at the Old Bailey in 1981, his vaguely Mephistophelian appearance and the nature of his crimes had eclipsed his faceless Victorian namesake in the UK public's consciousness.

As Alexandra Warwick admitted at her 2008 Ripper lecture, "The Yorkshire Ripper to me looks like the Devil, on his wedding photos and things like that. His incredibly dark looks and dark eyebrows . . . I think that mythology does attach to the Yorkshire Ripper. Partly because of the name, and the kind of heroic contest that takes place. He started to form the background of [David Peace's] novels the *Red Riding* quartet, he is this kind of Jack-the-Ripper mythological figure in the background of these stories about police corruption in the North of England in the Seventies."

But what he most certainly was *not* was Wearside Jack. Sutcliffe was a native of Bradford in Yorkshire, whilst the all-too-keen 'Jack' was a Geordie hoaxer who depleted valuable police time and resources, and was ultimately culpable in allowing the killer to remain at liberty long enough to inflict more harm. In 2005, 26 years after the event, the aptly-named John Humble was arrested for perverting the course of justice after new DNA identification techniques were applied to the envelopes he had licked.

Despite claiming he had (belatedly) tried to inform the investigation team that his communiqués were a hoax, Humble received a deserved eight-year prison sentence. An alcoholic loner, his apparent motivation was to become notorious – even if only under the secondhand moniker of 'Jack the Ripper'. In this, his motives were significantly different from those of Sutcliffe, who was pursuing his own primal needs and wanted to remain at liberty.

For why would a man who wanted to evade detection offer detectives clues as to his next moves? Why, when he was the grip of a dark compulsion that needed to be satiated, would he want to offer the law the chance of frustrating his personal fulfilment? Why would such a singularly self-absorbed and nihilistic man feel the need to play the tragic hero, offering to commit suicide if the law got close enough?

These may have been questions that occurred to Sutcliffe, the real 'Ripper', when he became aware of the hoaxer in his last couple of years of liberty. It may well have been similar to the bemusement experienced by the Whitechapel murderer of 1888 – if he did indeed find that the press and the public were ascribing their own motives to acts which arose out of his feral desires (desires which he himself could probably not articulate), and that the popular press had ascribed to him the unfamiliar, absurdly jokey nickname of 'Jack the Ripper'.

At his trial, Sutcliffe himself was inclined (consciously or otherwise) to play up to one of the various Ripper archetypes. Seemingly motivated by pure hatred and sadism, he nonetheless claimed that he had been put on a divine mission to kill prostitutes by the 'voice of God' that he heard emanating from a gravestone during his days as a gravedigger. The jury didn't buy the insanity defence and Sutcliffe was sent down for life – though he later became an inmate-patient of Broadmoor psychiatric hospital.

In effect, he was taking on one of the archetypes projected onto the original Ripper – that of the holy 'Avenger'. It was a motif that arose during the time of the Whitechapel crimes, when some suggested that the murderer may have been a religious fanatic. As we shall see, it is also one of the myriad Ripper images consolidated in the realms of pop fiction.

IV

Ripping Yarns

Jack the Ripper's fictional career began early. You might even say instantaneously. Indeed, the problem of separating fact from fiction has bedevilled the case from the start. Just as his 'trade name', Jack the Ripper, may very well have been the invention of an 'enterprising journalist', so reports on the events of the autumn of 1888 have been supplemented by supposition, speculation and naked invention ever since. As noted, the Ripper crimes mark the emergence of the New Journalism, where accuracy and integrity are frequently sacrificed on the altar of circulation and profit. Certain ripperologists (i.e. students of the Whitechapel crimes) have also been known to stretch the facts beyond breaking point. How much guesswork and conjecture is permitted before a book is exiled from the true crime shelves to the fiction section?

It's a question that divides opinion among experts. Donald McCormick's 1959 book, *The Identity of Jack the Ripper*, was instrumental in rekindling interest in the case, to the extent that Whitechapel murder expert Stewart Evans refers to him as "the 'father' of modern Ripper writing". However, McCormick is practically a dirty word among other ripperologists, who believe that his tendency to invent sources – including some jolly rhymes supposedly penned by the killer – has left many subsequent works riddled with inaccuracies. In their excellent book *Jack the Ripper: Letters from Hell*, co-authors Evans and Keith Skinner were in sufficient disagreement over the extent to which McCormick qualified as an author of non-fiction that only the former put his name to the chapters covering his theories. Evans describes McCormick's work as "essentially factual, although he wrote in an age where primary sources were not quoted and facts were not too strictly adhered to when they might have affected the appeal of the book". Some might suggest that he's a little naïve in thinking such an age is over.

Fact and fancy continue to intermingle in the fictional fog of 1888 Whitechapel. In 1996 Richard Wallace, in collaboration with his friend Thomas Vere Bayne, caused a minor sensation when he revealed in *Jack the Ripper, Light-Hearted Friend* that the Victorian children's author, Lewis Carroll, best known for his *Alice* books, was the Ripper. Wallace's 'evidence' consisted largely of anagrammatic readings of the books Carroll was writing at the time of the crimes, which he said translated into detailed descriptions of the murders. Few serious theorists were impressed. In response to the publication of part of the book in *Harper's Magazine*, cryptologists Francis Heaney and Guy Jacobson employed the same technique Wallace had subjected Carroll to on the first three sentences of the *Harper's* excerpt. They came up with: "The truth is this: I, Richard Wallace, stabbed and killed a muted Nicole Brown in cold blood, severing her throat with my trusty shiv's strokes. I set up Orenthal James Simpson, who is utterly innocent of this murder. P.S. I also wrote Shakespeare's sonnets, and a lot of Francis Bacon's works too."

Subsequent to Alice's adventures in Ripperland, Oscar Wilde's creation Dorian Gray found himself in the frame – at least metaphorically. Thomas Toughill's 2008 book *The Ripper Code* reveals that decadent poet and wit Wilde concealed clues to Jack's identity in his 1890 novella, *The Picture of Dorian Gray*. Apparently, when Wilde spoke of "feasting with panthers" he wasn't referring to the thrill of risky encounters with 'rough-trade' rent boys, but of sharing the company of one of history's most notorious killers. Toughill had first proposed his suspect – the colour-blind painter Frank Miles – decades earlier, but no amount of ingenious interpretation of fictional sources removes Miles from an asylum near Bristol at the time of the murders. Oscar would doubtless have been amused.

Such acts of literary detective work bring to mind the observation made by the BBC comedy character Blackadder, upon framing a pair of innocent actors overheard performing a play featuring a murder: "The criminal's vanity always makes them make one tiny but fatal mistake. Theirs was to have their entire conspiracy printed and published in plain manuscript."

The first obvious example of fiction inspired by the Ripper murders was *The Curse upon Mitre Square*. It was published with the kind of indecent alacrity that puts the most opportunistic modern publisher – waiting in the wings with the biography of a dying celebrity – to shame. Barely a week had passed between the discovery of the mutilated body of Catharine Eddowes (see Chapter Five) and the appearance of this grisly publication, penned by one John Francis Brewer. Premier ripperologist Donald Rumbelow dismisses it as "a piece of nonsense" in his *The Complete Jack the Ripper*, and it has been widely condemned as the first step on the case's steady descent into hysterical sensationalism. It received a brief, similarly unimpressed notice from the *Penny Illustrated Paper* on 3 November 1888: "A blood red splash at the head of a long, narrow poster is at this moment attracting some attention in town. It is the sensational advertisement of a sensational shilling brochure, called *The Curse upon Mitre Square*. I have glanced over it in the interests of my readers, and may say that it is a far fetched story by Mr. J. F. Brewer. The pith of it is that the mysterious murder of Kate Eddowes in Mitre square was the outcome of the Curse called down on that spot by a monk's assassination of a woman on the altar steps of Holy Trinity Church (which stood on the same site) three centuries ago, in the reign of King Henry VIII."

The lurid plot ingredients – hereditary curses, mad monks, incest, spectral visitations – are classic staples of the Gothic novel of the early 1800s, and the book is actually an effective potboiler – particularly if penned in under a week. The final chapter at least, which focuses on the deprivation in the district, is a heartfelt diatribe highlighting the neglect of Whitechapel's inhabitants, regardless of any supernatural nonsense in the preceding parts. Many of the authors subsisting on Grub Street could easily sympathise with the grind of poverty, as it could be a struggle to survive in the cutthroat world of the penny dreadful, which required a hugely prolific output.

The king of the penny dreadfuls was George M. W. Reynolds who, despite making a small fortune via his frighteningly industrious output, remained a political radical, condemning the clergy and aristocracy in his countless bombastic tales and essays.

His illustrated penny publications, later collected in volume form, easily outsold those of Charles Dickens, who huffed, "I hold his to be a name with which no lady's, and no gentleman's, should be associated." It wasn't just professional jealousy that prompted such disapproval, but the content of his rival's work, which heaves with sex and violence completely at odds with our stereotyped view of Victorian culture. Reynolds' most popular productions were the weekly *The Mysteries of London* (1844) and its sequel, *The Mysteries of the Court of London* (1848-56), both of which ran to several volumes and became international bestsellers in book form. They led the way in relocating the traditional Gothic tale from the medieval abbeys and secluded castles to the ghettos and slums of the industrial metropolis. He missed few opportunities to use this setting to denigrate the rich and powerful, whilst portraying the downtrodden poor in a sympathetic light, pulling few punches in his depiction of the squalid realities of life for the dispossessed.

"Shame and decency exist not among them – because they could never have known either," he writes of one unfortunate poverty-stricken family in *The Mysteries of London*. "They have all been accustomed from their infancy to each other's nakedness, and, as their feelings are brutalised by such a mode of existence, they suffer no scruples to oppose that fearful existence which their sensuality suggests. Thus – for we *must* speak plainly, as we speak the truth – the very wretchedness of the poor, which compels this family commingling in one room and as it were in one bed, leads to incest – horrible revolting incest!"

Reynolds' prurient sermons delivered sensationalist sleaze in order to condemn the political system he held responsible. In addition to his prodigious fictional output, he also found time to found and edit several news magazines, including *Reynolds' Political Instructor*, which in 1850 became *The Reynolds Weekly Newspaper*. This latter publication, then edited by the founder's brother Edward, was at the forefront of those sensationalising the Ripper crimes in 1888, in a tone designed to raise maximum radical political capital from the crimes. The paper would never lose its fascination with the case, carrying speculative coverage of the crimes well into the 20th century.

With the sheer volume of provocative material produced by Reynolds and his competitors for an eager marketplace, it's perhaps unsurprising that some had difficulty distinguishing between lurid fact and sensationalist fiction. J. F. Brewer does appear to have done his homework for his *Curse upon Mitre Square*; there *was* a priory on the site of the fourth canonical murder, even if his claims for the location of the altar which is the focus of the curse are rather less plausible. It isn't clear whether Brewer intended his booklet to be taken seriously – there is a long tradition of horror fiction weaving fact into its narrative to add impact – but it proved convincing enough for his tale of possession to appear in several modern paranormal encyclopedias under an entry for 'Jack the Ripper', as if its narrative bore some kind of supernatural relation to the actual events.

In his graphic novel *From Hell*, Alan Moore has a man selling macabre souvenirs – including monk-headed canes and pamphlets – in Mitre Square the morning after the Eddowes murder. "Since no historical record relates the alleged events of 1530 actually taking place, it seems likely that the story is a form of urban legend, revived and exploited in the wake of the Mitre Square murders by salesmen and pamphleteers of the type depicted here," Moore observes in his accompanying notes. There is almost certainly a wealth of East End myth and legend that fed into local views of the Ripper crimes, now lost to us because it existed only in oral form. In *East End 1888*, William J. Fishman reports an interesting show held during the period at Charrington's Assembly Hall on the Mile End Road: "On 13 October the recent sensation caused by the Ripper atrocities prompted a lecture there by a Professor Malden who 'gave one of his interesting dioramic entertainments on "London, its History and Mystery by Day and Night"' to a packed audience."

"The border line between the horrible and the grotesque has grown very fine in Whitechapel of late," noted George R. Sims in his column for *The Referee* on 21 October 1888. "There has probably been a revulsion of feeling, and the inhabitants have relieved their overstrained nerves by laughing. Certainly last Saturday night, although another murder was confidently expected, the general body of sightseers and pedestrians were making light of the matter. Along the pavement, which for many a mile is hedged with shooting-galleries and various arrangements based upon the six-throws-a-penny principle, plenty of hoarse-voiced ruffians were selling a penny puzzle in which the puzzle was to find Jack the Ripper. Jack was upon every tongue, male and female, last Saturday night. The costermonger hawking his goods dragged him in; the quack doctor assured the crowd that his marvellous medicine would cure even Jack of his evil propensities; and at the penny shows, outside which the most ghastly pictures of 'the seven victims', all gashes and crimson drops, were exhibited, the proprietors made many a facetious reference to the local Terror."

The Ripper's early artistic career remains somewhat elusive, his crimes the subject of treatments in the penny gaffs of the East End, ephemeral performances unlikely to be recorded in any shape or form. In *The Complete Jack the Ripper*, Rumbelow notes, "in February 1889, just four months after [final canonical victim Mary] Kelly's murder, comes a report that a music-hall was presenting an entertainment, possibly a sketch, about the Ripper and Mary Kelly." In his September 2008 lecture at the Museum of London in Docklands, Martin Willis, an expert on Victorian literature and science, offers an intriguing theory on how the stage and the supernatural may have overlapped in helping to mould popular views of the Ripper crimes. "While the Whitechapel murders were not of course theatrical events, the rise of theatre as a spectacle in this period –

from part of the 1860s, coming to great popularity in the Seventies – did provide a cultural context for what was happening in Whitechapel, and the beginnings of a process of mythologisation," he observed.

Willis makes reference to Pepper's ghost, a stage illusion that debuted in 1862, using lights and mirrors to make spectres appear – often very similar in appearance to the famous *Punch* cartoon depicting Jack the Ripper as 'the Nemesis of Neglect': "By the 1880s, Pepper's ghost was a central part of many different theatrical productions, and it's a keynote as well of magical performances by the great Victorian magicians . . . The Victorian public were used then by 1888 to seeing exotic individual actors manipulating ghostly spectres onstage, or indeed taking on the role of ghostly spectres themselves . . . the actual individual could leave the stage, with the optics leaving the ghostly presence onstage, the glass unseen by the audience because of lighting. Basically he can walk through walls, or you can walk through other individuals who are indeed themselves on the stage, creating extraordinary ghost effects."

Willis suggests that the illusions "performed at the Egyptian Hall during the period that we're talking about here, often using the ghost in conjunction with other tricks and major illusions – such as escaping from rope ties, walking through walls, or, very commonly and I think interestingly, sawing female assistants in half, 'disappearing' them in different ways . . . is one of the imaginative touchstones for the idea of Jack the Ripper as a ghostly, spectral figure, able, it seems, to move unseen through Whitechapel, evade capture, avoid police even when they appear to be very hot on his trail . . . Jack the Ripper was perceived as a figure of supernatural power, much as later Victorian magicians were for their illusions performed on the popular stages all around London." Willis argues that the conjurors of the era who cultivated mysterious occult stage personas – superstars of their day, with reputedly mesmeric power over the fairer sex – fed into popular ideas about the Ripper crimes.

It may seem a little tenuous, but almost from the beginning some commentators had put forward theories that the Ripper was a black magician, some going so far as to credit him with powers of invisibility. Other supernatural elements soon manifested in the sensation building up around Whitechapel in the autumn of 1888. The burgeoning interest in raising the spirits of the dead – which began in New York in 1848 with the famous Fox sisters, who claimed to have contacted the spirit of a murdered peddler – had become something of a mania in Victorian Britain. Numerous mediums – both professionals and enthusiastic amateurs – presented psychic solutions to the mystery of Jack the Ripper's identity. The most distinguished to offer his help was Robert James Lees, who claimed somewhat dubiously to be Queen Victoria's personal medium. In his diary, Lees records visiting Scotland Yard on 2 October 1888 to offer his psychic services, where he says he was "called a fool and a lunatic".

A survey of other such psychic insights into the crimes – a cavalcade of contradictory bunkum from attention-seeking crackpots – leaves you with much sympathy for Scotland Yard's attitude. It also illustrates how easily the barrier between fact and fiction was breached for many Victorians. The press were not alone in exploiting a tragedy like the Whitechapel murders for their own advantage. In *The Thrill of Fear* (1991), New York English professor Walter Kendrick's history of '250 years of scary entertainment', he describes horror as entertainment and what we'd now describe as 'true crime' becoming increasingly interchangeable in the Victorian era. By the time of the Ripper crimes, the idea of reading about violence and murder as a form of recreation was already well established.

"From the 1820s, to our own day, the purveying of real-life horrors has grown into a substantial industry," Kendrick writes. "It has thrived in every medium, and especially horrid cases have enjoyed remarkable longevity. In the autumn of 1888, for example, the murderer known as Jack the Ripper slaughtered at least five women in London's Whitechapel district, and newspapers gloried in the murders, with illustrations ... Most such stories could only be found in newspapers and pamphlets, which meant to shock if nothing else. The sharply stratified society of Victorian England came together in its fascination with these grim things. In 1861, the indefatigable Henry Mayhew reported that no fewer than 1,650,000 copies of a broadsheet on the Red Barn case had been sold; taken together with other screeds on similar horrors, Mayhew's total came to ten million over a span of about twenty years. Most estimates put the total population of England at under seventeen million during the same period."

"Given the reticence on such matters displayed by Victorian fiction and drama," Kendrick later adds, "it is rather surprising to find the period's true crime stories going in with such gusto for the clinical details of mutilation and dismemberment. The twentieth-century stereotype of Victorian home life makes no provision for family chats about missing heads."

In addition to his harrowing sagas of contemporary life in London's criminal underworld, George M. W. Reynolds also penned period horror serials like *Wagner the Werewolf*, but such Gothic fodder would never enjoy the respectability afforded authentic horror reportage. The reality of crimes like the Ripper murders gave them a certain respectability, something which Kendrick says effectively "exonerates the interest by making it intellectual, as the enthusiasm inspired by fictional murder mysteries is also taken to be. True-crime stories, however, characteristically focus on the gruesome details of their cases – how many times the razor slashed or the axe came down, and especially on how much blood was spilled and where it splashed."

The first example of full-fledged Ripper fiction appears to have been a Swedish short-story anthology entitled *Uppskäraren* ('The Ripper'), penned by one Adolf Paul. The Whitechapel murderer's involvement comes via the discovery of the Ripper's diary, but otherwise little is known of this reputedly unsavoury volume that was suppressed by the Russian authorities. Jack's literary career didn't really get into full swing until 1911, when a short story entitled 'The Lodger' by Marie Belloc Lowndes was published in *McClure's Magazine*. By the time she had expanded it into a novel in 1913, however, the plot's connections to the Ripper crimes were becoming increasingly tenuous. Like the novel *Dracula*, its afterlife would rest heavily on its reinterpretation for the big screen, when *The Lodger*'s links with the Ripper were gradually re-established.

The biggest literary milestone in fictional treatments of Jack the Ripper came via the pulp magazines, which inherited the tradition of the penny dreadfuls in early 20th-century America. These cheap and much-reviled publications dealt with a wide variety of sensationalist topics, primarily as short stories aimed at much the same target audience as their Victorian predecessors. One title in particular went on to become a legend among horror fans, now seen as the creative cradle of the genre, most notably for introducing the world to idiosyncratic cult author H. P. Lovecraft. *Weird Tales* began publication in 1924 and – whilst never a big commercial success – attracted a dedicated following for its characteristic blend of explicit horror and verbose, almost antiquated style. The author Robert Bloch was one of the last notable horror authors to emerge from the *Weird Tales* stable. Heavily influenced by the work of Lovecraft, he found his own voice with the publication of his short story 'Yours Truly, Jack the Ripper' in a 1943 issue.

Bloch would subsequently become best known as the author of *Psycho*, the 1959 novel that became a classic cinematic shocker when adapted by Alfred Hitchcock the following year. Like 'Yours Truly . . .', *Psycho* has its roots in an infamous murder case – that of the 'Wisconson ghoul', Ed Gein – though Bloch used the episode only as a jumping off point for his psychosexual thriller. In addition to employing true crime on occasion for inspiration, the author is also known for an irreverent style replete with gallows humour. 'Yours Truly, Jack the Ripper' contains little of this trademark black wit but, like many great short stories, is structured like a joke, with everything leading to a literally killer punchline.

Not everybody is a fan. In *Jack the Ripper: The Murders and the Movies*, Denis Meikle dismisses it as "a story still regularly anthologised and fondly referred to today by those with a low threshold for narrative originality". Meikle's book is much enlivened by his political perspective and he clearly finds Bloch's acerbic conservatism unattractive. He goes so far as to accuse Bloch of coining the term 'Red Jack' for the Ripper to try to put a communist spin on the killer's crimes.

Yet Meikle was obliged to cover 'Yours Truly, Jack the Ripper' because of its sheer ubiquity in fictional treatments of the crimes. Whilst never adapted for the big screen, mass-media adaptations – particularly those that take its theme of the Ripper as a black magician conducting human sacrifices in exchange for immortality – are legion. Radio provided a healthy market for horror stories in the mid-20th century, and 'Yours Truly . . .' worked well as a radio script on shows like *Stay Tuned for Terror*; it was also adapted for television by Barré Lyndon as an episode of the cult horror series *Thriller* in 1961. (Lyndon had scripted the best of the *Lodger* films in 1944.)

Bloch himself wrote a science fiction version of the idea for the legendary original *Star Trek* series in 1967. Entitled 'Wolf in the Fold', it depicts Jack as an immortal entity, crossing not just eras of history but the cosmos itself in his insatiable search for victims. Works such as this, and his futuristic follow-up to 'Yours Truly . . .', the 1967 short story 'A Toy for Juliette', established Bloch as horror fiction's foremost interpreter of the crimes, frequently commissioned to provide pithy forewords for future projects associated with the Ripper legend.

(Harlan Ellison, the caustic science fiction author who commissioned 'A Toy for Juliette' for his anthology *Dangerous Visions*, penned a sequel in turn. 'The Prowler in the City at the Edge of the World' is regarded by many as a minor masterpiece in its own right. Ellison also penned a Ripper script for the 1968 Western series *Cimarron Strip* entitled 'Knife in the Darkness', but Jack's Wild West excursion was a misfire and Ellison disowned it. He was on safer territory as conceptual consultant for cult science fiction series *Babylon Five*. A 1995 episode which brings the Ripper into the 23rd century, entitled 'Comes the Inquisitor', "boasts an outstanding script by writer/producer J. Michael Straczynski and a stellar performance by Wayne Alexander [as the interstellar Jack] in what may well be the Ripper's finest hour on the screen," according to the *Hollywood Ripper* website.)

It's an indication of the extent to which Jack the Ripper was almost seen as Robert Bloch's personal property that, when respected horror writer Richard Matheson was considering a similar scenario, he consulted Bloch first. Sensing his fellow author's reservations, Matheson revised his script to feature an immortal alchemist as his villain. The project became known as *The Night Strangler* and hit TV screens in 1973 as the sequel to *The Night Stalker*, a hit TV movie about a reporter named Carl Kolchak who discovers a vampire at large in Las Vegas. Jack the Ripper finally appeared as an immortal supernatural killer in the first episode of the subsequent TV series, *Kolchak: The Night Stalker*.

While looked back on fondly by many, the show was cancelled in 1975 after only 20 episodes. If nothing else, it was very much a product of its time. The central plot always consisted of Kolchak uncovering a supernatural threat, only to have it covered up by the authorities. In many respects, it was a paranormal parable for the Watergate scandal.

The Ripper crimes had always been political as far as radicals like George M. W. Reynolds were concerned. But while Meikle detects elements of a 'reds under the bed' subtext in Robert Bloch's writing, as a rule the fictions that propelled Jack far into the future or gave him an arcane agenda diminished the case's political undertones. (The inclusion of a 'General Jack D. Ripper' in the 1964 satire of nuclear diplomacy, *Dr Strangelove*, is largely a throwaway reference.) The event that gave the historical case a newly conspiratorial spin was a major six-part BBC series screened in 1973. Appropriately for a crime that was now firmly wedged in limbo between fact and fiction, *Jack the Ripper* had two fictional coppers from the BBC's popular police serial *Z Cars* investigating the case, abetted by reconstructions and actual expert witnesses. The dour duo ultimately failed to find their man – though, in the show's final episode, entitled 'The Highest in the Land', they did spark a whole new Ripper controversy.

The title referred to the testimony of one Joseph Sickert, who claimed to be not only the illegitimate son of the noted Victorian painter Walter Sickert, but also the grandson of Prince Albert Victor, heir to the British throne. Concealing the illicit marriage had involved a conspiracy, according to Joseph Sickert, which led to the Ripper murders being committed by elements in Queen Victoria's entourage. It was far-fetched stuff, but it captured the imagination of a young journalist named Stephen Knight who, in 1976, published *Jack the Ripper: The Final Solution* –

purporting to expose the Whitechapel murders of 1888 as the product of a Masonic conspiracy to protect the Crown. (See Chapter Eight.) Sickert subsequently retracted his story, but Knight's book was well written, tailored to paranoid times and a gift to the press. It quickly became a bestseller.

(As far as most ripperologists are concerned, little of Knight's thesis stands up to even cursory examination. It is arguably a classic case of a Ripper novel that found its way onto the non-fiction shelves under false pretences.)

It certainly inspired several fictional outings to 1880s Whitechapel, including the 1979 film *Murder by Decree* – which follows Knight's anti-establishment conspiratorial thread, but inserts an overtly fictional element in the shape of the detective Sherlock Holmes. "The horror story evolves into a *Chinatown* [the 1974 conspiracy thriller] or a Watergate situation," said director Bob Clark of how the script had evolved to fit the paranoid political tones of the time.

**

The Ripper archetype can be detected in the English literature of the last 50 years in its most elliptical forms. The Whitechapel murders are a lifelong obsession of Colin Wilson, the man who coined the term 'Ripperology' (see Chapter Seven). Before coming to prominence with his pop-existentialist study *The Outsider* in 1956, the 'Angry Young Man' (as he and many others were inaptly termed) was already working on a novel which dragged a similar spate of crimes into 1950s London.

Ritual in the Dark was finally published in 1959, the first of Wilson's novels about a semi-autobiographical researcher, Gerard Sorme, whose investigations draw him into the dark undercurrents of sex and the occult. In this instance, however, the young man finds himself distantly connected to a spate of bludgeoning and strangulation murders in Whitechapel and Spitalfields. In his acknowledgements, Wilson thanks his *Encyclopaedia of Murder* collaborator, Patricia Pitman, "for some stimulating (if unlikely) theories about the identity of Jack the Ripper"; in later years, he'd graciously concede that the Ripper figure in his novel, Austin Nunne, is equally unlikely. Both a wealthy aesthete and a homosexual, Nunne contravenes the behavioural rule of sex murderers preying upon those they find sexually attractive. (All Nunne's victims are female. As Wilson recently admitted to the authors: "I am far from satisfied with Austin. But there have been sex criminals who were woman-haters or as happy to kill men as women – e.g. Ivan Milat. Ripperologist Stewart Evans' candidate for JtR is Dr Francis Tumblety [see Chapter Thirteen], who was queer.")

More controversially, the story conflicts with the theory which suggests the socially comfortable do not erupt in bouts of sexual homicide; equally crucial to this writer is the fact that Nunne is way off his geographical patch when committing murders in the East End. But *Ritual in the Dark* remains a compelling portrait of the seedy 1950s gentility, and Nunne is an interesting character – a decadent but cultured man who believes that life will only be truly lived when the senses are fully awakened – by murder if need be.

Other notable Ripper-manqués include Jack Gurney, in Peter Barnes' absurdist satirical play *The Ruling Class*. Surrealistically filmed by Peter Medak, with Peter O'Toole in the 1972 title role, this black comedy about an unhinged scion of the British upper classes initially portrays him as a hippie-ish schizo who believes he is Jesus Christ. (When asked how he knows he is God – the father apparently one with the son – he disarmingly replies, "When I pray to Him, I find I'm talking to myself.")

In the film version, the stylised whimsy suddenly gives way to horror as the new Earl of Gurney is 'cured' with the entreaty to remember that he is 'Jack'. In the climax, images of corpse peers in the House of Lords and a baby menaced by a gorilla lend a taint of nightmare to Jack's polar shift towards the Ripper. Now a Tory peer of the old school, his belief in repression and keeping the lower orders in their place evokes the Victorian era (or, at least, the endlessly echoing Victorian hypocrisy of England's old elite), as he descends into misogyny and murder.

Iain Sinclair, London's literary 'psychogeographer', made a more direct use of the Ripper in his 1987 novel *White Chappell, Scarlet Tracings*, which was no less unconventional in its context (and indeed its title spelling). Merging past, present and street map in the style of his then-evolving novelistic oeuvre, Sinclair conflates the decades between a gaggle of avaricious booksellers seeking out a rare copy of Conan Doyle's *A Study in Scarlet* and the activities of the Ripper himself. The author's semi-hallucinatory prose style has a similar fragmentary effect to William Burroughs; more conventionally, the bloodstained portions of his narrative portray the Ripper as royal physician Sir William Gull – who by then was the consensus suspect for Victorian retro-conspiracy theorists. (See Chapter Eight.)

Sinclair's contemporary Peter Ackroyd was by that time finding success with his own psychogeographical biographies of London (both the city itself, its architecture and its Victorian literary luminaries, chiefly Dickens and Wilde). In his 1994 novel *Dan Leno and the Limehouse Golem*, Ackroyd assembles a roll-call of late Victorian London characters (Oscar Wilde and the Elephant Man make fleeting appearances) to much greater critical acclaim than Robert Bloch's similar trick in his latter-day pulp novel *Night of the Ripper*. Crossing the boundaries of fiction, historical fact and conjecture, it combines the world of the Victorian music hall – Leno was a famed comic performer of the period – with that of fantastic myth – the Golem was the monstrous clay protector of Prague's Jews, though the figure at murderous work here is a Victorian serial killer.

Though the allusions between the Golem and the Ripper are made fairly obvious, this is not Ripper fiction per se – set in 1880, it pre-dates the Whitechapel murders by the best part of a decade and concentrates on the old docklands districts of Limehouse and Poplar (where Rose Mylett was murdered – see Chapter One), rather than the more urban neighbourhoods of the East End that bounded the City.

***

Perhaps the most worthwhile exploration of the Ripper case to travel via Stephen Knight's conspiratorial route is *From Hell*, the comic series written by Alan Moore and drawn by Eddie Campbell which ran between 1991-6, was collected as a graphic novel in 1999 and filmed two years later. Moore doesn't endorse Knight's theories but employs them as a jumping-off point for his "horror story about the fateful patterns that exist in time; in human enterprise; even in the stones of the cities wherein we conduct our lives. It's the horror story buried at the roots of the twentieth century, and it just might conceivably be true."

"I think in *From Hell* Alan Moore unashamedly ripped off the Sir William Gull/Walter Sickert theory," observes forensic psychologist Laurence Alison, "but what's interesting about it is the psychology of how it's written." Using the internationally popular royal/Masonic conspiracy theory (see Chapter Eight) as its basis is merely a dark alleyway to somewhere else, opines Alison, himself a comics fan in his youth. "It creates a very unsettling, dislodged feeling – there's that very weird scene where Gull is going down the backstreets and looks through the window at that television screen with *Morecambe and Wise* on. When you're reading it, it just dislodges your brain from the narrative and creates psychological effects that are weird and kind of psychotic.

"And then of course you've got those awful scenes with the

dismemberment in graphic detail, frame by frame, and the psychology of the murderer portrayed visually and in the written word – which again is quite repellent. Scenes of dislocation, extracting pleasure from being in a different state of mind, feeling that almost godlike state, the psychology of the victimisation of women and the horror all make for a very effective picture novel."

Moore is widely recognised as a master of his art, a visionary who has helped transform comics from a form previously derided as trash. In many respects, comics took over from the pulps as literature's least loved incarnation when the former went into decline in the 1940s. Inevitably, Robert Bloch's 'Yours Truly, Jack the Ripper' has been adapted as a comic strip on more than one occasion, but Jack has also battled superheroes, including the DC characters Batman, in *Gotham by Gaslight* (1989), and Wonder Woman, who confronts history's most notorious misogynist in *Amazonia* (1997). In the universe of rival comics' publisher Marvel, Jack is akin to the Robert Bloch conception, originally a hunchback named Tom Malverne, who is given magical powers by a sorcerer and a cabal of vampires and reappears intermittently to possess the spirits of the unwary. Perhaps the quirkiest solution to the Ripper crimes is offered by the 2001 independent comic *Whitechapel Freak*, in which the murders are committed by a man with no legs, strapped onto the shoulders of a midget.

The familiarity of the character has inevitably invited parody. In 1971, British comedians Spike Milligan and Ronnie Barker co-wrote an episode of the *Six Dates with Barker* series entitled 'The Phantom Raspberry Blower of Old London Town', which became a serial in *The Two Ronnies* five years later. It features a mysterious figure haunting the streets of Victorian London, dressed in standard-issue Ripper top hat and opera cloak and terrifying the inhabitants with rude noises. Beneath the comedy of absurdity, 'The Phantom Raspberry Blower' parodies Victorian prudishness with the implicit suggestion that the Phantom's victims would as soon be murdered as 'raspberried'. A similar level of absurdity is employed in the 'Bullshit or Not?' segment of the 1987 film *Amazon Women on the Moon*. A satire of the paranormal investigation shows still popular today, it investigates the theory that Jack the Ripper was the Loch Ness Monster – who duly appears, complete with cravat and bowler hat, to lure an unfortunate East End harlot into the shadows.

Using Jack the Ripper to poke fun at Victorian values remains a popular sport. The underrated BBC adult cartoon series, *Aaagh! It's the Mr Hell Show*, featured a regular slot entitled 'Diary of a Victorian Lady

Detective', in which the titular sleuth's attempts to solve various mysteries is thwarted by the repressive misogyny of the 1800s. In the third episode, broadcast in November 2001, our heroine gets on the trail of Jack the Ripper, finds him in the phonebook under 'butchers', but is prevented from apprehending the fiend when she dies in childbirth. The 'Victorian Dad' strip from adult comic *Viz* plays on a similar level, featuring a father in the modern day who subjects his family to the full force of hypocritical Victorian values. Inevitably, in one story he is revealed as the Ripper. In 2009, in one of its spoof news features *Viz* identified the character Blakey, from feeble 1970s sitcom *On the Buses*, as the Ripper, changing his catchphrase from, "I 'ate you, Butler!" to, "I 'ate you Victorian prostitutes!" (As a satire of the increasingly silly Ripper theories publicised to promote the latest sensationalist books, the *Viz* piece is right on the money.)

In what those without a robust sense of fun may see as the ultimate in trivialisation, the Ripper has become the subject of a number of board games: "As the events unfold, day by day, can you find the missing reporter from the *Queen's Park Sporting Gazette*? Why was a bomb thrown at the cricket match? What happened to the escaped prisoner? What secrets does the discovery of a decapitated corpse portend? These are only a few of the mysteries that will challenge your deductive reasoning as you spend five investigative days trying to solve the mysteries of *The Queen's Park Affair*." In *London 1888*, the players take on different roles, one of whom may be Jack's accomplice or even the Ripper himself. The similarly-titled *Whitechapel 1888* casts one player as the killer and the remaining contestants as the victims endeavouring to evade his grasp.

Mystery Rummy: Jack the Ripper replaces conventional playing cards with those depicting Ripper suspects, sites and clues. In *Mr Jack*, the Ripper must dart through the shadows to avoid identification and apprehension. In *Who Is Jack the Ripper?* the players become intrepid reporters, anxious to be first with the scoop on the latest atrocity, whilst in *Jack the Ripper* one player takes on the role of Metropolitan Police Commissioner Sir Charles Warren and attempts to change history by nailing his opponent, Saucy Jack. There is also a *Jack the Ripper* storytelling game, where the case unfolds as characters ask each other questions in character, and *Ripperology*, an unofficial variant on *Monopoly*.

The Ripper's debut in digital entertainment came just before the centenary of the crimes, in a 1987 text-based adventure entitled *Jack the Ripper*, in which players find themselves wrongly accused of the murders. (The victims are portrayed in digital graphics, reputedly modelled by the author's sisters!) In the 1992 scrolling platform adventure, *Masters of Darkness*, the player becomes a swashbuckling psychologist on the trail of Dracula himself, with the Ripper as one of the fiends that stands in the way – though he turns out to be a wax doll subsequent to his defeat. (The adventure game *Waxworks* – see Chapter Nine – was released the same year.) In 1994's *World Heroes 2: Jet*, one of the popular range of beat-'em-up fighting games, Jack is the punk-style British contender in an international tournament.

Ripper (1996) is an altogether more serious affair, a futuristic adventure where the player becomes a journalist tracking down a Ripper copycat killer stalking the streets of New York in 2040. *Duke Nukem: Zero Hour* lowered the tone again in 1999, with Jack the Ripper getting a walk-on part in a light-hearted gunplay romp set in Victorian London. The following year saw the skeletal hero Sir Daniel Fortescue battle Jack, a top-hatted green monster with long claws, in the platform adventure *MediEvil 2*. *Shadowman* (2002) is an altogether grimmer affair, based upon the voodoo-powered comic hero Jack Boniface. Jack the Ripper is an architect named John G. Pierce, one of a quintet of supernatural serial killers the hero must defeat in this action-horror adventure.

In the 2003 game *Jack the Ripper* the player takes on the role of James Palmer, a reporter for *New York Today* who discovers in 1901 that the Whitechapel killer has crossed the Atlantic. *Mystery in London: On the Trail of Jack the Ripper* (2009) is a 'hidden object' game in which the player must find clues hidden in photographs to advance the story, unravelling connections between the murders and Stevenson's *The Strange Case of Dr Jekyll and Mr Hyde*. The Ripper's most recent digital outing is *Sherlock Holmes versus Jack the Ripper*. The latest of a popular interactive game franchise that allows the player to don the detective's deerstalker, the designers have attempted to recreate 1888 Whitechapel in full virtual 3D.

***

It was in the 1970s that the shadow of the Ripper escaped the era of the Victorian East End music hall and entered the West End's musical theatres. *Jack the Ripper: The Musical* was first performed by the Players Theatre in 1974, with book and lyrics by Ron Pember and music by Dennis DeMarne. Much-parodied as a comically sick concept (on a par, say, with 'Auschwitz on Ice'), its influence would long outlive any minor controversy. Improbably perhaps, it would also become the progenitor of a whole subgenre of Ripper musicals.

As the organiser of the Whitechapel Society (the UK's only dedicated 'ripperology' association), the delightfully-monikered Frogg Moody recalls, "It's kind of based around a music-hall scenario, and the [music-hall chairman's] table was set in the audience for maximum audience participation."

The music itself was a hybrid of 1970s MoR balladry and more ballsy musical fair in the tradition of a show like *Cabaret*, which evokes a dark period of history with a few powerful show tunes. Unashamedly melodramatic, the show does not entirely ignore the social degradation that led the women to their ends. "Annie, I have something for you in my pocket," the Ripper promises the doomed Chapman at one point, "I'll see you right!"

The most notable songs are 'I Am the Man They Seek' and 'Who Am I?', both brooding ballads that might have been done justice by Scott Walker in his crooning days, with dark lyrical metaphors such as, "An ocean of blood separates me from mankind," and a city of "ravished virtue . . . purple bruises". Other scenes touch upon Gilbert and Sullivan, with 'Something Nasty in the Mail' evoking the Lusk letter ("Half a kidney and a note that taunted!" – see Chapter Five) and a police chorus promising, "The Ripper will not prevail!"

"The 1970s musical is fine but it's not really the kind of thing that I'm into," demurs Moody, himself the composer of a rock musical called *Yours Truly, Jack the Ripper*. "I know it won an award, but its oom-pah-pah type stuff didn't really gel with me; I think it got quite panned as well. But that type of music's got a place out there and it's been successful, because numerous amateur dramatic societies have taken on Ron's musical and it's still being performed to this day, so good on him."

Moody agrees with the authors that the Pember-DeMarne musical most likely had an influence on Stephen Sondheim's later *Sweeney Todd: The Demon Barber of Fleet Street*, with its cockney Gothic and darkly misanthropic lyrics. But his personal favourite piece of Whitechapel musical mummery has a quite different source.

"I've recently actually heard, for the first time, the Spinal Tap 'Saucy Jack' track. I thought it was going to be something that was really taking the rise in typical Spinal Tap fashion." In the celebrated 1983 mock-rock documentary *This Is Spinal Tap*, the pastiche Brit-rock band's claim that they're writing a Ripper musical is posited as the ultimate crass insensitivity. "But when I heard it, it's actually quite a serious musical song of a Ron Pember type."

Recently posted online, more than a quarter of a decade after the Spinal Tap film, and featured as part of their 2009 'reunion tour', the song clips the signature of the 'Saucy Jacky' postcard sent to Scotland Yard (as with all the others, its authenticity is disputed). Perfectly parodying the whimsical music-hall pastiche of artists like the Beatles and the Kinks in their psychedelic periods, the harpsichord-trilling 'Saucy Jack' accuses, "You're a naughty one . . . you're a haughty one . . ."

Of his own *Yours Truly, Jack the Ripper*, first performed in 1996, ripperologist/rock musician Moody explains, "I'd seen the film *The Lodger* by Hitchcock some years ago, fell in love with it and toyed with the idea of writing a soundtrack." Moody would later be beaten to the punch by Divine Comedy keyboard player Joby Talbot, who performed a live score to Hitchcock's silent melodrama. By now though, Moody had a more traditionally rounded musical narrative in mind.

"I purposely set out to make it as dark as possible – even the song titles reflected contemporary sayings that were around at the time. I wanted to have a musical that portrayed the facts as best as I could possibly get them, and the music and the lyrics were to push along the story."

Veering from music-hall stylings to social realism to Americanised rock histrionics, Moody and lyricist Dave Taylor's show is narrated by a sympathetic everyman character whose significance becomes unambiguous in the closing scenes: "Some say it must be a cannibal, someone else a Russian Jew . . . everyone was a suspect for a while . . . They'll never catch him in a hundred years. Don't ask me how I know – I just know."

"Here was a man, the story's narrator, who knew far too much about the story and kept dropping hints all the way through," says Moody of his narrative device. "But also he went into a dark decline, so therefore you thought no, he can't be the Ripper – particularly on the Kelly murder, he really breaks down and starts almost crying.

"Because we've had princes, royal physicians, all sorts of people being drummed up as the Ripper, we wanted to highlight the fact that he was an ordinary man, which serial killers are. When the Yorkshire Ripper was found he was just a lorry driver; just a chap who was up and down, with mood swings."

Aiming for period detail to complement the melodramatics, the show features staged tableaux of the famous *Illustrated Police News* illustrations and copies of the original *Star* headlines on the Whitechapel murders as props. "Getting cut up was an occupational hazard," the narrator describes the lot of the East End's fallen women. "There were plenty of honest, hard-working men who had to close their eyes and pretend their wives weren't whores."

One nicely melancholic touch is the use of the traditional ballad 'Only a Violet from Mother's Grave', which Mary Kelly purportedly sang in the pub on the night before she was murdered. More Grand Guignol in its effect, 'Catch Me When You Can Mr Lusk' continues the tradition of setting the infamous Lusk letter to music.

"I think it's the only letter that's authentic," says Moody, at variance with his Whitechapel Society peer Jon Ogan. "I read somewhere about the actual handwriting, a handwriting expert [C. M. McLeod] said that out of all the letters, because of the way in which some of the loops were like daggers, that betrayed to him that it was authentic. I think if anything's going to be kosher then that letter was; I think that the kidney *was* from the Ripper victim. We actually credit that lyric to Jack the Ripper."

Yours Truly, Jack the Ripper has played in several runs over the last decade, on both sides of the Atlantic. As Frogg Moody is aware, its basic concept is no longer unique but now part of a Ripper musical tradition. "I've heard of quite a few that have run very shortly – there was actually one based on Mary Jane Kelly. It had a lot of publicity but I think it just got performed a few times and then shelved."

As recently as April 2009, a show called *The Ripper* (once again concentrating on the victims) played for one night only at Soho's New Players Theatre. "The thing that I'm most proud of is that every single Ripper author, from Don Rumbelow to Stewart Evans, has endorsed our show," stresses Moody, setting his project apart. "Because we played the First UK National Conference on the East End Murders of 1888 and Jack the Ripper [in 1996], and most of them were there. Stewart Evans actually organised the conference, he booked me and I went to stay with him at his house – he's got the biggest Jack the Ripper collection in the world."

As the resident musicologist of the Whitechapel Society, Moody has tipped his hat in the *Whitechapel Journal* to figures as diverse as the late rockabilly guitarist Link Wray. Wray's minimalist 1959 instrumental, 'Jack the Ripper', is a sequence of echoing, Ennio Morricone-like riffs with a light, Duane Eddy-ish touch. Covered many times, the early 1960s version by the Surfaris evokes the *Pulp Fiction* theme and, more pertinently here, opens with the hammy mad laughter and woman's scream that became generic with Screaming Lord Sutch's 1963 near-hit, 'Jack the Ripper'.

"Pretty basic," Moody assesses the underrated Link Wray and his influence on rock guitar, "but I love all that kind of stuff. I know people who criticise Screaming Lord Sutch's 'Jack the Ripper' – you've got to remember it's of that time. At the time it was way ahead of what anybody else was doing. They should be remembered for that and not ridiculed."

'Jack the Ripper' by Screaming Lord Sutch and the Savages is actually a piece of 1960s beat-boom corn, redolent of the rock 'n' roll pastiches that Benny Hill used to pepper his early shows with. With its basic R&B riff and its lyric about the Ripper's "little black bag and his one-track mind", it marks the point at which the mythical Ripper no longer has anything to do with the actual Whitechapel murders. Its refrain, "Is your name Mary Clarke?" is taken from the fallen-woman scenario of 1959 British exploitation film *Jack the Ripper*, from the producer-director team of Baker-Berman. (The film also pre-dates the popular theory that claims the Ripper was a member of the upper classes, fixated on finding only one woman – Mary Kelly, not Mary Clarke. See Chapter Eight.) The movie is responsible for a whole generation of Brit cinemagoers (including the co-author's mother) believing that the Ripper had really been pursuing a woman named Clarke, but showman-rocker Sutch's tribute would find a strange immortality.

Cover versions of the Sutch song by Western US garage bands Jack & the Rippers and the Sharks would improve upon the blueprint, with an edgy early 'psychobilly' sound replacing the English Sutch's faux-American tones. Most importantly, they were conscientious enough to change the offending line to, "Is your name Mary *Kelly*?"

"I've got a lot of time for Screaming Lord Sutch," protests Frogg Moody. "When you play that song today – because it was in the Sixties, it was produced by Joe Meek – it's quite scratchy." Legendary producer Meek is himself now infamous for the murder-suicide that ended his career. "But I loved what Screaming Lord Sutch was doing at the time. He was a big influence on people like Alice Cooper, that kind of gore rock. I think he called it 'rock 'n' gore'. People like the White Stripes and the Black Lips and the Horrors have all covered that song."

In his increasingly hammy horror stageshows of the early 1970s, Sutch, founder of the Monster Raving Loony Party, backed by various members of Deep Purple (once his young protégés), introduced his predatory antihero as "the *one*, the *only* Jack the Ripper!"

"Someone told me he actually saw Screaming Lord Sutch onstage singing 'Jack the Ripper'," recounts Moody. "He came onstage with rubber hearts and lungs – he used to do this kind of autopsy and pull these organs out of a body in front of the audience. People in the audience actually fainted. I don't know if he used synthetic blood or anything, but he was pulling all this stuff out and he had the knife going into the body, just throwing all these organs around the stage."

Sutch's camp standard continues to appear in ever more distorted forms. The White Stripes play a live version which is pure cacophonic garage rock. Goth band the Horrors' version is a pounding, post-industrial revision, with a melodramatic vocal that suggests Nick Cave drained of all subtlety. Its one-dimensional Rocky Horror-isms were illustrated by an amateur promo video directed by one Emma Smith (presumably no relation to the Old Nichol Gang victim); it shows 'the streets of London' as a back alley in the rural provinces and a young Ripper in white boots, uncharacteristically burying an unrepresentatively young victim – before ending with the composition of the 'Dear Boss' letter.

Post-Sutch, in the mid-1960s Bob Dylan incorporated Jack the Ripper into his surreal, marijuana and speed-suffused lyrics of the time, when the killer sat "at the head of the chamber of commerce" in 'Tombstone Blues'. In his 1970s sleeve notes to the Velvet Underground's posthumous *Live 1969* album, critic and songwriter Elliot Murphy (one of many once cited as 'the new Dylan') refers to "Lord Byron, Jack the Ripper, F. Scott Fitzgerald, Albert Einstein, James Dean, and other rock 'n' roll stars". Far away from being just a sordid mutilator of women, the Ripper was now a cultural iconoclast. He was rock 'n' roll.

Perhaps it's inevitable that, with the genre's insatiable appetite for bloodshed and sleaze, Jack finally found his musical home in heavy metal. Kings of high-octane camp Judas Priest released a 'Ripper' on their 1976 *Sad Wings of Destiny* album (and employed a vocalist named Tim 'Ripper' Owens for a period), cult British metal band Praying Mantis recorded their own 'Ripper' in 1979, whilst Irish hard rock legends Thin Lizzy reported a 'Killer on the Loose' in 1980 – causing some offence with the absurdly macho line, "Honey I'm confessin', I'm a mad sexual rapist," at a time when the Yorkshire Ripper had just been apprehended.

In latter years, it's a fair assumption that the Tennessee deathcore band Whitechapel didn't pick their name at random from a London A-Z. The Texas metal band Ripper have recently returned to action subsequent to almost 20 years on hiatus, appropriately helmed by Rob Graves, whilst the Swiss metal band Meridian's vocalist, Jack D. Ripper, has departed for pastures new – as has Ripper, vocalist with the uncompromisingly titled Brazilian band Sodomizer.

In the less decibel-charged sphere of 'independent' or 'alternative' rock, the years following the murders' centenary saw an interesting spurt of Ripper-related activity. On their 1990 *Crushed Velvet Apocalypse* album, underground band the Legendary Pink Dots told of 'The Death of Jack the Ripper'. Opening with echoing footsteps in the Sutch tradition, it heads into a sparse, neo-psychedelic industrial soundscape with lyrics that fantasise about feminine revenge and "suicide in Menstrual Lake". "Jack is dead," the whining refrain tells us, "and nobody knew."

That same year saw the most understatedly atmospheric and accurate evocation of the crimes in rock music. Former Smiths vocalist Morrissey has belied his former 'delicate bloom' image with a fixation on classic British crimes; the Moors Murders and the Kray twins have both appeared in his lyrics, and his ambiguously compassionate 'Jack the Ripper' is a ballad addressed to the victims: "Your face is as mean as your life has been," he tells one of the unfortunate women, but, whilst the lyric never names him, there's little doubt as to who the narrator is. "I know a place where no one will pass," he entices the doomed woman, to a backing of stripped-down guitar riffs in the Link Wray tradition. (The song was covered raucously by young metal/'emo' band My Chemical Romance, effectively destroying its atmosphere.)

Garage band leader, figurative artist and former boyfriend of 'Brit art' icon Tracy Emin, Wild Billy Childish had already covered Wray's 'Jack the Ripper' with his former band Thee Headcoats. His own 'Saucy Jack', on the 2003 LP *1914* by the Buff Medways, takes the (then apocryphal) Spinal Tap title and marries it to a noisy, reverb-filled evocation of early Who classics. "Lying on her back . . . throat cut from front to back," runs one elegant couplet, as the backing vocalist trills the refrain, 'Saucy Jack'.

But perhaps the most likely latter-day balladeer to evoke the Whitechapel murderer did nothing of the kind. Nick Cave and the Bad Seeds' 'Jack the Ripper' – from the 1992 album *Henry's Dream* – contains no homicide beneath its layers of sonic psychodrama, just sexual metaphor: "She screams out, 'Jack the Ripper' . . ." Cave testifies about a claustrophobically intense relationship. The pain and fear of mortality that were his obsessions would be thoroughly exorcised on the blackly comic 1995 *Murder Ballads* album, before the artist decided that the subject was an all-too-literal "dead end". But the Ripper's appearance in his lyrics – if only in metaphorical form – is testament to the choking hold the faceless killer still has on the windpipe of popular culture.

V

The Double Event

The pony and trap clip-clops its way down the cobblestone back street. The tired little horse is driven by an even more fatigued man. Louis Diemschutz has been out touting his wares in the markets of Kent, and is only just now – at one in the morning of Sunday 30 September – returning to the back entrance of the International Working Men's Educational Club, of which he is steward.

As a street hawker of cheap decorative jewellery, Diemschutz might be seen as an aspirant low-level capitalist. But as a Jew struggling to stay afloat in a sea of drifting gentiles, Louis understands the need for community, for solidarity, among the dispossessed. He is not too enthused by politics itself – for him, the pipedream of universal brotherhood has to make way for the reality of earning a living – but is not too much at odds with the theme of tonight's lecture at the club, which he has missed: The Necessity of Socialism.

"Go on, boy . . ."

The silly nag won't shift any further. As he drives his trap into Dutfield's Yard – a small turning off of Berner Street, where the Educational Club is situated at number 40 – the beast has frozen as if in silent trepidation. Not even a stroke of his master's horsewhip can persuade it to budge.

In the deepening darkness, Diemschutz detects an obstacle in their path but is too far from gaslight to perceive its shape or size. He mutters an imprecation in Yiddish and reverses the whip in his hand, holding the whip end and reaching forwards with the handle to the spot from which his pony refuses to proceed.

It doesn't take too long before he pushes against something soft but immoveable.

Alighting from the trap, he strikes a match. Several feet before the stilled hooves she lays in chaotic repose. Sprawled out with her right arm behind her, she clutches tight at something her grip refuses to relinquish – even in her present state.

Louis Diemschutz dithers for a moment. There's no doubt that the universal brotherhood of man owes something to its sisters, but he doesn't want to be responsible for this drunken woman's welfare. The streets contain too many like her – many not even natives of the East End, but drawn here like Louis and his brethren. But theirs is no search for religious tolerance or for a Diaspora community, just a magnetised lunge toward the Abyss that swallows so many of its people whole.

Diemschutz leaves his pony and trap to run inside, seeking physical and moral support to help him take care of the wretched woman lying in his path . . .

***

They call her Long Liz round here. Not that she's any kind of a giant, but at nearly five and a half feet tall she's the equal of most men in the East End. How much longer she looks now, draped out over the cobblestones and bleeding. Shedding her life as her consciousness sinks into oblivion, barely aware of the fuss and bother that's about to erupt around her.

In her dying moments, Liz's mind recaps the fractured memories of her last couple of hours. How she'd picked up a right gent in the Bricklayers Arms . . . he'd walked her along arm in arm, like a courting couple . . . bought her some black grapes and sweetmeats . . . but then . . . and then . . .

. . . it all started to go wrong such a short while ago . . . such a short lifetime ago . . . he, drunk and angry with her, pushing her to the floor, not letting her rise to her feet . . . when it attracted the concern of a young Jew in the street, he shouted at him, "Lipski!" – the name of the Jew they hanged this last year just gone, for poisoning his mistress in Whitechapel . . .

***

As Long Liz's blood trickles onto the stones from a throat wound, she no longer has any awareness of the concerned Jews who are attempting to come to her aid. All is lost to her now.

As they shine a light on the deep, gushing wound in her upper throat, Diemschutz sighs inwardly with relief that his comrades have joined him. It is as bad as he feared; they are not dealing just with a drunken whore but with bloody murder. None wish to touch the dead or dying woman, so one of their number hurries off up the street to seek a constable.

Still Louis feels unease. The grisly deed seems so new, so fresh, that the dark red is only just stopping its flow as her heart ceases beating. So where is he, this butcher of women? "I fancy he was still here, lurking about in this yard somewhere." Diemschutz's eyes dance about him. His comrades reassure him that, whoever this was, he has long since taken to his heels, probably scared off by Louis and his pony cart. They know that, when he came running to them in the club, he was really fleeing the desperate presence he believed to be hanging about in the nooks and crannies of Dutfield's Yard and Berner Street.

When the good Doctor Bagster Phillips is summoned to the scene of the crime, he notes that the dead woman has been killed by a deep, almost straight cut to the throat below the jawline, severing her windpipe and cutting deep into the muscle. Bleeding has erupted spontaneously from the carotid artery, her death occurring relatively rapidly. Clasped in her hand are a bag of perfumed cachous and what appears to be a grape stalk, the attack occurring so rapidly that her hand has not released them.

At St George's Mortuary the next day she is formally identified as Elizabeth Stride – a local woman, though not indigenous. Hailing from near Gothenburg, Sweden, the former Elizabeth Gustafsdotter had married a carpenter named John Stride and both had gravitated toward east London. As his health and their marriage failed, she was drawn – like so many other fallen woman – towards the most assured method of earning a bed to rest herself and a few drinks to console herself.

On the mortuary slab, in her deathly repose, Long Liz displays a most comely facial structure for a murdered 45-year-old whore. Indeed, they regard her as quite a sad and soulful figure hereabouts. It's hard not to feel for a woman fallen on hard times, who lost her husband and two children in the wreck of the Princess Alice, when the steamer sank with the loss of up to 700 at Woolwich ten years prior.

Except that a little searching by the police will turn up a surprise for those who were taken in: Liz and John Stride never had any children that the records bear witness to; at the time that Liz was so cruelly butchered, John was not dead but living in penury in the workhouse. Long Liz was little but a romancer, so it seems, though everyone knew she could use her tongue in other ways beside spinning a yarn; just this past year alone, she was up before the beak about eight times for drunken disorderliness and the use of obscene language.

But all this will be forgotten in death. Elizabeth Stride, compulsive liar and inveterate streetwalker, soon to be buried in an unmarked pauper's grave, has achieved a tragic immortality. She will be third in the unofficial canon of victims of the Whitechapel murderer, the unknown man that the press are now calling 'Jack the Ripper'.

***

For reasons best known to themselves, the esteemed gentlemen behind the Metropolitan Police investigation considered Liz Stride to have died by the same hand as Polly Nichols and Annie Chapman. Dr Robert Anderson, as Assistant Chief Commissioner of the Met's Criminal Investigation Department, headed the Whitechapel enquiry and claimed later to have known the identity of the murderer whilst being somehow unable to put a collar on him. Most interestingly, in the light of our knowledge about our own contemporary Rippers, he would write in *Blackwood's Magazine*: "One did not need to be a Sherlock Holmes to discover that the criminal was a sexual maniac of a virulent type; that he was living in the immediate vicinity of the scenes of the murders . . ."

Inspector Fred Abberline – the emigrant from the West Country who, according to his superiors at Scotland Yard, knew the underworld of the East End better than any local plod – has gone down in history as a similarly shadowy figure to the Ripper himself. Not a single photograph of this crucial figure in the investigation is known to survive. Always explicitly linked with the case that he (and his colleagues) manifestly failed to solve, Abberline would later echo Anderson's belief that the police of the time knew who the Whitechapel murderer was, and would lend credence to several diametrically-opposed theories about his identity.

But the 'canonisation' of the five recognised victims would be ultimately sealed by a senior Met officer not even present in the force when the Whitechapel murders were occurring. Melville Macnaghten was a son of empire and the British Raj. In 1881, he had suffered a vicious assault by Indian rioters whilst overseeing his family's tea plantations in Bengal; it brought about his friendship with James Monro, then Inspector-General of the Bengal Police, who later sought Anderson's appointment to the Met CID in 1887. Initially rejected by the Home Office, Macnaghten would be instated as Assistant Chief Constable in June 1889, seven months after the last of the recognised Ripper murders.

But it is to Macnaghten's typed and handwritten notes – the 'Macnaghten memoranda' – that we owe the identification of the 'canonical five', including Liz Stride, the marginalisation of four other possible Ripper victims (including Martha Tabram), and the listing of three contemporary police suspects who would not become common knowledge for some years (and which we will duly cast a curious eye over). Their contentions would later be compounded – and to some degree contested – by the so-called 'Swanson marginalia', notes written in the margins of Robert Anderson's autobiography (*The Lighter Side of My Official Life*) by Chief Inspector Donald Swanson of the CID, who had been in overall day-to-day charge of the Whitechapel investigation.

So what are we to make of the inclusion of Long Liz Stride in this pitiful canon? Is the conventional wisdom that the Ripper was interrupted by Louis Diemschutz – and thus didn't subject her to the same post-mortem mutilations inflicted on his previous victims – unassailable? Given the local crimes that both preceded and followed the autumn of 1888, would it not be realistic to assume there was more than one offender committing crimes of violence against women in the vicinity?

"I would contend that this depends on your inclusion/exclusion of Liz Stride," answers investigative psychologist/ripperologist Jon Ogan. "There are a few aspects of the case that differ from the remainder of Macnaghten's five. So if she was not killed by JtR then two were responsible for this set of five or six murders, though I do think that there was only *one* JtR in a picqueristic/mutilative mode of killing."

We will come to the Ripper's possible motivation for the mutilations soon enough. But as for the lost Long Liz, it seems equally valid to assume she may have been the victim of a 'domestic'. The eruption of drunken violence was a given in the post-Hogarthian streets of the Victorian East End, and a witness seems to have seen Liz pushed to the ground by a drunken bully in Berner Street, immediately prior to her death. There is also a suggestion that she may have been murdered by the man she was cohabiting with at the time, Michael Kidney. (This is posited in A. P. Wolf's 1993 book, *Jack the Myth* – almost solely supported by the factual assertion that many more murdered women fall victim to partners than to strangers.)

But Liz Stride is included in the Ripper canon not so much because of her own sad fate, but because her death is seen as the prelude to a more forensically typical Ripper murder that took place that same night (or early in the morning). If it seems unlikely that a sexual mutilation and homicide should take place simultaneously, and in close geographical proximity, to a violent domestic killing – the latter using an apparently shorter, blunter blade than the six-to-eight-inch knife used on the other canonical victims – then perhaps we should consider later instances of coincidental murder.

The coincidence of extremely violent criminals at work in the same locale is illustrated by two infamous US cases from the 1970s. On 7 May 1972, two female co-ed students from the Fresno State College in Berkeley disappeared from the northern Californian city of Santa Cruz; their bodies would never be found intact, their dissected remains buried in the mountains overlooking the desert region. A young Asian girl hitchhiker suffered a similar fate on 14 September. On 13 October, an old vagrant was beaten to death with a baseball bat in the Santa Cruz mountains. On 2 November, a Catholic priest died by multiple stabbing in his church, in the local town of Los Gatos. On 8 January 1973, the dissected remains of another college girl were thrown in plastic sacks from the cliffs of the nearby town of Carmel. On 25 January, a Santa Cruz couple were repeatedly shot and stabbed to death at their home. That following evening, a mother and her two young sons sleeping in a nearby log cabin were similarly wiped out. On 6 February, four teenage boys camping in Santa Cruz State Park were massacred by gunshot. On 15 February, the decapitated, sexually-abused corpses of two girls – one Caucasian, one Asian – were discovered in a canyon in nearby Alameda. That same month, the skeletal remains of another college girl were found on a desert road outside downtown Santa Cruz; before the vultures got to her, she had been cut open and disembowelled.

It was a terrifying crime spree by any standards – or at least it would have been, if the local state police had identified this nine-month homicidal orgy as a connected series. But the 1970s saw America ascending to the peak of her formidably-high murder rate, afflicted by a pestilence of 'Rippers' – some of whom, it seems realistic to say, may remain unidentified to this day.

With hindsight, the numerous Santa Cruz murders of 1972-3 stand revealed as the deeds of two men quite unconnected with each other. In April 1973, necrophile Ed Kemper – a veritable giant of a man at six foot nine – would murder his hated mother and her friend, dismembering their bodies for his sexual gratification. When he gave himself up to a bemused Santa Cruz Police Department the following week, he began a series of confessions to the sexually sadistic May, September and January crimes listed above, plus the double murder of the two girls in February. These crimes' apparent similarity to the murder of the girl whose skeleton was found the same month was pure coincidence; she had fallen victim to Herb Mullin, a multiple murderer responsible for all the other diverse random killings listed over this period. Mullin, a paranoid schizophrenic whose condition was aggravated by bad LSD trips, was caught by pure chance and rationalised his many crimes as a series of sacrifices made to avert another San Francisco earthquake. But it's unlikely he had any real insight into his actions, and the entirely separate motivation for his and Kemper's crimes illustrate the nebulousness of the catch-all term 'serial killer'.

Closer to the scene of the Whitechapel murders, a number of interconnected London cases would prove a source of lasting controversy.

Timothy Evans, a professedly illiterate simpleton, handed himself in to the police for the murders of his young wife, Beryl, and their one-year-old daughter, Geraldine, in December 1949. At trial he retracted; his final defence was that the child murder was committed by his fellow tenant of Rillington Place, Notting Hill, one Reg Christie. Evans was convicted and hanged for the murder of baby Geraldine.

When Christie was wanted several years later for the necrophile murders of a number of young women, it threw the Evans case into sharp relief. Journalist and TV presenter Ludovic Kennedy later argued in his influential *10 Rillington Place* that Evans' committing either of the murders under the same roof as a multiple sex killer was too much of a coincidence – in fact, Christie confessed to the murder of Beryl Evans at his own trial, though not to that of Geraldine. And so Timothy Evans became the exemplar of the tragic miscarriages of justice which surely occurred when the British still practised capital punishment.

Kennedy was taking his lead from a 1955 work published in the wake of Christie's execution, entitled *The Man on Your Conscience* by Michael Eddowes; this in turn was countered by a contemporary work entitled *The Two Stranglers of Rillington Place* by Rupert Furneaux, which argued that, as a bully who knocked his wife around, Evans was certainly capable of violence against her. (His simplicity of mind has sometimes been used to exonerate his reputation – but since when was stupidity incompatible with violence?) Much later, in 1994, after Eddowes' death his son John published his own continuation of Furneaux's theme – *The Two Killers of Rillington Place*. His aim, he stated, was to refute his father's version of events because he knew him to be "mentally ill, a fantasist and liar". There seemed to be unresolved filial issues at work, but the younger Eddowes did at least succeed in throwing into question what had been the consensus view for many years.

It's possible that serial sex murder and domestic murder may have occurred at the same premises. When Evans changed his story to "Christie did it", he allegedly told fellow prisoner Donald Hume that Christie had strangled little Geraldine but that he was present during the deed; Evans apparently didn't want to be responsible for the child's welfare, after Beryl had supposedly died during an abortion performed by Christie. However, Hume – as a psychopath who later admitted to a murder-for-gain that he was acquitted of – is admittedly not the most reliable of sources.

It's been little remarked upon as to how Christie's murder rate clearly accelerated after the Evans deaths. After Tim Evans' execution, Christie would kill his wife and then embark on an intensifying, Ripper-like spree that led to his own destruction. It's possible that, as a necrophile, Christie had been excited by the violent deaths that occurred in his block of flats. It's also likely, however, that he *did* use the Evans' marital problems as a ruse to get his hands on Beryl – they were poor and she was pregnant, the same situation that led one of his final victims to him. Given that unspecified marks on Beryl's genitalia may suggest post-mortem rape, it seems most likely to this writer that she was the victim of a sex murderer – as at least the majority of the Whitechapel victims also appear to have been.

***

By the time a gaggle of onlookers and police gather around the prostrate body of Long Liz Stride, a much stranger scene has already begun to unfold less than a mile up the road, in Aldgate – adjoining Bishopsgate and the financial centre of the City of London. If the same man is continuing the bloody spree that began in Berner Street, then he is truly deserving of the title 'Spring-Heeled Jack'.

On this evening of 29 September, Katie has only been back in London this last couple of days. Returning from hop-picking in Kent, the destitute woman boasts to the superintendent of the casual ward at Shoe Lane, "I've come back to earn the reward offered for the apprehension of the Whitechapel murderer. I think I know him." The super tells her to mind how she goes, in case she too becomes a victim. "Oh, no fear of that," she tells him, all brazen.

Or at least that's the way it will play out in the press when Katie Eddowes – just another among the flotsam and jetsam of the London poor, sucked into the gravitational vortex of the East End – becomes a more significant figure in death than she ever was in life.

Out on the streets, in the hand-to-mouth existence lived daily by Katie and hundreds of others like her, her speech is not so correct and her behaviour even less so. By this morning of the 29th she has turned up at Cooney's common lodging house with her bloke, John Kelly, an Irishman sometimes working casually as a porter at Spitalfields market. She's not there long before they decide to pawn a pair of John's boots, to give 'em the wherewithal to get through another day. It buys 'em tea, sugar and a breakfast at Cooney's, but by two o'clock that afternoon all the money is gone – the rest of it poured down their necks by Katie and John, accustomed as they are to a daily drink to get 'em through life's woes.

We find Katie again at a half past eight that evening, pissed as a pudding and making a spectacle of herself in Aldgate High Street. When a rozzer comes to see what all the commotion is about, she's drunk out of her mind and doing a vocal impression of a fire cart. As she concludes her performance and lays down to sleep on the paving stones, Sir Robert Peel's finest rouses her from her slumber and runs her down to Bishopsgate nick.

It takes a while for Katie Eddowes to return to her normal senses. At a half past twelve she asks when she's to be let out; "When you're capable of taking care of yourself," retorts the peeler. Katie protests that she can do that now, but it's another half-hour before they let her go. "I shall get a damn fine hiding when I get home," she tells her benevolent captor, speaking of her latest dosshouse as 'home'. "And serve you right," he tells her. "You have no right to get drunk." In his quietly-assured righteousness the policeman reflects the morality of the day. When violence erupts out on the streets it's the business of either the Metropolitan or (in this case) the City Police. But if a man disciplines his wife by tanning her hide, it's no concern of the law.

"This way, missus," he tells the inebriate woman as he leads her back out onto the street. "Good night, old cock," she tells her uniformed guardian.

Such are the last recorded words of Catharine Eddowes. When the rozzer asks her name and address, she gives him the false identity of 'Mary Ann Kelly'. The name is a strange portent of the extreme fate she will share with another doomed woman.

Nothing more will be heard of Katie Eddowes until they find her ripped asunder. But several men will claim that they saw her a little after a half past one at the passage entrance to Mitre Square, between Houndsditch and Leadenhall Street. Chatting away, they see her happily accompanying a gentleman into the square whose chest she strokes with a boozy familiarity. As for him, he's a broad-shouldered bloke, a bit taller than average, with fair skin and a moustache; he's wearing a peaked cloth cap and has the look of a sailor about him. If they're never to clap eyes on him again it may be because he's returned to sea, where other desperate women are available for his use at every port.

What the witnesses imply is obvious, but after her personal tragedy unfolds there will be few with much bad to say about Katie; she may have drunk a bit but you rarely saw her roaring drunk – they say of the woman pulled in by the police well past the point of inebriation. Nor was she a whore, they say. Katie was just a woman down on her leather uppers and, if she'd fallen in her attempts to get through another day, then she was no more a prostitute than anyone who earns a pittance for a hard day's work.

When looked at like that then everyone becomes a prostitute, and Katie's sin is no greater whether committed once or a thousand times. Such will be the sentiment sustained by the crowds who line the streets of the East End to watch her horse-drawn glass hearse carry her to an unmarked grave at the City of London Cemetery, situated in the east London outskirts of Little Ilford (now Manor Park).

***

He's going to take what he's paid for now. Even though the transaction's only verbal, with no coins changing hands. A few minutes of quiet opportunity is all that's needed . . .

Her eyes pop wide open but there's no noise. Nothing. Just the feel of her old windpipe turning to mulch in his hand. It's only a few moments before she drops, but by then all his senses are aroused. The rage has been building within him and the excitement is about to overflow. Whether he's waited a half-hour for this or whether he's waited weeks, the result is the same – he can barely control the extremity of the attack which is now taking place.

Her throat is slashed, deeper, deeper, left to right, as he descends upon the supine doxy. Just the overture, just the prelude. Now, panting heavily, he will compose his symphony. He will create his masterpiece . . .

Some fools opine that the police should be using the new technology of photography to take a close-up picture of the women's eyes – there, they assuredly claim, lies the image of the Whitechapel murderer, the last living thing the unfortunate victims ever saw.

Well then, let them picture this! One sweep of the blade cuts through an eyelid, but it is only an opening to a grander event. She will be truly his. Skin. Scars. Flesh and blood. His canvas, his materials. All his. He cuts down through the bridge of the nose, working quickly through gristle and mucus. Her face is coming apart in his hands, he is carving down into her very being, but he needs to remain conscious of time.

There, inside the square, time is slowed down to a pace where every ecstatic moment drives his spirits upward into a frenzy of ecstasy. But his mind must remain aware that, outside the square, time passes more quickly and the prospect of intruders to his private ecstasy grows greater with every moment.

The blade passes down the face to the cheek, pulling away the tip of her nose entirely. He pushes behind her blood-matted hair and cuts at the lobe of her ear, his wish to destroy her entirely, to reduce her to mere scraps of scrag end, aggravated by the nagging sense of passing time.

He is going further now, exploring, appropriating, stealing. Down he cuts in a jagged line all the way from her white meat to the entrance to Cock Lane. Compelled to invade her inner space, her reaches through the despoiled old belly into the deeper reality of her organs. How easily it all comes away! Muscle. Cartilage. He rips at her and drags her insides out. The bloody, gaping hole is now a battered gateway, torn open by force.

Woman. Meat. Hole. All is his.

***

It's no later than a quarter to two when the peeler comes running to the warehouse man on Mitre Square. "For God's sake mate, come to assist me!" The rozzer is pale in the face, shaken. When the watchman asks the matter, he almost sobs, "Oh dear, here's another woman cut up to pieces!"

And so she is. Whoever this 'ripper' may be, he's gone further this time. Katie Eddowes lies viscerally exposed, to the eyes of the world and to the elements, in the southwest corner of the square. By the time the immediate neighbourhood is roused there's almost a familiarity and a sense of expectation in the air, tempered though it is by a sickening dread. In the regional press of the day, they will describe her injuries thus:

"The sight was a most shocking one. The woman's throat had been cut from the left side, the knife severing the main artery and other parts of the neck. Blood had flowed freely, both from the neck and body, on the pavement. Apparently, the weapon had been thrust into the upper part of the abdomen and drawn completely down, ripping open the body, and, in addition, both thighs had been cut across. The intestines had been torn away from the body, and some of them lodged in the wound on the right side of the neck."

So runs the report in the Southend Standard, *published in the furthest coastal point of Essex, the county that directly adjoins the East End. It is a time when the newspapers run no photographs and words alone must be sufficient to move the reader. But if the contemporary reports seem unsparing, worse is to follow in the privacy of the City Mortuary at Golden Lane.*

It is here that Katie is belatedly identified, having first been reduced to a list of wounds, clothing and meagre material possessions. The police report runs: "black cloth jacket, three large metal buttons down the front, brown bodice, dark green chintz dress, with Michaelmas daisies, golden lily pattern; three flounces, dark linsey skirt, thin white skirt, white chemise, brown ribbed stockings – feet mended with white material, a large white neckerchief round neck, pair of men's old lace-up boots, tattoo marks on right forearm, 'T.C.', the whole of the clothing being very old. She wore also a black straw bonnet, trimmed with black beads."

As with the other women, all Katie owned was all that she stood up in. Layers of frayed Victorian fashions clung to her wounded femininity, protecting her from the elements but offering no protection from the predator on the streets. Her tattoo – a surprisingly common feature among working-class Victorian women – comprised the initials of Thomas Conway, her ex-husband, their relationship ruptured by alcoholism and violence. It is only a pawnshop ticket for men's working boots – similar to those she was forced to wear herself – that leads Kelly, her man of the past seven years, to the mortuary to identify her. For the murderer has left little of her face, and so her features alone will not suffice.

***

The assumption that the same man had killed both Long Liz and Katie was fed by an ink-smudged postcard received by *The Star* on 30 September and printed the following evening:

I was not codding
dear old Boss when
I gave you the tip,
you ll hear about
saucy Jacky s work
tomorrow double
event this time
number one squealed
a bit couldnt
finish straight
off. had not time
to get ears for
police thanks for
keeping last letter
back till I got
to work again.
Jack the Ripper

Posted in the early hours of 30 September, the postcard's arrival in the first post led some to believe it came from the same hand as the 'Dear Boss' letter – which also promised to "clip the ladys ears off". The fact that Katie's left earlobe had fallen out of her clothes as she was carried to the morgue seemed like further proof. But the postcard was written in a discernibly less ornate style to the letter, while its publication in that evening's *Star* bred healthy suspicion among the police, given that 'Dear Boss' had finally been printed in that morning's *Daily News*. Suggestions of a circulation war involving bogus letters should perhaps be tempered by the writer's apparent knowledge that a previous letter had been suppressed – or perhaps compounded by how the news of a double murder, and the basic forensic details, would have been all over the East End by the time its residents rose to meet the pre-dawn working day.

But this sinister correspondence contained sufficient prescient detail for Scotland Yard to take a second look. The police took the fateful decision to publicise the letters; reproductions were pinned up in police stations and printed in the daily press. This is the moment that 'Jack the Ripper' was truly born. The decision proved a controversial one for the police, and a profitable one for the press. The immediate consequence was a torrent of 'Ripper letters' addressed to the police, the press and anybody else with a high-profile connection to the case.

"The newspapers, ever ready to take occasion by the hand and make the bounds of fooldom wider yet, have allowed Colney Hatch, Hanwell, and Earlswood [lunatic asylums] to empty the vials of idiocy upon the head of the general reader," wrote George R. Sims, one of a number of contemporary commentators who took a sceptical view of both the letters and the decision to publish them. "Every crackpot in the kingdom who has a whim, a fad, a monomania, a crotchet, or a bee in his bonnet is allowed to inflict it upon the public under the heading of 'The East-end Horrors'." Sims sardonically styled Jack the Ripper 'the hero of the hour'.

***

What the killer *had* definitely left behind this time, however, seems to be the only material clue he has bequeathed to history. Catharine Eddowes' murder had apparently been committed within the space of ten minutes, her cooling blood still warm when she was discovered. Just over an hour after the most extreme attack thus far, a torn piece of fabric from her bloodied apron was found in the doorway of a charity housing estate, Wentworth Model Dwellings, in nearby Goulston Street. Above it, on a brick wall, was a chalked graffito that the policemen who discovered it believed to have been written only recently: 'The Juwes are the men That Will not be Blamed for nothing.'

Or so it has passed into legend. In fact, the actual wording of the graffiti (apart from the misspelling of 'Jews') has been disputed ever since, as the Metropolitan Police had erased it from the wall by 5:30am that same morning, on the orders of the Commissioner, Sir Charles Warren. It seems an extraordinarily incompetent move to do so without photographing the evidence (as was requested in vain by the City Police), given that this might have been the killer's handiwork, seeking to deflect blame onto an already scapegoated ethnic group. Clumsy as the glaring accusation was, its awareness of a growing anti-Semitic mood and its ungrammatical use of a double negative (standard speech among some East Enders right up until the present day) may just have denoted that it was authentic.

"Neighbourhood watch committees put the blame on immigrants, on socialists, on anarchists, on anyone who didn't fit in," said Christopher Frayling in his centennial documentary, *Shadow of the Ripper*. "That autumn saw the closest thing to a pogrom in the East End before the rise of fascism. And ever since then many people have continued to believe that the Ripper must either have been a Jew or an outcast of some description. The events of 29 September seemed to reinforce these prejudices." Warren was concerned about fanning the flames of anti-Semitic violence when most of the Wentworth's tenants were Jews.

Not all of his police force shared his concerns, however. In 1910, Sir Robert Anderson (knighted as he was by then) would echo what had apparently been his contemporary thoughts about the killer's ethnicity, in his *Blackwood's* article: "the conclusion we came to was that he and his people were low-class Jews, for it is a remarkable fact that people of that class in the East End will not give up one of their number to Gentile Justice." Nothing in Anderson's suspicions has ever been substantiated.

As Frayling later acknowledged, "Sir Charles Warren's attempt to protect the Jewish community backfired, as the newspapers began to criticise him for hastily rubbing out what was thought to be a piece of material evidence. The *Pall Mall Gazette* pitched in by listing all the main theories, asking why he believed in any of them when Warren and the police failed to come up with hard fact."

Despite the theories of those like Dr Thomas Bond, who detected a sexual psychopathology in the Whitechapel murderer, many of the most popular theories seemed to comprise social prejudices. As curator Julia Hoffbrand elucidated at her *Jack the Ripper and the East End* lecture, "At the time it was very much groups of people within society that were suspected, so you got the obvious – you got lunatics, you got butchers, you got doctors, Jews very early on were suspected and scapegoated, [there was a] huge influx of Jewish immigrants from Eastern Europe fleeing persecution and restrictions in the previous chaotic years . . ."

In Frayling's documentary film, William Bordell, the former curator of Scotland Yard's Police Museum (the 'Black Museum'), was inclined to be more sympathetic toward the police investigation of the time: "There was no way of using the sort of skills we have today. No fingerprinting, no forensic science, and with the Ripper what did he leave behind? The bodies and very little else. You could say that if you handed down the clothing and had a look at that you might have found out something, but no knives were ever found, none of the weapons were found . . ."

It's also claimed that, by the time that the murders of Liz Stride and Katie Eddowes occurred on the same night, the Met had saturated the streets of Whitechapel and Spitalfields with officers, some uniformed, some plainclothes, some even, it's alleged, in drag. It's a tragic irony then that the murder of Katie should take place up the road in Aldgate, which was under City Police jurisdiction.

"If you go back to the Ripper case," opines investigative psychologist Jon Ogan, "the police worked incredibly hard and it's very unfair to say they were failures. A lot of times these offenders are caught by chance. With the Yorkshire Ripper, whizzing forward in the timeline, obviously the police had some inkling that he was involved in some way, due to the number of times he was interviewed, but sadly couldn't put that together. I wouldn't be surprised if your Jack the Ripper was interviewed in a similar way. Maybe just because he knew somebody or lived near or something like that, maybe there was no direct evidence. I wouldn't be surprised if he was interviewed more than once, though obviously we don't have the police records now."

But the Ripper – as he was becoming more commonly known to readers of the popular press – was also about to deliver an item of forensic evidence that has been controversially disputed ever since. It's hardly an exaggeration to say that its authenticity (or otherwise) may be the ultimate criterion for adjudging whether the media entity known as 'Jack the Ripper' ever truly existed.

***

"The peritoneal lining was cut through on the left side and the left kidney carefully taken out and removed. The left renal artery was cut through. I should say that someone who knew the position of the kidney must have done it.

"The lining membrane over the uterus was cut through. The womb was cut through horizontally, leaving a stump of three quarters of an inch. The rest of the womb had been taken away with some of the ligaments . . .

"I believe the perpetrator of the act must have had considerable knowledge of the positions of the organs in the abdominal cavity and the way of removing them. The parts removed would be of no use for any professional purpose. It required a great deal of medical knowledge to have removed the kidney and to know where it was placed. Such a knowledge might be possessed by some one in the habit of cutting up animals."

So runs City Police surgeon Dr Frederick Gordon Brown's post-mortem report on Catharine Eddowes (as quoted in Begg, Fido and Skinner's comprehensive reference work, *The Jack the Ripper A-Z*). Brown immediately put himself at odds with the views of medical experts who had examined the earlier victims, and with one Dr George Sequeira, who sat in on the post-mortem but believed the killer had extracted the uterus and kidney almost accidentally, as a result of his frenzied butchery.

The fact remains that these vital organs were taken from the scene by the killer. The tendency of such an offender to relive his crimes, by the taking of trophies and by mnemonics which evoke strong memories, was largely unknown to the Victorians. However, if the killer had also taken Annie Chapman's missing rings – or possibly even extracted both hers and Polly Nichols' front teeth – then it was unlikely to have been a petty act of theft. Like the effete hero of French litterateur Marcel Proust's *In Search of Lost Time*, who suddenly relives the substance of childhood when he tastes a madeleine cake dipped in tea, some sexual murderers are known to recreate their most intense emotions via the use of *aides memoire*. But their 'trophies' evoke memories of an altogether less ethereal nature.

Small items of clothing; snippets of hair; photographs of the victim; perhaps even body parts; all have gone missing from serial murders in the decades since the Ripper crimes. Perhaps the epitome of this syndrome is John Crutchley – an offender not apprehended for murder, but convicted of rape (aggravated by a vampiric blood-drinking ritual) in Florida in the 1980s. According to former FBI profiler Robert Ressler, Crutchley was deserving of a particularly long sentence due to his status as a potential serial killer (the coining of that now-familiar term attributed to Ressler). As dubious as it is to sentence an offender on the basis of what he *might have* done, there seems to be little other explanation for the collection of stolen women's credit cards and female fashion accessories that Crutchley had stored in his home. Perhaps most ominously, he had videotaped the rape of his victim and the draining of her blood, intending to experience the emotional high of replaying his crime again and again.

Crutchley's tape is redolent of the idea of the 'snuff movie', a filmed or videotaped atrocity that so far remains in the realm of urban myth. However, whilst the idea of an underground market for snuff movies is unrealistic (the logistics of risk against likely profits making the idea untenable even to the most depraved criminal), there is no doubt that some sexual murderers have tried to preserve their transgressions forever via consumer technology.

In early 1950s California, convicted rapist and amateur photographer Harvey Glatman abducted, raped and strangled three young women, after forcing them to pose in bondage for photographs; their murders were probably only pragmatic acts to evade capture, but the photos resembled the 'cheesecake' covers of vintage true detective magazines. In 1960s England, Ian Brady would record the ordeal of his and Myra Hindley's child victim, Lesley Ann Downey, on a reel-to-reel tape recorder; his complete emotional detachment became apparent when, at the 'Moors Murderers' 1966 trial at Chester Assizes, the prosecution forced the begrudging admission from him that the traumatising tape was 'unusual'. In 1998-9, one of the authors attended the opening and closing of the trial of Charles Ng, a Hong Kong Chinese, in California; the chief plank of evidence against Ng was the infamous 'M Ladies' video, which showed two female victims in their late teens terrorised by Leonard Lake (who had since committed suicide) and Ng. The tape had been suppressed for years, and rumours of a snuff video were ultimately confounded – though thus far it comes closest to such an obscene legendary artefact.

Some criminal historians have linked the mindset of such offenders with the letter that was sent to George Lusk, the builder who had been elected head of the Whitechapel Vigilance Committee in the wake of the murder of Annie Chapman, on 16 October 1888:

> *From hell*
>
> *Mr Lusk*
> *Sor*
> *I send you half the Kidne I took from one women prasarved it for you tother piece I fried and ate it was very nise I may send you the bloody knif that took it out if you only wate a whil longer*
>
> > *signed*
> > *Catch me when*
> > *you can*
> > *Mishter Lusk.*

Whether or not the letter's various illiteracies are genuine or camouflage, the package did deliver on the spidery, right-leaning scrawl's promise. Accompanying it in a cardboard box was half a kidney, preserved in spirits of wine. Lusk at first took it as a macabre prank, but when he presented it as evidence it immediately excited controversy. The curator of the Pathology Museum at London Hospital in Whitechapel announced that it was the 'ginny' kidney of a middle-aged woman suffering from Bright's disease, which had been excised from the body within the previous three weeks. The pathologist of the City of London countered this, stating that a person's age and gender could not be determined from their kidney alone, that gin left no traces in the kidney and that the organ's surviving twin, as viewed in the autopsy on Catharine Eddowes, was perfectly healthy. This is in turn may be refuted by part of Dr Brown's post-mortem notes, which some commentators claim suggests evidence of Bright's disease.

As with so much about the case, the question remains open. But could this have been an instance of the Ripper remembering his crimes with gruesome relish, his powers of recall stimulated by the imagined shock of the letter's recipient?

"In any sense authentic?" Jon Ogan ponders the authors' question. "No. When the Lusk letter was first received, the press were convinced it was from Jack the Ripper, the police were convinced it was from Jack the Ripper. Then, as the investigation into the kidney and the letter progressed, they seemed less and less sure until the endpoint where they seemed to suggest it was just a hoax. A lot of people miss that out. I remember reading up on it years ago in *The Ripperologist*, in a piece called [in Holmesian style] 'The Adventure of the Spurious Kidney'. Obviously we don't have it left to know where it was from. There was this thing about the Bright's disease, if it was a diseased kidney. That's the kind of sample specimen that medical students might have been playing around with. She may have been a hard drinker, because commercial sex workers in those days were hard drinkers, now it's just different kinds of drug and substance abuse.

"If the Lusk letter was genuine it would narrow down the suspects in some way: because if it was a guy who knew that this bloody object was a kidney, that would have been some kind of technical competence on the defendant's behalf. I wish I could convince myself it was genuine. But if it's a hoax then it's obviously not worth worrying too much about the psychology of the offender, because it isn't by him. If it *was* him, then you'd probably want to look at the parallels with the Zodiac Killer. It's quite strange and rather ironic, as quite possibly the Lusk letter was faked and I think the 'Dear Boss' letter was faked, but that sort of writing has stimulated the Yorkshire Ripper tape – which was a fake – and the Zodiac Killer to do the same kind of thing. [See Chapter Three.] The FBI go into this in great detail because they look at the psychodynamics of the offender, which is rather old-fashioned. I'm not really into this kind of stuff, because it's not rooted in any kind of empirical work – but the FBI guy would say it would be somebody really 'low-powered' who is using these crimes to help his self-esteem. But there again it's all predicated on one fact: is it real? It probably isn't. And the other thing about the Lusk letter is the aspect of cannibalism."

Cannibalism is not a recognised disorder in *DSM* [*Diagnostic and Statistical Manual of Mental Disorders*] *IV*, the professional bible of the western psychiatric industry. However, 'anthropophagy', as it was termed by Krafft-Ebing, is described in his 1896 *Psychopathia Sexualis* as one of the most extreme manifestations of sadism. In more recent years, it was described by a US forensic psychologist to one of the authors as the ultimate sexual transgression, exceeding that of necrophilia – the desire to absorb the flesh or organs of the object of desire surpassing even the great taboo of raping his or her corpse. If the Lusk letter *can be* assumed to be possibly authentic, then it seems the Ripper quickly descended to the most extreme realms of transgression occupied by those we now recognise as serial sex murderers.

"Unlike other forms of crime, serial killing seems to have an exactly identifiable point of origin in the Whitechapel murders," noted Alexandra Warwick at her Museum of London lecture. "Most studies simply assume that Jack the Ripper represents the first example of this particular criminal type; despite the fact that he is certainly not the first person to carry out a series of murders of strangers for no material or personal profit, he has been called 'the benchmark by which all sex killers are judged', who 'stands at the gateway of the modern age'. These comments are typical. The Whitechapel murders are seen to usher in what has been called [by Colin Wilson] the Age of Sex Crime, and they are identified as being both an effect of, and a response to, modernity."

But how accurate is such a hypothesis? We have already noted how there are very few records of sex murder prior to the Ripper, with the notable exception of the Fanny Adams case only two decades prior. However, crime historians in general – and Wilson himself in particular, in apparent contradiction of his own theory – have worked their way back into dusty written archives to dig up certain key cases that would be regarded in a very different light today.

Towards the end of the first decade of the 19th century, Andrew Bichel was beheaded for the murder of two young women in Bavaria. Described in the late Victorian publication *Mysteries of Police and Crime* as a married man and father, "esteemed for his piety", his motives seemed a mystery at the time. In 1807, he ensnared his first victim by posing as a fortune teller; pouncing on her as she stared into a supposedly magical looking glass, he bound her before stabbing her through the throat. After a second girl met a similar fate in the following year, a police dog eventually led the local constabulary to Bichel's barn, where the skeletal remains of his victims were found buried, bisected in two. Both girls' clothes had already been found intact in Bichel's home. The only rationale he could offer was that he had robbed the girls of their clothes to supplement his family's meagre income – it seems unlikely at best, particularly as the clothing remained intact, though it was accepted at the time. With hindsight, it seems more likely he was a sex murderer who'd taken trophies in order to relive the emotional heights of his crimes.

In Paris in 1872, a string of five prostitute killings apparently prefigured the Whitechapel murders by 16 years. According to later newspaper reports, a Ukrainian named Nicolai Wassili (also spelled Nicolas Vassili) was found to be responsible, and was sent to a lunatic asylum rather than being guillotined – unusual in itself for the time. Wassili was said to be a member of an extreme sub-sect of the Skoptsky religious cult, whose aversion to worldly sexuality led its male adherents to practise castration of their own genitals. If these largely legendary reports are in any way accurate, then he may be an extremely rare instance of a 'harlot killer', actually motivated by puritanical morality rather than his own twisted sexuality.

Wassili was supposedly released from the asylum in January 1888, and his movements remain unaccounted for from this point. At the height of the Whitechapel murders he would be named by the French press as a potential suspect, but this is speculation based on hearsay that he intended to travel to London. It should be noted that the five prostitute murders attributed to him involved stabbing the unfortunate victims in the back, without any further mutilation. It should also perhaps be taken into account that no definitive records of the time substantiate Wassili's existence, and all that is known about him comes from the press reports. As surgeon and criminological researcher N. P. Warren has pointed out, the character of 'the Avenger' in Marie Belloc-Lowndes' novel *The Lodger* is just as likely to be inspired by the Wassili legend as it by the Ripper – for whom the archetype of avenging religious fanatic is just one of many prospective motives projected onto the blank screen of his identity.

Returning to the subject of the newly identifiable serial killer, Alexandra Warwick notes, "there are basic contradictions in these views; because as much as Jack the Ripper is seen as extraordinary, he is also regarded as in some way expected. On the one hand he is seen, by 19th-century commentators and contemporary ones alike, as the inevitable product of urban anonymity, a figure of the brutalised working-class mass, and as the technologised killing machine that is the logical outcome of industrialisation."

It's undeniably true that the Ripper has served as a historical signifier, a fork in the road whereby those professionals or laypersons with sufficient interest became gradually better able to identify the crime of serial sex murder. But the claim that this somehow originated with the urban alienation that followed the Industrial Revolution seems increasingly dubious. In 1897, not quite a full decade since the Whitechapel murders, an ex-soldier named Joseph Vacher was arrested in rural France for a thwarted attack on a young peasant woman. Eventually charged with the local murder of a shepherd boy, he was believed responsible for up to 14 sex murders of young people of both genders.

By the time Vacher was guillotined that following December, he had earned the soubriquet 'the Ripper of the Southeast'. The classic polymorphous pervert, it's ironic that his story has faded into obscurity whilst his apparently less prolific London counterpart continues to capture the imagination via his very anonymity. Vacher's young victims were mutilated, disembowelled and raped after death. Some had been visibly bitten by the brain-damaged ex-soldier. Contrary to the post-industrialism thesis, all the murders took place in agricultural and farmland settings.

In this, at least, Vacher was part of a grim tradition; for France had a history of rural sex murderers who had been tried over the preceding several centuries as 'werewolves'. (One of the last, Jacques Garnier, had been adjudged insane and granted asylum by monks – a remarkably tolerant judgement for its time.) This was also the case in other European countries, particularly Germany, where such men were claimed to be 'hairy on the inside' – in other words, they effected no external physical transformation.

After the Enlightenment, the word 'werewolf' disappears from all church and court logs of the time. But it seems that it was once used as a folkloric label to describe men tried for bestial crimes – men who would now be termed 'serial killers'. By the time of the Whitechapel murders and Vacher's crimes, there was no longer any recognisable cultural term for such transgressors.

"The incipient bases of psychology and psychiatry were around in the time of the Ripper," confirms Jon Ogan in his response to the authors, "if the murders were committed two or three hundred years earlier, I think he'd have been down as a werewolf or there would have been some other animalistic interpretation to his behaviour, rather than as the sexual picquerist that we'd call him now. In terms of the rubric of the time, how you'd construct someone's personality, with no psychology and no psychiatry you'd use 'werewolf'."

To paraphrase Dickens' description of the poor, it seems that we have always had – and always will have – the Rippers among us.

VI

Victorian Values

In late 1980 an unwelcome example of what some might have called 'Victorian values' hit the headlines, with the final murder by the Bradford trucker Peter Sutcliffe. The similarities between Sutcliffe's crimes and those of Jack the Ripper – he targeted prostitutes, mutilating the bodies of his victims – had led the press to dub him the 'Yorkshire Ripper'. The Ripper analogy was a salient reminder that the Victorian era may not have been the moral golden age that the era's leading British politician suggested.

In 1983, Prime Minister Margaret Thatcher would spearhead her second successful election campaign with the call for a return to what she described as 'Victorian values'. Whilst the slogan was initially chiefly a reference to economic virtues which she associated with the era – self-reliance and hard work – it soon also came to embrace the conservative moral values Thatcher advocated. Among the most ardent crusaders in the cause was opinionated Christian housewife Mary Whitehouse, who'd been campaigning against what she saw as moral degeneracy in the media since 1963, forming her National Viewers' and Listeners' Association two years later. In the early years, Whitehouse was largely ignored by figures in authority, who considered her an eccentric irritant or a figure of fun, but Prime Minister Thatcher took her views very seriously. (In 1980, Mrs Whitehouse had been awarded the CBE.)

In 2006, the Conservative shadow attorney-general, Dominic Grieve, attempted to reignite the crusade for Victorian values, inspiring the author Lee Jackson – who specialises in crime novels set in the era – to pen a piece for the BBC News website entitled 'What Were Real Victorian Values?': "One need only read the full life histories of Jack the Ripper's victims – that's the real story of the Victorian East End," he observes. "It's not a uniform history of shared moral values and responsible parenting."

Mrs Whitehouse was a prominent supporter of the Bright Bill, aka the 'Video Nasties Act' of 1984, which banned dozens of cheap horror movies on videocassette, making their possession or sale tantamount to possessing or selling drugs. The same reactionary newspapers that supported Thatcher had been running lurid scare stories about the sex crimes and violence supposedly inspired by such films, under banner headlines like 'How High Street Horror Is Invading the Home'. The hysteria was fed by the fact that VCRs were a new addition to most living rooms. The new technology had caught the UK government unprepared, and no certification system was in place, meaning anybody could theoretically rent any film regardless of age and the film's content.

Some kept their heads amidst the hysteria. "To blame books and films for your crimes is a frequently heard mitigation in court," wrote barrister and popular author John Mortimer QC in 1983. "It may be that the roots of criminality lie far deeper and the possibility exists that neither Jack the Ripper nor Heinrich Himmler had ever seen a video nasty." Conversely, 'The Scandal of the X-Cert Rippers' was penned as a 'special report' by journalist Liz Gill in the *Daily Express*. "The idea," she wrote of early 1980s thrillers such as *The Shining* and *Dressed to Kill*, "is to make women afraid and vulnerable." As if hoping to achieve the same effect herself, alongside stills from these films the piece publishes photographs of authentic victims of violence, including 20-year-old student Jacqueline Hill, the final victim of the Yorkshire Ripper. "Could their killers have been aroused by horror films?" asks Gill.

Feminism isn't generally associated with a rightwing newspaper like the *Express*, but the reactionaries were singing from much the same hymn sheet as radical feminists on this topic. Peter Sutcliffe's reign of terror, particularly the murder of Hill, had inspired a wave of activism among self-styled revolutionary feminists, and groups like the Angry Women began 'Reclaim the Night' marches designed to make the streets safe for women and – more controversially – institute a nocturnal curfew for men. They targeted video libraries and sex shops, vandalising buildings and staging sit-ins in an attempt to close down businesses they saw as promoting violence against women. One TV documentary also propagated the radical feminist thesis of a very direct connection between Sutcliffe's crimes and 'video nasties', whereas for the most part VCRs had appeared on the UK domestic scene in the early 1980s, in the months and years following Sutcliffe's last murder. (There has never been any serious suggestion that the killer possessed one himself.)

The idea that entertainment could be blamed for inspiring crime was nothing new. Despite Margaret Thatcher's rosy-tinted view of the era, a mere 100 years earlier there were violent offences to be accounted for and the media wasn't slow to point a finger of blame at the more disreputable diversions of the day. The Ripper murders of 1888 inspired *Punch* magazine to blame the Victorian equivalent of video nasties – sensationalist stage plays and the music-hall theatre – in very similar terms: "Is it not within the bounds of probability that to the highly-coloured pictorial advertisements to be seen on almost all the hoardings in London, vividly representing sensational scenes of murder, exhibited as 'the great attractions' of certain dramas, the public may be to a certain extent indebted for the horrible crimes in Whitechapel? We say it most seriously; – imagine the effect of these gigantic pictures of violence and assassination by knife and pistol on the morbid imagination of unbalanced minds. These hideous picture-posters are a blot on our civilisation, and a disgrace to the Drama."

To be fair to *Punch*, it also drew attention to deprivation and poverty as possible contributory factors towards crime in 1888 (something Thatcher's supporters in the press were at pains to avoid), and, as we shall see, it was far from alone in implicating popular entertainment in the Whitechapel atrocities. In 1856, the newspapers had been dominated by the case of William Palmer, a doctor accused of poisoning numerous acquaintances and relatives in order to facilitate his extravagant lifestyle of womanising and gambling. Some 30,000 people came to see him hang on 14 June of that year (Palmer is reputed to have eyed the gallows nervously, asking his executioner, "Are you sure it's safe?")

The Lord Chief Justice presiding over the trial had been John Campbell, also an active politician, and in 1857 he took an active part in a House of Lords debate over new legislation designed to regulate the sale of poisons, inspired by the Palmer case. "I am happy to say that I believe the administration of poison by design has received a check," Lord Campbell told the House. "But, from a trial which took place before me on Saturday, I have learnt with horror and alarm that a sale of poison more deadly than prussic acid, strychnine or arsenic – the sale of obscene publications and indecent books – is openly going on."

One suspects that Dr Palmer's victims would much rather have been subjected to smut than strychnine, but the Lord Chief Justice had made his point. The motive for his sensationalist comments was the launch of the first ever Obscene Publications Bill to be put before a British Parliament, co-ordinating the previously piecemeal prosecution of sexually-stimulating material into a coherent policy.

Lord Campbell had allies in his quest. The Society for the Suppression of Vice was the National Viewers' and Listeners' Association of its day. "This society, instituted in 1802, has laboured unremittingly to check the spread of open vice and immorality, and more especially to preserve the minds of the young from contamination by exposure to the corrupting influence of impure and licentious books, prints, and other publications, its difficulties have been greatly increased by the application of photography, multiplying, at an insignificant cost, filthy representations from living models, and the improvement in the postal service has further introduced facilities for secret trading which were previously unknown," ran a breathless 1872 article in *Leisure Hour* magazine.

The same article trumpeted some of the Society's successes: "This society has been the means of suppressing the circulation of several low and vicious periodicals. Within the last two years it has also been the means of bringing to punishment, by imprisonment, hard labour, and fines, upwards of forty of the most notorious dealers, and within a few years has seized and destroyed the following enormous mass of corrupting matters: – 140,213 obscene prints, pictures, and photographs; 21,772 books and pamphlets; five tons of letterpress in sheets, besides large quantities of infidel and blasphemous publications; 17,060 sheets of obscene songs, catalogues, circulars, and handbills; 5,712 cards, snuff-boxes and vile articles; 844 engraved copper and steel plates; 480 lithographic stones; 146 wood blocks; eleven printing presses, with type and apparatus; 81 cwt. of type, including the stereotype of several works of the vilest description."

It's an impressive haul that tells two divergent stories about Victorian values. On the one hand it testifies to the vigour and tenacity with which some Victorians lived up to their image as puritans. But it also tells us that there was this much material to seize – presumably only a fraction of the amount actually in circulation – and that people were willing to risk the hefty penalties orchestrated by Lord Campbell in order to trade in it, suggesting a thriving market in erotica and pornography. The Society for the Suppression of Vice primarily used sting operations, where agents would approach appropriate establishments posing as customers looking for something "a little spicy", then initiate a prosecution after securing a suspect publication. Like the National Viewers' and Listeners' Association, the Society was far from universally popular and, if identified, its agents risked attack from unsympathetic passers-by. In 1888, a correspondent who signed off as 'Justice' suggested to *The Star* that the perpetrator of the Whitechapel atrocities was a member of such a society, presumably taking the suppression of vice to the next level by butchering prostitutes.

At the other end of the spectrum, some inevitably blamed the pernicious influence of pornography for the Ripper murders. One of the contemporary suspects for the crimes was an eccentric American quack doctor and conman named Francis Tumblety; some commentators of the day noted ominously how the teenaged Tumblety began his career selling erotic reading matter to barge passengers in Rochester, New York. "The books he sold were largely of the kind Anthony Comstock suppresses now," recalled Captain W.C. Streeter, who owned one of the boats Tumblety used to trade on, speaking to the *Rochester Democrat and Republican* in December of 1888. (Comstock was 19th-century America's answer to Mary Whitehouse, who boasted of being responsible for 4,000 arrests and 15 suicides in his crusade to eradicate smut Stateside.) It was Captain Streeter's considered opinion that Tumblety's "mind had been affected by those books he sold, and I am not at all surprised to hear his name mentioned in connection with the Whitechapel murders" – a sentiment that would doubtless be applauded by both the National Viewers' and Listeners' Association and the Angry Women.

Those modern crusaders who wished to draw a connection between pornography and crime were delivered a star witness in the shape of rapist and necrophile Ted Bundy, whose brutal 1974-8 campaign of murder across the US left at least 29 young women dead. After his apprehension, conviction, and incarceration awaiting execution, Bundy became the subject of intensive study by psychologists and criminologists, as the media began to treat serial murder as a burgeoning epidemic. There were some parallels between his crimes and those of the Whitechapel murderer – and indeed the Yorkshire Ripper – specifically post-mortem mutilation of an apparently sexual nature, focusing on the genitalia. So what had turned this articulate, intelligent, charming young all-American into the most notorious psychosexual monster of his generation, in his own words, "the most cold-hearted son of a bitch you'll ever meet"?

Robert Ressler, the FBI agent responsible for coining the term 'serial killer', began a project to interview such offenders in the late-70s as part of his work with the Behavioural Sciences Unit. According to Ressler, interviewing Bundy was an exercise in futility and, after a preliminary session, he "realised that Bundy would never talk, that he would attempt to con people (as he had done so successfully) until executed, and I went home." Others continued to visit the killer behind bars right up until his execution date in 1989, in the hope of gleaning some insight into his crimes – or at least a definitive final tally of his victims and the location of any undiscovered bodies.

At the last minute Bundy arranged to see a dozen or so police officers, claiming he was ready to unburden himself and reveal all; it soon became apparent this was just a ploy to get his execution deferred. The ruse failed, and on 24 January Ted Bundy died in the electric chair. The identity of his last interviewer – who spoke to Bundy on camera the day before his execution – surprised many. Dr James Dobson was a psychologist best known as the founder of Focus on the Family, an Evangelical Christian organisation that took up where Anthony Comstock left off. Was this some desperate last-ditch attempt by the killer for clemency, or a cynical scheme to attain entry to heaven by the backdoor? Dobson was in little doubt that Bundy, after a career of evil, was finally doing God's work.

"As a young boy of twelve or thirteen, I encountered, outside the home, in the local grocery and drug stores, soft-core pornography," the condemned prisoner told his benevolent inquisitor. "Young boys explore the sideways and byways of their neighbourhoods, and in our neighbourhood, people would dump the garbage. From time to time, we would come across books of a harder nature – more graphic . . . I wasn't some guy hanging out in bars, or a bum," he added. "I wasn't a pervert in the sense that people look at somebody and say, 'I know there's something wrong with him.' I was a normal person. I had good friends. I led a normal life, except for this one, small but very potent and destructive segment that I kept very secret and close to myself. Those of us who have been so influenced by violence in the media, particularly pornographic violence, are not some kind of inherent monsters. We are your sons and husbands. We grew up in regular families. Pornography can reach in and snatch a kid out of any house today. It snatched me out of my home twenty or thirty years ago."

According to Michael Newton in his book *Serial Slaughter*, an FBI study established that 81 per cent of sex killers were stimulated by pornography, which they'd first encountered in childhood, "but a cautionary note is necessary here. The anti-pornography crusade got a shot in the arm from Ted Bundy's eleventh-hour confessions in February [sic] 1989 – and crusader James Dobson reportedly banked $1 million hawking videotapes of the Bundy sermonette – but there are risks involved with taking such statements at face value. Bundy biographer Ann Rule describes the Dobson tape as 'another Ted Bundy manipulation of our minds. The effect of the tape is to place, once again, the onus of his crimes – not on *himself* – but on us.' It is also worth noting that Bundy's definition of 'soft-core pornography' included pulp detective magazines, replete with crime photos and staged 'jeopardy' scenes which also fuelled the masturbatory fantasies of killers Eddie Cole and John Joubert. It comes as no surprise that rape-slayers enjoy pornography, but that enjoyment does not brand any one given magazine or film as a 'cause' of violent crime. Strangler Earle Nelson apparently limited his reading matter to the Holy Bible, and Heinrich Pommerenke killed his first victim after a viewing of *The Ten Commandments* convinced him women were the root of all evil."

Among the objectionable material that Dr Dobson's group, Focus on the Family, campaigned against was the depiction or discussion of nudity (even nude statues), disobedience, tight clothing, alcohol consumption, masturbation, bad language, oral sex and a whole host of other aspects most us might consider comparatively everyday, or at least largely innocuous. (They also railed against the cartoon *Spongebob Squarepants*, which they believed to be promoting homosexuality.) Dr Dobson's outfit fits firmly into the stereotype of what we mean by 'Victorian values'. Of course, it is a stereotype and, just as Focus on the Family represents just one extreme modern viewpoint, treating the attitudes and behaviour of Queen Victoria's subject between 1837-1901 as a single, uniform entity neglects numerous shifts in British society during that 64-year span.

Just as in any era, attitudes fluctuated as the pendulum of public opinion swung one way and the other across the moral landscape. Lord Campbell's Obscene Publications Act of 1857 may suggest an atmosphere of sexual conservatism that reflects the tone of the buttoned-up 1950s, but, just as the 1960s saw a youth rebellion fuelled by sex, drugs and rock 'n' roll, some see a similar mood in the 1860s, when elements of the younger generation were inspired by the scandalous verse of Algernon Charles Swinburne, a poet who revelled in his reputation as a degenerate. Attitudes varied according to class, geography and personal proclivity. Everybody's experience and perspective was as different then as it is now. Nineteenth-century England, Victorian London, 1888 Whitechapel all had their prudes and perverts, their sexual predators and prey, too diverse to defy easy categorisation. But a survey of the most extreme and interesting examples is essential to set the scene, painting the backdrop to the Ripper murders.

According to prolific cult author and popular criminologist Colin Wilson, the murders represent a key moment in the swing of the moral pendulum. In his mammoth 1984 *A Criminal History of Mankind*, Wilson's central thesis is that there are different eras of crime, analogous to the 'hierarchy of needs' theory espoused by the psychologist Abraham Maslow in the mid-20th century. Put crudely, we are motivated by different desires that escalate as each is satisfied; the most basic is for survival; after that security, then communal belonging and affection, followed by esteem and ultimately self-expression. According to Wilson, the history of crime follows a similar pattern; the majority of pre-modern crimes were committed out of sheer desperation; by the early 1800s, murders were being committed to protect respectability (the activities of Dr Palmer might fit into this category). For Wilson, the Ripper murders represent a milestone in the transition from the criminal urge for self-respect and the deviant acts of violent self-expression that characterise modern serial murder.

He flags the Whitechapel killings as a distinctively "new type of crime": "The Jack the Ripper murders of 1888 were among the first of this type, and it is significant that the killer's contemporaries did not recognise them as sex crimes; they argued that the Ripper was 'morally insane', as if his actions could only be explained by a combination of madness and wickedness." It can be argued that, if murdering and mutilating unfortunate women isn't 'wicked', then what is? More pertinently perhaps, the desperate of the modern world may still be forced to extreme measures in the pursuit of survival – just as the most notorious of Ancient Rome's emperors were indulging in bizarre homicidal whims some 2,000 years ago, where the only sane motive might be described as perverse self-expression. In print, the 'hierarchy of needs' makes perfect sense; in reality, it's all a little too pat.

When Dr Thomas Bond made his assertion that the killer "must in my opinion be a man subject to periodical attacks of Homicidal and erotic mania . . . in a condition sexually, that may be called satyriasis," the authorities of the day may not have had any more idea than we do what to do about people with such grotesquely-twisted libidos. But there seems to have been little doubt that the Ripper crimes had horrific sexual undertones. Contrary to the popular clichés cherished by Mary Whitehouse, the Victorians most certainly did talk and think about sex as much as we do today – though in different ways. The French philosopher and historian Michel Foucault suggests, in *The Will to Knowledge* (1976), that, rather than repressing sexual knowledge, the Victorians were transforming it from the realms of religious morality presided over by black-clad priests into the white-coated realms of the physician and scientist.

Dr Bond may have had access to a burgeoning new genre of scientific literature on sexual deviance; in particular, he may have referred to *Psychopathia Sexualis* by the Austro-German doctor Richard von Krafft-Ebing, one of a growing number of academics subjecting the sex urge to scientific scrutiny. Whilst the use of Latin to detail the more sensationalist passages was employed to deliberately discourage the lay reader, the fact that the book went through numerous editions suggests it was reaching an audience beyond its intended readership of lawyers and scientists. The later editions also included a reference to the Ripper crimes. "He does not seem to have had sexual intercourse with his victims, but very likely the murderous act and subsequent mutilation of the corpse were equivalents for the sexual act," concludes Krafft-Ebing.

Corresponding to Wilson's theory, Krafft-Ebing refers to the work of a number of his European colleagues, noting a worrying statistical rise in sex crime beginning in the 1840s. "The moralist sees in these sad facts nothing but the decay of general morality, and in some instances comes to the conclusion that the present mildness of the laws punishing sexual crimes, in comparison with their severity in past centuries, is in part responsible for this," he comments in *Psychopathia Sexualis*. "The medical investigator is driven to the conclusion that this manifestation of modern social life stands in relation to the predominating nervous condition of later generations, in that it begets defective individuals, excites the sexual instinct, leads to sexual abuse, and, with continuance of lasciviousness associated with diminished sexual power, induces perverse sexual acts."

From analysing the atrocities in Whitechapel in the autumn of 1888, the medical profession soon found itself the subject of scrutiny as a likely breeding ground for the perpetrator. "O have you seen the devle with his mikerscope and scalpul a-lookin at a kidney with a slide cocked up," ran the postscript to a letter written to the doctor who examined the piece of kidney mailed to George Lusk, president of the Whitechapel Vigilance Committee. The letter may have been a hoax – as it's likely that all of the Ripper letters were – but the sentiment is wholly authentic. In taking a central role in matters of life and death – sex and surgery – doctors were increasingly becoming mythic figures of the 19th century, carrying a strange frisson of dread in an age when effective anaesthetics were in their infancy and there were frighteningly high mortality rates on the operating table.

"The image of the doctor as someone capable of intense cruelty and immorality was certainly available in popular novels in nineteenth-century literature. So when the Ripper story came along there was a readily available image," according to Dr Maryanne Hailstone, an academic who has studied contemporary concerns about surgery and vivisection, interviewed in the 1988 BBC documentary *Shadow of the Ripper*. "You can see it actually in the theatre," she adds, referring to the Victorian operating theatre where the interview was being conducted, "that women were brought in here and exposed to the gaze of medical students, undergoing major operations, and the allegation was that many of these women were undergoing this major surgery unnecessarily, that it was to promote the careers of the surgeons and to give the medical students practice, and not at all for the benefit of the women themselves. This idea of the special vulnerability of women, and of the cruelty of medical men in their work on animals and on patients, comes together in a view that's being very strongly articulated by the late 1880s – which is the idea that doctors and experimenters in general get a kind of sexual satisfaction from inflicting cruelty." Into this new archetype stepped the featureless silhouette of the Whitechapel murderer and his little black medical bag – the legend of 'Dr Jack' was born.

Vivisection on live animals was as contentious a topic then as it is now, a key battleground for those suspicious of the motives and morality of the men in white coats. The Society for the Abolition of Vivisection was founded in 1875 and achieved some success, with legislation to regulate the practice passed the following year and recorded instances of experiments on live animals sharply declining in the following decade. "The experimenters were their own worst enemies," according to Ronald Pearsall – one of the most prolific 20th-century commentators on the underbelly of Victorian values – in *Night's Black Angels*; "they were arrogant, self-satisfied, and clearly took pleasure in their calling. When they moved outside their field and poured scorn on the use of anaesthetics for childbirth or even ordinary surgery, then the general public were justified in stamping many of the experimenters as inhuman sadists who were using vivisection as a cover for their own diabolical pursuits."

Pearson provides a lurid example in the shape of the Continental physiologist Elie de Cyon, who wrote in the 1880s that the "true vivisectionist must approach a difficult vivisection with the same joyful excitement, with the same delight, with which a surgeon undertakes a difficult operation . . . He who shrinks from cutting into a living animal, he who approaches a vivisection as a disagreeable necessity, will never become an artist in vivisection . . ." Pearson comments that "paranoiac dissertations of this type are far more common in Victorian pornography and in the casebooks of Stekel and Krafft-Ebing than in medical literature

. . . [The likes of Cyon] were, inadequately hiding their propensities under jargon, classic sadists." For his part, the vivisectionist dismissed his English critics as frustrated old maids. "Let my adversaries contradict me," he wrote, "if they can show among the leaders of the agitation one young, rich, beautiful and beloved, or one young wife who has found in her home the full satisfaction of her affections."

Cyon's subconscious association between vivisection and sex speaks volumes about his own psyche, where the scalpel as phallic substitute casts a shadow as long as that of the newborn Dr Jack archetype. "The surgical knife is the longest and most potent idea in the canon of Ripper beliefs," observed Professor Clive Bloom in his lecture, 'Jack the Ripper: A Legacy in Pictures', delivered at the Museum of London in Docklands in 2008. "It opposes the insidious and the benevolent and makes them twice as creepy. The doctor who is a killer, a bad and by definition mad physician, is a favourite of the [horror] genre. The Ripper can join Dr Frankenstein, Dr Jekyll, Dr Fu Manchu, Dr No, the real Drs Crippen and Shipman . . . in the pantheon of medical men who have been spawned since the nineteenth century. The doctor is an ambiguous figure, at one and the same time a benefactor of mankind and a serial killer; an intimate stranger and pervert; a professional and butcher . . ."

The ambiguity Bloom alludes to includes an aura of taboo sexuality that surrounds the medical profession to this day. With factors such as intimate inspections by strangers and the obvious (often literally) naked power relationship between physician and patient, it's easy to see how medical fetishism might take a hold. From innocent youthful games of doctors and nurses to the enduring popularity of naughty nurse outfits in adult emporia and more extreme examples that employ medical equipment, it must surely be one of the commonest modern fetishes. This also appears to have been true in the 1800s, as evidenced by erotic books such as 1881's *The Amatory Experiences of a Surgeon*. "Throughout Victorian pornography, the riding master with his whip and the doctor with his scalpel exchange roles," according to the Australian author and literary historian Coral Lansbury.

Doctors could also find themselves the subject of erotic obsession outside the pages of pornographic fiction. In 1853, the physician Robert Brudenell Carter published his study *On the Pathology and Treatment of Hysteria*, detailing his research on the psychological illnesses that seemed to beset women of the day. In an age when well-to-do women were frequently relegated to the status of walking ornaments, Carter observed that some feigned hysterical fits simply to attract attention. He was particularly troubled by the number of ladies who insisted that their conditions demanded the most intimate of examinations. Carter observed that he had "seen young unmarried women of the middle class of society, reduced by the constant use of the speculum, to the mental and moral condition of prostitutes; seeking to give themselves the same indulgence by the practice of solitary vice; and asking every medical practitioner . . . to institute an examination of the sexual organs."

The fact that the Victorian doctor could be a cruel yet sexy stereotype doesn't tell us that Jack the Ripper was a doctor – but the common popular assumption that he probably *was* does tell us something about the evolving Ripper mythology. There have been a few medical serial killers in the medical profession – such as the British doctor Harold Shipman and various 'angels of death' in the nursing profession – whose body-counts run into the hundreds, making them among the most prolific murderers in criminal history. But subsequent to their trials and convictions there is little enduring fascination, unlike the enigmatic Whitechapel murderer.

After his lecture at the Docklands Ripper conference, Clive Bloom was asked why he thought Shipman had failed to attract the ambivalent anti-hero status of 'Saucy Jack'. "Shipman is a problem because we know Shipman's face; Shipman would have to have something different about him," speculated the Professor. "He's a benevolent-looking, pleasant man with a beard. And plus the fact, to be honest, [that] he knocks off too many people, in bureaucratic circumstances. He's the National Health gone mad. Whereas the nineteenth-century poisoner is always a woman, of course, so poisoning is the choice of women and therefore he's sort of emasculated before he starts.

"Shipman is interesting because he hasn't gone into popular mythology, not at all," added Bloom, "whereas plenty of American killers – the Boston Strangler, Son of Sam – have. And I think it's the method. If you're going to poison someone, unfortunately you have to be a woman . . . And I have to say it: the women aren't very glamorous because they're old ladies. So there's no sexual activity there . . . We don't *know* that [the Ripper crimes are] sexual, because there's no forensics from the time to tell us that – [but] the *implication* is they are, or of course, they were." In other words, the medical aspects of the Ripper myth only become significant in conjunction with deviant sexual overtones.

The first new suspect offered by the 20th century's first fully-fledged ripperologist was a medical man, the mysterious (and pseudonymous) 'Dr Stanley'. In *The Mystery of Jack the Ripper* (first published in 1929, expanded from his magazine article of 1926), Leonard Matters proposes an eminent London surgeon and cancer expert as the killer. According to Matters, Stanley's son Herbert, the apple of the doctor's eye, contracted syphilis from the prostitute Mary Kelly in the summer of 1886. After Herbert died of the disease, two years later, the grief-stricken Stanley swore revenge, butchering Kelly and her associates in rage before fleeing to South America. Subsequent ripperologists have rubbished the theory. Two years is an improbably short time for syphilis to prove fatal; there's nothing to support the idea that Kelly was infected; and documentary evidence to substantiate the theory is in short supply. In particular, the article from a 1918 Argentinean newspaper in which a pupil of the suspect describes Dr Stanley making a deathbed confession to the crimes (and upon which Matters based his book) continues to elude researchers.

For all that, the story endures – both as the theory of a respected journalist and in the vaguer realms of fiction and folklore, where links between surgery and syphilis continue to haunt popular perceptions of the crimes. A recent medical Ripper was proposed in the 2005 book *Uncle Jack* by Tony Williams, who identifies his ancestor Dr John Williams (an echo of the Ratcliffe Highway murders, perhaps?) as the killer. A highly successful Welsh surgeon appointed as official physician to the court of Queen Victoria in 1886, according to *Uncle Jack* he led a double life in which he conducted a clandestine affair with Mary Kelly. Moreover, Dr Williams became preoccupied by his wife's infertility, and took to stalking Whitechapel, murdering prostitutes and taking their reproductive organs back to his laboratory for experimentation. It's highly speculative, and reads more like a Gothic pot-boiler than a plausible theory. But, if nothing else, *Uncle Jack* is evidence that the link between psychosexual deviance and sadistic surgery remains strong in the Ripper story.

Whilst Dr Williams was most likely innocent of misemploying his scalpel, medical practitioners such as the pioneering gynaecologist Dr Isaac Baker Brown more than made up for it. Dr Brown was a fully qualified member of the London medical establishment, with a thriving private clinic in Notting Hill. Its business was primarily clitoridectomy – the surgical mutilation of female sexual organs. Brown preached that female masturbation – which he referred to as "peripheral excitement" – lay at the root of the vast majority of intractable 'problems' with the fairer sex, and many influential voices agreed. *The Times* reported that the good doctor had "brought insanity within the scope of surgical treatment"; the *Church Times* agreed, recommending his 1866 book, *On the Curability of Certain Forms of Insanity*, to the clergy. Dr Brown's theories make for disturbing reading, inclining even the most committed chauvinist to cross his legs and mount the barricades with the Angry Women.

"If medical and surgical treatment were brought to bear, all such unhappy measures as divorce would be obviated," he declared. In following this unspeakable philosophy, Brown removed the clitorises – "I always prefer the scissors," he wrote – of scores of Victorian women. Some hated their husbands, others "would not marry" and enjoyed "serious reading", or were thought peculiar for taking long walks in the country.

Dr Isaac Baker Brown's death in 1873 takes him out of the frame as a plausible Ripper suspect – though his legitimate career of sexual mutilation for profit makes him a more odious character than any of his contemporaries accused of the crimes. To be fair to the medical establishment, his theories were criticised in the leading journals and he was soon expelled from the Obstetrics Society. The practice of clitirodectomy ceased in England thereafter, but the likes of Brown must have left deep scars in the Victorian psyche.

His career also illustrates the shift of power from religion to science in the era, as sins became syndromes and degeneracy was increasingly categorised as a disease. Genital mutilation of the kind practised by Brown was undertaken in Ancient Egypt, and Amnesty International estimates that two million such procedures are currently undertaken every year. The perpetrators and victims are predominantly African, though it is also common in parts of the Arabic peninsula and the practice has been imported by immigrant communities into the US and Europe.

The motive is overwhelmingly religious, reflecting local lore which dictates that women whose sexual organs are not mutilated are unclean or morally suspect. (Dr Baker justified very similar conclusions with specious medical jargon.) The mutilation of female genitalia is sometimes referred to as 'female circumcision', linking it to the less pernicious male equivalent where the foreskin is surgically removed. Today, around a third of the planet's male population have undergone the procedure, but it has become increasingly controversial. Outside of religious grounds, most modern medical advocates of the operation emphasise possible hygiene benefits, but their 19th-century predecessors were also convinced that circumcision discouraged masturbation.

Masturbation was one of the preoccupations of the main medical ideologues of the day. The American doctor John Harvey Kellogg ran a highly successful clinic in Michigan, advocating a mixture of Christian clean-living, vegetarianism, enemas, and abstention from sexual activity. He wrote several popular medical guides, including *Treatment for Self-Abuse and Its Effects*, published in the year of the Whitechapel murders. "The operation should be performed by a surgeon without administering an anaesthetic," says Kellogg on the topic of male circumcision, "as the brief pain attending the operation will have a salutary effect upon the mind, especially if it be connected with the idea of punishment, as it may well be in some cases. The soreness which continues for several weeks interrupts the practice, and if it had not previously become too firmly fixed, it may be forgotten and not resumed.

"In females," adds Dr Kellogg, "the author has found the application of pure carbolic acid to the clitoris an excellent means of allaying the abnormal excitement." According to Kellogg, for a significant minority masturbation could prove fatal and "such a victim literally dies by his own hand". In 1896, he developed a breakfast cereal designed to curtail sexual feelings – cornflakes – which remains his legacy to the world.

Dr Kellogg had plentiful medical authority to draw upon from across the Atlantic to support his theories on masturbation. A popular British family medical encyclopaedia of the 1880s has the following advice to offer: "Some of the most lamentable instances of youthful decrepitude, nervous affections, amaurotic blindness, and mental debility and fatuity in early life, which come before medical men, are traceable to this wretched practice. Whenever young people, about the age of puberty, exhibit unaccountable symptoms of debility, particularly about the lower limbs, with listlessness and love of solitude, look dark under the eyes &c., the symptoms should not entirely be lost sight of."

It's tempting to observe that those medical authorities not fuelled by religious mania were almost certainly themselves a bunch of wankers. For all its ambiguities, there is a spirit of hypocrisy that hangs heavy over the Victorian era, which the popular image of Jack the Ripper embodies in many respects: a respectable man – often a doctor – by day, who by night unleashes his darkest, primal urges.

In *The Erotic Arts*, Peter Webb describes the era as "a non-permissive age in which, however, pornography flourished underground, brothels catering for every extreme proliferated, and child prostitution was commonplace. It was an age of sexual repression, in which hypocrisy seems to have characterised the sexual attitudes of the majority, and nowhere is this more clearly reflected than in the art of the day." The hypocrisy Webb refers to chiefly relates to the proliferation of nudes in Victorian art galleries. In an age when surgical mutilation was seen as a legitimate – even scientific – response to feelings of erotic stimulation, unabashedly sensual paintings and naked statues were on open display in every major British city.

The unwritten rule was that so long as the subject was classical it wasn't obscene. So a vogue for salacious scenes from Ancient Greek and Roman life and legend gripped the art world, and, as long as no obvious indications of modernity intruded, such art remained within the boundaries of good taste and beyond the reach of the Society for the Suppression of Vice. Concerned clergymen frequently complained, but as a rule were wary of appearing philistines in an age when the classical cultures of Greece and Rome were considered the foundation of modern civilisation. Artists like Lord Leighton and Sir Lawrence Alma-Tadema were celebrated for canvases that often featured flagrant titillation, sensuous nude figures swathed in a thin veil of antiquity, pert nipples and curvaceous buttocks against a backdrop of marble columns and pagan temples. Whilst only the wealthy could afford to commission or purchase such works, people of every walk of life could view them in public galleries.

On a more private level – as the hauls taken by the Society for the Suppression of Vice attest – smut of every description proliferated. In 1872, an enterprising sweet manufacturer named Samuel Parkinson was arrested for "exposing for sale a number of indecently stamped pieces of confectionery in the Victoria Market". A police inspector bought some cough lozenges and reported a "number of cakes of boiled sugar, on which were stamped the figures of men and women in the most disgusting positions". Parkinson was imprisoned for a month with hard labour. Other inventive erotic merchandise available to the Victorian consumer included 'Bachelor's Scarf Pins' – "containing secret Photographs of Pretty Women" – and watches where the mechanism activated tiny figures in compromising positions.

Photography was in its infancy, but the new medium was soon employed to depict sexual subjects – just as the Venus of Willendorf suggests that our Paleolithic ancestors were inspired to their first attempts at sculpture by the erotic impulse, and modern developments like the VCR in the 1980s or the internet in the 1990s became purveyors of salacious content. The 1880s' answer to *Playboy*, *Knave* or *Hustler* were periodicals like *The Cremorne*, *The Boudoir* and *The Pearl*, which, according to Ronald Pearsall, were "salacious products, in which every conceivable perversion, position, and anomaly are presented with brusque candor, whether it is sodomy, incest, buggery, or the fashionable 'French' vice clinically called *cunnilicto* and its corresponding variation, *fellatio*."

Unlike modern equivalents, such entertainments were an expensive indulgence that put them well beyond the budget of the average Victorian. This was even truer of the erotic books of the era, which were largely the preserve of the well-heeled collector. The bibliophile Henry Spencer Ashbee left some 15,000 volumes to the British Museum in his will in 1900, the majority of which were pornographic; the Museum had its reservations, but Ashbee stipulated that if the institution wanted the priceless early editions by the likes of Cervantes, they must also preserve the more disreputable volumes in his collection. The Museum by and large complied with his instruction, making this august institution the reluctant repository of the largest library of antique porn in the world, securing titles like *The Story of a Dildoe* (1880) and *Kate Handcock, or a Young Girls Introduction to Fast Life* (1882) for the nation. Ashbee took a particular interest in the extensive literature relating to flogging, such as *The Romance of Chastisement*, subtitled *Revelations of School and Bedroom by an Expert* – which proved popular enough to justify editions in 1870, 1873 and, indeed, 1888.

Ashbee was far from alone in his fascination with flagellation. Indeed, the popularity of whipping as a sexual kink led this strain of sadomasochism to be dubbed 'the English vice', and some have suggested that at least part of *The Romance of Chastisement* was penned by Swinburne. The foremost poet of his era made no secret of his predilection, which colours much of his scarlet verse: "No propensity to which human nature is addicted, or lech to which it is prone, holds firmer roots than Flaggelation," he wrote in *The Whippingham Papers*, another collection of sadomasochistic porn he is popularly believed to have had a hand in (published again in 1888). Swinburne leaves little doubt as to the roots of his obsession, making repeated references in letters to the great pleasure he took in being punished at school, where he claims his favourite tutor – a keen disciplinarian – nicknamed him 'pepper bottom'.

Whilst the children of the poor routinely led wretched lives, the offspring of the privileged also had their crosses to bear, and public schools prepared their pupils for the rigours of running an empire with a blend of insitutionalised bullying and savage discipline. It left many with strange scars on their libidos that long outlasted the welts on their buttocks. Swinburne's interest was not confined to theory or nostalgia, and he was a regular at a brothel in St John's Wood where "two golden-haired and rouge-cheeked ladies received, in luxuriously furnished rooms, gentlemen whom they consented to chastise for large sums of money."

"Sub-divisional Inspector Roberts said that the place was furnished in the usual way of a disorderly house . . ." ran a revealing report about a raid on another brothel in *The Daily Telegraph*. "In the centre of the studio was a large arm-chair with brass rings fixed to the top of the frame. In a wardrobe he found two birches and several wrist and ankle straps, which could be fixed to the chair; in a room on the second floor another birch, and in a box in the lumber-room two other birches or flagellettes."

The Victorian hostility to pornography owed much to its inevitable association with masturbating. An unspoken moral sentiment was that prostitution was preferable to the hazards of 'self-pollution'. It was prostitution that was Victorian England's guiltiest secret, defiantly overlooked in all polite discourse but obviously proliferating in plain sight to all but the most innocent eyes. The Victorians were keen statisticians, but attempts to assess the number of women 'on the game' vary a great deal – with figures of between 7,000-80,000 in the capital alone cited for the mid-1800s – though several experts confessed that they suspected their best efforts were inevitably underestimates. Part of the problem lay in definition, particularly at the top and bottom ends of the vice trade's social spectrum. Whilst the army of women who lived and worked in brothels throughout the kingdom obviously qualify, their numbers were supplemented both by ladies of easy virtue who lived off the favours of the wealthy elite and the poverty-stricken who supplemented their meagre incomes with the wages of sin, when circumstances dictated or the opportunity arose.

In the former category, the most celebrated courtesan of the age was Catherine Walters, popularly known as 'Skittles'. Skittles was the equivalent of the modern celebrity, pursued by the wealthy and titled (she counted among her admirers the future King Edward VII), her fashion statements emulated by stylish young ladies, her exploits eagerly followed in books like *Skittles, a Biography of a Fascinating Woman* and *Anonyma, Fair but Frail*. The widespread popularity of the magnetic Ms Walters illustrates how selling sexual favours in Victorian England could be a path to luxury for the glamorous few – admired, envied and desired by legions of what can only be described as fans. The Ripper's victims represent the other side of the coin, wholly devoid of glamour and driven by immediate need. Unlike the cliché propagated by countless films, these weren't 'golden-haired and rouge-cheeked ladies', but desperate, careworn women touting for business to raise the price of a roof over their heads or another drink, servicing their customers against rickety fences or down filthy alleyways, quite unlike the luxuriously furnished rooms where the champagne never stopped flowing.

Ronald Pearsall gives a pragmatic view of Victorian vice in *Night's Black Angels*: "The Victorians accepted prostitution with a good deal more commonsense than the present age credits them with, he wrote in 1975, at the height of the 'Jack the Ripper' revival. "Many prostitutes chose their trade dispassionately; it was easier, more profitable, and even healthier than being a needlewoman, a mill hand, or a factory worker. There were risks from venereal disease, but these were no greater than from consumption or from cholera and scarlet fever that periodically came to ravage the slums. Prostitution was one of the few ways, except marriage, that a poor girl could escape from her class and her background. Such girls could scarcely go down in the social scale, and an intelligent pretty girl could, if she decided to be a prostitute, graduate to become a *poule-de-luxe*, a well-treated mistress, or even retire at an early age and live a respectable life in Maida Vale or Notting Hill."

None of the Ripper victims enjoyed such prospects. Their varied stories tell of women who found themselves selling their bodies in the backstreets and alleys of the East End by a combination of bad luck and bad judgement, of broken marriages and personal tragedies, of individuals doing their best to survive in the face of desperation and poverty. Aspects of their world echo strongly today. Just as many of the hookers walking England's red-light districts today have drug problems, so all of the Ripper's victims were alcoholics. The same substance – be it crack or gin – that numbs the senses enough to endure such a soul-destroying job ends up becoming the very reason to do it once addiction takes hold.

Even when danger rears its bloody head, and official warnings join common sense in deterring streetwalkers from plying their trade, for those whose precarious day-to-day subsistence relies upon soliciting in unsafe streets it must be difficult to heed such advice. Add to this the craving of a habit to feed, and the temptation to brave the streets must become all but unconquerable. Their circumstances made the Ripper's victims acutely vulnerable.

According to Michael Newton in *Serial Slaughter*, although only five per cent of the serial killers in a 20th-century FBI study targeted sex workers, "All of Europe's classic serial stalkers have been harlot killers, from Jack the Ripper to Yorkshire's Peter Sutcliffe, Italy's Giancarlo Guidice, Stockholm's cannibal team of Harm and Allgren, and London's 'Jack the Stripper', presumed a suicide but still unnamed after nearly three decades." Newton draws no conclusions from this, however, and it would be rash to identify any national trends from such statistics.

In his book *Jack the Ripper: The Murders and the Movies*, film journalist

Denis Meikle makes the interesting observation that, "Jack the Ripper was not a sex-killer in the commonly understood sense of the term, in that there is no evidence to support the notion that his crimes were sexually motivated, any more than the crimes of Yorkshire Ripper Peter Sutcliffe were sexually motivated . . ."

Meikle has a point. On the one hand there is the assumption that the Ripper murders include a heavy sexual component, particularly in the light of the overbearing influence of Jack's contemporary, Sigmund Freud, who's had us looking for phallic symbols under the bed for over a century. But the post-mortem mutilations of the victims concentrated on the uterus, and also sometimes the kidneys, which scarcely qualify as sexual organs. In the final canonical murder, when the killer had the opportunity to conduct a more lengthy destruction of the female form, pretty much every part of Mary Kelly's anatomy was subjected to post-mortem mutilation. What, we would be justified in asking, is so inherently sexual about any of this?

The sexual aspect of the Ripper crimes remains the elephant in the drawing room of Ripperology. Whilst the consensus has it that the case's enduring fascination originates from the fact that the killer was never successfully identified, it is surely equally true that the murders wouldn't have sustained our interest so keenly had the victims been porters or ploughmen, rather than prostitutes. The reality of life as an East End streetwalker was unquestionably sad and seedy. But the aura of illicit sex that suffuses the story – the backdrop of illicit 'kneetremblers' in a twilit world – is enough to lend a certain lurid glamour to proceedings, however distasteful. Many ripperologists may prefer to ignore this sordid sensuality – but, in doing so, do they echo the hypocrisy of those who preferred to draw a veil over the trade in flesh at the heart of Victorian England?

Chapter VII

Ripperology

"At 7.30 this evening, and every evening, a walking tour of Whitechapel will visit the sites where the bodies of the women killed by Jack the Ripper were found. During today, and every day, hundreds of people will visit the Jack the Ripper tableaux in Madame Tussaud's and the London Dungeon. A century-old crime scene is reanimated every day, and the immediate question is obvious: why? What is the continued attraction of these sites and scenes?" – Alexandra Warwick, 'Inventing the Serial Killer', a lecture at the Museum of London, 13 September 2008.

The question remains: What makes the faceless mutilator of destitute women in the squalid East End of the late Victorian era such an endless, timeless source of fascination?

From their seedily sinister origins, the wax death-masks at Madam Tussaud's Chamber of Horrors and the plague- and pox-ridden mannequins of its 1970s descendant, the London Dungeon, have metamorphosed into a Gothic theme-park experience for the family audience. Jack the Ripper, as a product of the late 19th century, may have lived through the beginning of what we still regard as modern times but, in his representation as a cloaked demon akin to Dracula, or as a Victorian 'slasher' prefiguring Freddy Krueger, he has become a one-dimensional figure of folklore.

Over the last 35 years, however, a subculture has quietly developed in which enthusiasts see themselves not as guardians of a myth but as historical investigators. Viewed from outside as 'ripperologists', the mixed ranks of criminological professionals and diligent amateurs are so named for a remark by pop-philosopher/criminologist Colin Wilson.

Briefly coming to fame as one of Britain's misnamed 'Angry Young Men' in the mid-1950s, much of Wilson's prolific oeuvre has been based upon his examination of the 'Outsider' (the archetypically alienated figure who provided the title of his breakthrough book) – with an increasing focus upon the criminal outsider. Jack the Ripper was cited in this context in an excised chapter from *The Outsider*, which later appeared in *Encyclopaedia of Murder*, the first of many such imaginative analyses of the subject by Wilson. For all his philosophising about the psychology of crime, the veteran author admits to a more folksy origin to his interest: "My granddad told me about Whitechapel when he was a child and how he hurried home from school in case the Ripper got him."

As the old fellow may have gathered if he'd lived to read his grandson's criminological writings, a male child was probably among the safer members of the local community. Wilson himself became what he would call "a clearing house for ideas" on the Ripper, making comment upon the flow of theories which later developed into a flood whilst refraining to commit fully to any of them. In 1976, he coined the umbrella term 'ripperology' in a review of Stephen Knight's hugely influential (and highly contentious) *Jack the Ripper: The Final Solution* (See Chapter Eight).

One of the present day's more respected ripperologist-authors is William (or Bill) Beadle, a genial east Londoner living in the London/Essex suburb of Dagenham. As he explains of the ripperology group of which he's a prominent member, "The Whitechapel Society was originally founded in 1995 by Mark Galloway, who is life president. "It was basically a club for people interested in the Ripper murders and included quite a number of authors. It was originally founded as the Cloak and Dagger Society, publishing a magazine called *Ripperologist*."

Initially meeting at the Alma pub off Brick Lane, in a function room filled with Ripper-connected art and ephemera, these morbid Victoriana buffs soon diverged in their interests. "*Ripperologist* basically split from Cloak and Dagger in about 1999," says Beadle, "and a new club, the Whitechapel Society, was founded. We also founded another journal, called *The Whitechapel Journal*. I think it's fair to say it's the only society now. *Ripperologist* still publishes but it's basically an internet publication, and there is a bigger magazine called *Ripperana* which publishes several issues a year, but I don't think it now has a very large circulation."

One of the Whitechapel Society's other prominent members, investigative psychologist Jon Ogan, has made noted contributions to the journals, particularly *Ripperana*. He also gave a lecture at the First UK National Conference on the East End Murders of 1888 and Jack the Ripper, organised by Mark Galloway in 1996.

(By a grim irony, the conference was held nowhere near the East End but, rather, in the East Anglian town of Ipswich – where one of the

Ripper's psychological descendants would conduct a reign of terror ten years later. See Chapter Twelve.)

"The gist of my talk was to take an objective approach to examining the crimes," relates Ogan. "I placed this in the context of investigative psychology and looked at other mutilative murders in the similar time period to produce a rudimentary model of such offenders."

Also taking the podium were Ogan's colleague Nick Connell and the original ripperologist himself, Colin Wilson. "I feel that, whilst he is an entertaining writer," opines Ogan of his co-lecturer, "the subject requires a systematic approach to build up models or typologies of offenders to tell us about what types of offender will carry out a crime. For example, Ripper folk tend to read up on all types of serial killers rather than those who commit murders in a similar manner to JtR. Colin's work is much more 'clinical' – in that he goes into details of offenders without a systematic approach to classification. Clinical psychologists are different from us! We take a statistical approach to build up these models, but then again," he good-naturedly quips, "we tend to be boring number crunchers!"

Ogan's preoccupation with the subject did not arise, however, from his academic background at the University of Liverpool's School of Psychology.

"I guess I moved into the topic because in the early Eighties it was (and still is) *the* most infamous of unsolved murder cases," he acknowledges. "I wish I could say it was some form of psychological insight that I could bring to bear upon the case. But funnily enough, it was JtR that brought me into contact with investigative psychology, and not the other way round. Instead, it formed a natural progression for me from my interest in other mysteries such as Loch Ness, sea serpents, Atlantis and the like."

Beadle, now in his early sixties, is a generation older than Ogan, the origins of his fascination stemming from the era in which he grew up. "I was about thirteen when I saw the Dan Farson programme on Jack the Ripper in November 1959," recalls Beadle, "two quarter-of-an-hour programmes, one the next week, one that week, in which he examined both the murders and the suspects. Farson seemed to get a lot into each quarter of an hour, he was very good.

"He did *Farson's Guide to the British*, which were basically half-hour weekly programmes about all things British. He was a broadcaster, journalist, and of course he wrote a book about Jack the Ripper about thirteen years after that, published 1972."

Indeed, in his own less infamous manner, Daniel Farson is himself a significant figure in subterranean Britain. A prominent presenter on the

UK's first commercial TV channel, Associated-Rediffusion (forerunner to ITV), he was the first in the medium to interview Colin Wilson, at the time of *The Outsider*, and unhesitatingly acclaimed him a genius.

Farson was also a complex and troubled character: great-nephew of *Dracula* author Bram Stoker; sometime publican and lifelong alcoholic; an active but tormented homosexual, and an acolyte of post-expressionist painter Francis Bacon's gay Soho underworld. According to survivors of the 1960s criminal underworld interviewed by this writer, he also frequented the Regency Jazz Club in Stoke Newington with gangster Ronnie Kray, where they would pick up teenage boys. (Before his death in 1997, Farson would decry the government's lowering of the gay age of consent as doing "untold damage to the vulnerable young". One can only assume his memories of Kray's predatory tastes lingered long in his mind.)

But it's for his contributions to ripperology that he appears here – principally in scouring the 'Macnaghten memoranda' for the identities of three men Scotland Yard considered viable contemporary suspects, and ascribing emphasis to the suspect he most favoured himself. "Dan Farson wasn't given permission to quote the actual name Montague John Druitt," explains Bill Beadle, "so he put a copy of the birth certificate on TV with the name blurred out. The initials were 'MJD'. I think it was six years after that Tom Cullen came along, and did publish the full name of that particular suspect [in his 1965 book *Autumn of Terror* – Farson would follow this with his own *Jack the Ripper* in 1972]. The Dan Farson theory has not really survived – Montague Druitt is really losing impact as a Ripper suspect." (See Chapter Fourteen for our look at the recurring suspects.)

But the obsessive research and theorising that result in the naming of favoured suspects are mainstays of ripperology. "In the early days of my interest there was no *Ripperana* or *Ripperologist*," reflects Jon Ogan, "so the only place to get out your info would be via a book. I was disinclined to writing a book-length treatment of the case, so Nick Warren's *Ripperana* made a great forum for folk to contribute their findings and their suspects.

"I remember writing on John William Smith Sanders and that it took a long time to collate his family background. I also remember looking over some press coverage that had not been featured in other books. I think at that point that was the key: most authors just reprised the same old facts on the case, adding their particular slant by introducing their own suspect. At that time I was able to highlight coverage that was often overlooked, such as supposed eyewitnesses. Nick Connell and I also collated some info on Mary Jane Kelly's background [see Chapter Eight]; we also found three other murders committed on the infamous Dorset Street."

The latter research would later be echoed in book-length form in Fiona Rule's lauded *The Worst Street in London*. Ogan's groundbreaking research into Sanders as a potential suspect was based on Scotland Yard's concerns about tracing three former medical students who suffered mental breakdowns, apparently in acceptance of disputed rumours about the Ripper's supposed surgical knowledge. The formerly mild-mannered John Sanders was known to have become psychotically violent and to terrorise family and friends, the type of behaviour often associated with damage to the brain's frontal lobe. His incarceration in a lunatic asylum at Virginia Water, Surrey, led to a tradition that the basement was 'Jack the Ripper's room', one of many such oral legends.

Indications that Sanders was institutionalised since 1887 apparently discount the possibility of him as the Ripper (as does his residence in Maida Vale, west London, from this writer's point of view). As an empirical researcher, Ogan was inclined to accept that his line of enquiry had led to a dead end – although his historical investigation into Sanders also focused on possible confusion with Dr Jon William Sanders, a gynaecologist who died under anaesthetic in January 1889.

"As for, do I think Dr Sanders is a suspect? Well, no," concedes Ogan. "Though I do think this illustrates the relative ease with which folk can conjure up suspects."

"People are turned on by different things," observes his colleague Beadle. "For example, I was at the Kennedy [conspiracy] conference at the weekend and I'm a supporter of the Mafia theory. But others are not remotely interested, to them it's all CIA and military." ("Lee Harvey Oswald killed JFK!" laughs conspiracy sceptic Ogan.)

"Once again you've got a whole plethora of theories with the Ripper," continues Beadle. "I think it's what people are comfortable with; I think if somebody is very much a conspiracist then in terms of the Ripper they're going to go with the Gull and the Masons theory, or any other sort of theory connected with the royal family. [See Chapter Eight.] If people think the Ripper is an insignificant little man they're going to go with my guy, William Bury, or Aaron Kosminski. [See Chapter Thirteen.] They may on the other hand be fascinated by the idea of the Ripper being a member of the upper classes, in which case they're going to go for somebody like J. K. Stephen, or perhaps Montague John Druitt. It depends on what sort of person you find fascinating. Jack the Ripper can be anybody you want him to be, whatever your personal likes, dislikes or fascinations tend towards."

From his more academic perspective, Ogan is in total agreement. "Now my psychology studies have placed a different focus upon the crimes, not in terms of the offender, but on why folk want to believe in a particular suspect. More specifically, how they build up cases against this or that suspect. 'Confirmation bias' is a phenomenon that should be referred to as 'Ripper Syndrome'. It is amazing how enthusiasts will seize upon the elements of someone's background that support their candidature of Ripper suspect while ignoring those aspects that don't!"

But whither the basic fascination of the Ripper crimes? After all, as feminist commentators have reminded us over the last 20-odd years, they were the ultimate debasement of unfortunate women already living at the sharp end of desperation. The means by which the feminist reading was communicated may have been shrill – the most strident of the sisterhood equated an interest in murder as on a level with the crime itself – but still, they had a point. Even the most cynical misanthrope would be hard-pushed to depict the Whitechapel murders as a deliverance from misery, however intolerable the state of the victims' lives when viewed from the outside.

We ask Bill Beadle if ripperology differs significantly from the morbid latter-day cult of the serial killer.

"Not really, no, not for me," he disarmingly admits. "For me, Jack the Ripper is purely and simply a serial killer. His identity and his exact motives are the great mysteries. Other people have suggested that he's not a serial killer per se, that he was part of a conspiracy, or he had a particular motive like monomania."

"To some extent, I think folk will view the JtR murders differently as there is also an emotional buffer inasmuch as JtR's crimes were carried out so long ago," demurs Jon Ogan. "So they feel they can investigate them without it feeling 'sordid'. Though, of course, some students of the crimes will dip into text covering other serial killers in an attempt to gain some form of understanding of the offender responsible. But this neglects the point that all serial killers are not alike. Nor can we make hard and fast rules on offender behaviours."

But isn't there something inherently sordid about the subject, a little sick even? Whether or not we accept the Whitechapel murders as 'sexual', given that the main target tended to be the victims' abdomens rather than their genitalia, they were still impoverished sex workers whose willingness to do anything for a few pennies led to their evisceration. Is this not then a corruption of carnality?

Above: This cartoon from *Punch* illustrates the idea that lurid and violent entertainment partly inspired the Ripper murders. The entertainment industry has long served as a scapegoat for criminal behaviour among reactionary elements in media and government. *Authors' collection*

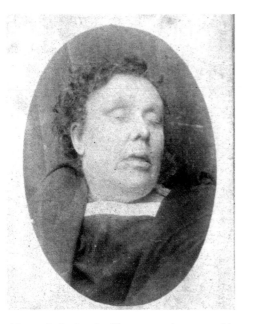

Above left: Annie Chapman, the second 'canonical' victim. She was glamorised by British sex kitten Barbara Windsor (**above right**) in *A Study in Terror* (1965), the first film to mention the victims by name. *National Record Office / Authors' collection*

Right: *Punch* also recognised the role poverty played in the Ripper crimes. But the 'Nemesis of Neglect' is more than metaphorical to some, for whom the elusive Ripper conjures the image of an almost spectral entity. *Authors' collection*

Right: Spring-Heeled Jack evolved from a folk devil to a sinister vigilante in the Victorian penny dreadfuls. Mentions of the character in correspondence sent to police and press after the Whitechapel murders suggest he played a part in creating 'Jack the Ripper' in the popular consciousness. *Authors' collection*

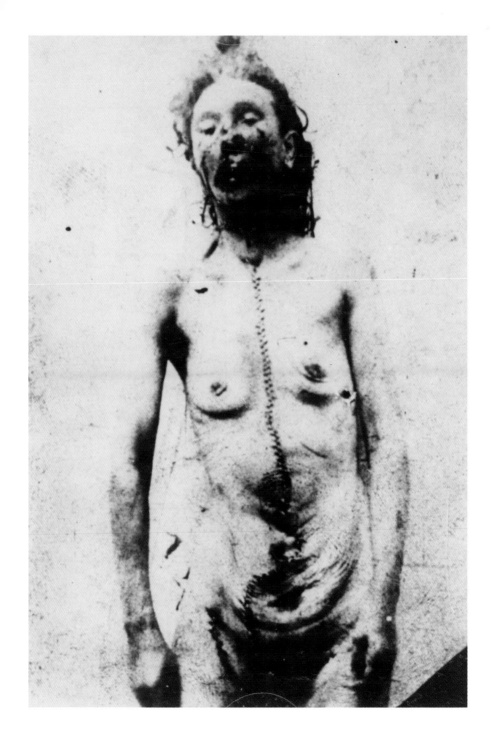

Above: The body of Catherine Eddowes, the fourth canonical victim, in the mortuary after post-mortem examination. The mutilations she suffered – particularly those inflicted on her face – were the most extreme before the all-out attack of the final recognised murder. *National Record Office*

BLIND-MAN'S BUFF.

(As played by the Police.)

"TURN ROUND THREE TIMES,
AND CATCH WHOM YOU MAY!"

THE ROMANCE
OF CHASTISEMENT;

OR, REVELATIONS OF SCHOOL AND
BEDROOM BY AN EXPERT

Above: The inability of the police to apprehend the Ripper was exploited both by satirists – such as the *Punch* cartoonist whose work is reproduced here – and political radicals, who suggested greater efforts might have been made if the victims had come from the respectable West End. *Authors' collection*

Above right: Despite its reputation for sexual propriety, the Victorian era was a golden age for pornography, particularly of a sadomasochistic nature. An edition of this classic flogging anthology, *The Romance of Chastisement*, was published in 1888. *Authors' collection*

Right: The murder of Mary Kelly, as reported in the *Illustrated Police News*. The report refers to her as the seventh victim, reflecting the common conviction of the time that two earlier 'non-canonical' murders – those of Emma Smith and Martha Tabram – were also the work of the Ripper. *Authors' collection*

Mary Jannette Kelly
Millers Court
9.11.88

Above left: The body of Mary Kelly, probably the Ripper's last victim. She was so badly mutilated that it has been suggested she could only be identified by her hair. (More fanciful theories have claimed the victim was someone else altogether, with Mary supposedly gone to ground after the event.) *Authors' collection*

Above right: Ripperologist Bill Beadle conducts a Ripper tour on 16 November 2008: "The photo was taken at the site of what used to be 13 Miller's Court, scene of the murder of Mary Jane Kelly on 9 November 1888. The grating which you can see on the left is where her bed is said to have been located. Miller's Court is now a sports goods warehouse." As in Moore and Campbell's *From Hell*, Beadle transports us from modernity to the ghostly shades of atrocities past. *Mark Galloway*

Left: A waxwork of the poisoner George Chapman – aka Severin Klosowski – which remained on display at Madame Tussaud's for 60 years, subsequent to his execution in 1903. He has been suggested as a suspect for Jack the Ripper – most notably by Inspector Abberline, a leading figure in the investigation. *Authors' collection*

On the invitation card:

Bobby & Micky

invite you to the

Jack the Ripper

Good Entertainment, Jovial Atmosphere

Manager: Len Harvey

Above: The guvnors invite you to the Jack the Ripper, Whitechapel, 1975. Publican Bobby Wayman transformed the Ten Bells, where Annie Chapman and Mary Kelly are believed to have drunk, into London's first theme pub. *Bobby Wayman*

Below left: The bar staff are shown outside – their apparel ranging from 1970s to Victoriana – with an actor dressed as the Ripper. *Bobby Wayman*

Below right: Actor Peter Dawson – then playing the title role in a Whitechapel Theatre play about Jack the Ripper – menaces the barmaid in the eponymous pub. Note how she continues pulling a pint as the Ripper's blade closes in on her throat! *Bobby Wayman*

Above: The cover of the script to the 1971 play, *Jack the Knife*, by Oscar Tapper, published by ELAM (*East London Arts Magazine*). The artwork by Jimmy Johns is redolent of 1960s Marvel Comics, while the featured rhyme is taken from an alleged 'Ripper letter' rubbishing contemporary Victorian theories.

Left: A wax effigy of Peter Kürten, the Düsseldorf Ripper, from the Madrid Wax Museum. Kürten dubiously suggested that visiting the waxworks and reading about Jack the Ripper as a child inspired his murderous career.
Authors' collection

This page and top, opposite page: Victims from the London Dungeon's Jack the Ripper Experience. Jack the Ripper has become an integral part of London's identity, fascinating visitors to the UK's capital city. *Authors' collection*

Above: A dapper guest attends a Halloween party dressed as Jack the Ripper. The Ripper's image is now fixed in the popular consciousness, even though it bears little resemblance to any of the witness descriptions of the murderer. *Authors' collection – photo Marc Williams &* *Jason Heeley)*

This page: *Assault! Jack the Ripper* is one of the most unusual and unpleasant Ripper films. A Japanese 'pink film', its only connection with the Ripper crimes is its unflinching depiction of sexual arousal by bodily mutilation.
Mondo Macabro

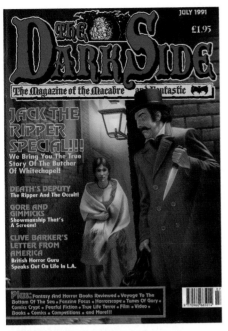

Above: Horror magazines *The Dark Side* and *Rue Morgue* both dedicated special issues to Jack the Ripper: *Dark Side* cover artist Simon Dewey avoids the top hat and opera-cloak clichés, whilst *Rue Morgue*'s Vincent Marcone capture's the character's chimerical qualities. *Authors' collection*

Below: Jack the Ripper cards from Mother Bomb Press's two *Murderers* sets – early examples of 'murderabilia', collectible ephemera featuring serial killers.

Above left: Jack the Ripper has enjoyed a musical career of sorts: Screaming Lord Sutch almost had a hit with 'Jack the Ripper' in 1963, before it was banned by the BBC.

Above right: At the other end of the spectrum, experimentalists Radio Werewolf read aloud excerpts from the purported Ripper letters for *The Fiery Summons* (1989) – an album designed as an occult ritual to unleash the inner beast. *Authors' collection*

Right: Jack the Ripper has featured in numerous comics; among the more idiosyncratic is *Whitechapel Freak*, which puts forward the theory that the Ripper was actually a man with no legs, strapped onto the shoulders of a midget!
Authors' collection

This page: Jack has entered the digital age with enthusiasm, with numerous websites such as the excellent *Ripper Casebook* and a number of computer games. In the most recent he matches wits with Victorian England's master detective, in *Sherlock Holmes versus Jack the Ripper*. *Focus Home Interactive*

Above: The Whitechapel Messiah – an incarnation of the Alchemist character employed to promote the UK's leading alternative jewellery studio, Alchemy Gothic. In their version, the Ripper's victims were actually vampires, perversly turning Jack – or Sir Mortimer Windsor FRS in this fictional incarnation – into a hero. (Author Kim Newman came up with a similar idea in his Anno Dracula series of alternative history novels.) *Authors' collection*

"I don't think the sexual murder type has a lot to do with it," insists Beadle. "Sometimes everything comes together, it meshes to create something which is massively of interest. By 1888 most of the population could read and you had the New Journalism, like the *Globe* and the *Sun* – not today's publication of the same name, but tabloid journals with daily news. And they saw the Ripper murders as exactly the sort of subject that they wanted to cover, it was a put-bums-on-seats sort of thing. Now you've got this wonderful vision of Victorian London and a stalking figure cutting his victims down – as Tom Cullen, one of our better Ripper authors, has remarked, 'The Canaanite figure with the knife.' I think that whole ambience, of fog-shrouded streets and gaslights, has created the great legend of Jack the Ripper – not necessarily the fact that he killed prostitutes, or that the murders were of a sexual orientation."

As one of the keepers of the flame, Beadle takes his subject deadly seriously and prefers to keep it away from the kind of extreme commercialisation that's seen serial-killer ephemera (including 'murderabilia' autographed by homicidal offenders) being sold online.

"We don't go in for it, not at the moment. That tends to be from the Ten Bells pub, places like that," he says with a muted distaste. But, on the other hand . . . "We probably tend to do little things like key rings and badges, maybe caps and things like that – so yeah, we'll do a certain amount of memorabilia, but mainly it's for the tourist market. Personally I think it trivialises it."

As Bill Beadle suggests, Whitechapel's Ten Bells pub – on the corner of Commercial Street and Fountier Street in Spitalfields – has long traded on its association with the murders.

"I went in there many times," he acknowledges. "I'm not a great fan of it. They had a lot of stuff in there, and then there were the claims that all the Jack the Ripper victims used to drink in there. We've no evidence to support that, though they probably would have done because it was one of the many pubs in the area. Probably one of the Ripper victims would have been in there from time to time, but the Ten Bells used to try to give the impression that it was their specific local."

In fact, over the 13 years from 1975 to 1988, the pub threw in its lot with this dark period of history and was rechristened the Jack the Ripper. For a protracted period, East End drinkers were able to imbibe in a boozer that was one part Scotland Yard's Black Museum to several parts Barnum & Bailey carnival.

***

"When George Davis came out of the nick, they actually called me up to Truman's brewery in Hanbury Street because of all the undesirables that I was friends with," says ex-publican Bobby Wayman of another piece of East End history. For this was May 1976, and petty crook Davis had just been released on the Queen's Prerogative of Mercy from a sentence for an armed robbery many believed he had not committed. (He would blot his copybook somewhat when caught red-handed as the driver on a bank raid, 18 months later.)

As Wayman says, it's something of an irony that the brewery objected to his drinking cronies, when they'd allowed him to rename the Ten Bells after the East End's ultimate undesirable. "They actually bought the main cartoon in the London *Evening Standard* from Jak: he had 'em all standing outside the Jack the Ripper with all the flat noses and cauliflower ear'oles, with all the chaps in the bowler hats and the pinstriped suits from the City. I said to Wally Hinds at Truman's, 'You're rucking me, but without it you wouldn't have had that publicity.'" In his newspaper cartoon, Jak parodied the slogan of the campaign to free Davis by embellishing the legend 'Jack the Ripper' with 'Is Innocent – OK?'

Wayman recalls the origins of the Jack the Ripper pub and his own time as the P. T. Barnum of the licensee trade: "How it started with the Ripper was, in about '74, me and my friend Mickey Taheeney were with Truman's and we had other pubs together. Spitalfields fruit market was in its bloom then, it was really rock and rolling, because they had an early morning licence. So I went to Truman's and they said, 'We're not going to give you any money, you'll have to put your own money in it.' All they had to pay for was the swing signs, though they had the door of number 29 Hanbury Street in their museum."

The brewery, based in the same street where Dark Annie had met her bloody fate in the backyards, had sequestered the door of her murder site as a historic artefact. "I knew the area, because my wife, Franny, lived there; I found out that Annie Chapman was seen leaving the Ten Bells. She was actually supposed to have seen standing there, in Fountier Street, looking down to Brick Lane and Hanbury Street."

As for the pub itself, Bobby describes it as existing then in a pre-1888 Dickensian twilight: "When we went in there it was run by a man and woman, and they think she murdered him, pushed him down the stairs. When you went down to the cellar you had a spiral staircase – it was in the 1800s that it was built. Upstairs it was just a shambles and they used to get all the meths drinkers in there, and winos. They'd be down the market nicking stuff, giving it to them for their drink. It was like a Fagin's den."

From there, at a personal cost of £15,000 – no small sum at mid-1970s values – Wayman and Taheeney embarked on a renovation programme informed by the former's personal research into the Whitechapel murders. Bobby describes the newly transformed Jack the Ripper:

"There used to be an old silk market, where the boats came in from overseas to bring the silks in, and on the back wall of the Ripper was a big mural all done in tiles of the ships coming into London Docks. They used to have a horseshoe-shaped bar, so we had the bar taken out and put in the old Victorian type which is still there today, with all the old-fashioned spindles. Little things like that – we had all the décor put back to the era of 1888. I got in touch with a designer named Neil Bartrick, who worked for Truman's and designed a couple of other pubs; I had a great big board done by a signwriter, edged with gold leaf, and a big Perspex sign put up outside with all the names of the people who Jack the Ripper murdered, and the dates. We had the big old-fashioned lamps outside – until someone came and nicked 'em and I had to get some more. Then Bartrick put me in touch with the geezer from the Black Museum at Scotland Yard; we wanted those types of drawings that you used to see in the court sketches, we had 'em done on block boarding.

"We had the tourist trade for nearly as long as I was there, nearly seven years. When [broadcaster] Monty Modlin came down to see me in August 1975, it was the most glorious, sunny evening you could wish to have, and he's got me outside the pub with his sound recordist saying, 'It's a foggy night in London.' You couldn't buy that publicity." As Wayman is well aware, despite the legend all the Ripper murders took place on clear nights.

"See, what I've always said is you could be a publican, you could have the George and Dragon, he could have the Lion and Lamb, but there's only one Jack the Ripper and I've got that!" he asserts, staking his claim for the immortality of what may be the first theme pub.

Among the Whitechapel Society today, Frogg Moody, creator of the *Yours Truly, Jack the Ripper* musical, has fond memories of Wayman's showmanship. "They started serving Ripper hotpot at lunchtime," he recalls. "They had strippers in there as well, and Ripper tipples that you could buy. I actually went down there years and years ago, when I first became interested in the subject, and I was just completely hooked on the area. It was when you could buy a Jack the Ripper t-shirt at the bar and it had a copy of the *Illustrated Police News* on it."

"Then we used to have coaches come down from Wallace Arnold's," reminisces Wayman. "They used to go into Tower Hill and I knew a chap there, I used to speak to him nicely and when he was doing a tour of London he'd bring the coach to the Jack the Ripper. That is when I got involved with Peter Dawson, the actor from Whitechapel Theatre, 'cos I let him stage a play on the Ripper one night for the American tourists."

Frogg Moody believes he knows the origins of the show: "There was a guy called Oscar Tapper and he started off a society in the East End in the Sixties, based around Toynbee Hall. He wrote a play called *Jack the Knife* – I've actually got the script to it, I bet it was the same one. They released a magazine called *ELAM* [East London Arts Magazine], it was on the front cover. It was very well illustrated by a guy called Jimmy Jones, it's got the typical Jack the Ripper with the top hat and the black bag, with prostitutes, done in caricature form."

"We'd have an influx of people coming in all the time," Bobby reminisces, "even if they just had an orange juice. You'd see the Japanese people taking the names on the board outside, with all the dates. I should have charged 'em for it, but there you are! They'd want to know the ins and outs, you'd think that we were born back then: 'Ah gee whiz, is this what he did?' Then you'd gild the lily a little bit, of course. You had to – I was a better actor than Peter Dawson!"

Ever the showman, Wayman gave the tourists not just a tangential murder site but a traditional British haunted pub: "There was a ghost there one night, we could feel it. I'd gone over there to help 'em, it must have been quite late; I felt a cold presence. There was some hardboard on the floor and it kind of lifted itself up; I went and got a priest in to exorcise the place.

"This is the truth, I was there – the radio came on and turned off. I could not go in that pub and go down that cellar. When our manager Jimmy Murphy was going on holiday and I was going over to stay there, I committed the almighty sin which you should never do, I locked it up and came home. I used to tell that to the tourists when they came in: they'd say, 'Have you seen anything?' I'd say, 'You want to be here sometimes . . .' They used to think I was fannying 'em."

Whether the unquiet spirit was that of Dark Annie or Mary Jane Kelly – or indeed the previous unfortunate landlord – was never established. An even darker portent was the pub's financial downturn caused by increasing overheads, which led Wayman to abandon his personal project in 1982. He kept in touch with the new licensees, but the death knell would sound – perhaps ironically – at the time of the centenary of the Whitechapel murders.

"I think it's strange, the bitchy comment about the feminist critique of the centenary," remarked Alexandra Warwick, co-author of *Jack the Ripper: Media, Culture, History*, to a member of the audience after her Museum of London lecture. "I live in Bethnal Green and I remember when the Ten Bells was briefly the Jack the Ripper pub, with the grim pictures in there, I remember the first kind of commemoration. I think in the exhibition downstairs [*Jack the Ripper and the East End*], the issue of thinking about the victims, of thinking about how they're brought in, how you can think about something like their place in the story, has become much more sophisticated, much more sensitively done than it was twenty years ago, at the time of the centenary."

Perhaps one of the most remarkable aspects of the 2008 exhibition would be how it assimilated such a wide range of historical materials – including the post-mortem photos, much more harrowing in their impact than any of the *Illustrated Police News* pages reproduced at the pub. To those who took offence at the pub's carnival atmosphere, it was a matter of context rather than raw material. As Frogg Moody notes, "They did have a lot of feminist protests, they eventually had to change the name back [to the Ten Bells]." All the more remarkable, perhaps, that the pub should trade under the Ripper's name for a dozen years, before the historic anniversary attracted the attention and the ire of feminists.

"Really, the pub back in the Seventies kicked those ideas off, Ripper walks and things like that," says Bobby Wayman's son Levene, himself now something of a ripperologist. It certainly seems that the first guided tours of the murder sites responded to the pub's theme, and to the tourist trade it attracted. "I think it was in '88 that it had to go back to the Ten Bells, due obviously to women's protests and feminist groups saying it was exploitation of heinous crimes back in the late 1800s."

"I remember saying to Levene, 'If I'd have been there when these women were standing outside with their banners, there was no way I'd have stood for it,' they'd have had to fight me tooth and nail," his father reflects with a melancholic defiance. "But I suppose Truman's were coming out of it and it'd been sold anyway. Someone phoned me up and said, 'Bob, you're not going to believe it, at your old pub they've got them dopey women with banners, whatever you want to call 'em – I know what *I'd* call 'em – marching up and down: "How can you name a pub after a notorious woman killer?"' Blah blah blah."

As a former native of the old East End and its no-bullshit climate, Wayman is unlikely to perceive any moral difference between his Ripper theme pub and the Anne Boleyn pub in Plaistow – named after the decapitated victim of a merciless English king. One may have been a victimiser and one a victim, but the pubs' names still testify to the bloodstains on each era of human history.

"If it was a money earner, and the people who were in it were drawing the crowds in like Dad was doing back in the day, perhaps they would have said, 'Well no, we'll stick with it,'" reasons Levene Wayman, "especially as it was the centennial anniversary. It doesn't matter who you talk to around the world, everyone knows about Jack the Ripper. So to have a pub in London – in the area from where he's supposed to have poached his victims – and then to change it back is crazy."

"I think the pub took a nosedive when they put it back to the Ten Bells," laments his father. "It went from riches to rags. It was soiled looking, it looked sad. I couldn't drive by there for five years – if I was going down Commercial Road I would go down Shoreditch way rather than drive by it. I could not see it in its sorry state."

But the Ripper theme was kept up at the newly reverted Ten Bells, as Frogg Moody recalls: "I was in the East End one day and I went to the Ten Bells, it used to be run by a publican called Dave. He told me that they'd been bought out and he was about to get the push. So I said to him, 'Look, we've got to capture this pub as it is at the moment.' So I managed to get him to let us shoot a video. We put old Victoriana stuff in there, an old piano, candles in wine bottles, and one of our actresses actually sang the 'Violet' song that Mary Kelly was singing on the night she died. It was probably the first time the song was sung in that pub since that actual night."

***

At the end of her Museum of London lecture, Alexandra Warwick answered an audience member's question as to whether ripperology "has actually come in from the cold" by stating she saw the subject as "the study of the Whitechapel murders, the conditions, the investigations, the evidence and so forth" – as opposed to fascination with a mythic archetype called 'Jack the Ripper' – "there's become a kind of depth and range in the way those events are looked at."

"Ten years ago," responded the audience member, "if you'd have looked at any journal that was dealing with the Whitechapel murders, they would have been writing about [forensic psychologist David] Canter and all that kind of stuff from the FBI. Today, the *metier* is more like [Cambridge University historian] Gareth Stedman-Jones, sociological and historical stuff."

"That was possibly our journal editor, Adrian Morris," Bill Beadle tells the authors, "because that is very much a view of Adrian's. We've moved away from actually identifying who the murderer was to examining the historical, political and social significance of the murders. People have said, 'Well, *why* did the murders take place, *why* were the victims where they were, doing what they were, on those nights?' And now you have a society which is full of, if you like, social historians."

"I book the speakers for the Whitechapel Society," confirms Frogg Moody, "and I said the remit's got to change: not *who* was Jack the Ripper, but *why* was Jack the Ripper? And once you say *why*, you open up a whole spectrum of new lecturers – because you've got Booth's poverty map, you've got the trades of the area, you've got the social conditions, what was happening in the East End at the time, the docks, all these come into it. When the Whitechapel Society first started off as the Cloak and Dagger Club, sure, every speech was on Jack the Ripper because they had the choice of all the authors. But you can't keep having the same people. There were a lot of upset people when we said we were going to change the remit: 'We're coming to hear about Jack the Ripper!' 'Well, how much do you want to know? You know the story. Surely there are other elements . . .'"

"We've had a number of very good speakers," confirms Beadle. "Last year we had Sarah Wise who wrote this new book on the people who lived in the Jago, the 'Old Nichol Gang', as they were called. It was a real tour de force for us. We've had Professor Bill Fishman, noted academic and social historian, author of the book *East End 1888*. We've had various Ripper authors who are more than *just* Ripper authors – they are crime historians like Martin Fido, Stewart Evans, Don Rumbelow, Robin Odell. Paul Begg is one of our most distinguished members – he co-wrote *The Jack the Ripper A-Z* with Fido and Keith Skinner, and three what you might call 'overview' books on the Ripper murders."

These writers are the doyens of ripperology, if not for whom the increasingly arcane study would not exist. And the Whitechapel alumni contain at least one seemingly incongruous name.

"Jeremy Beadle was one of our foremost members," says Bill Beadle of his unrelated namesake. "We're doing a series of lectures in tribute to him, which we call the Jeremy Beadle Lectures." TV's late practitioner of *Candid Camera*-style pranks was also – some may be surprised to hear – an obsessive bibliophile who owned possibly the greatest crime library in the British Isles. A man of apparent contradictions, the populist buffoon with the withered claw-hand was also an earnest criminology buff who could have debated the Whitechapel murders with anyone cited in this book.

"In the Whitechapel Society we've got about two hundred and twenty members and about two hundred and twenty different reasons why people have become members," opines Beadle. "Many people are fascinated entirely by the research. They will spend their weekends, their evenings, going around conducting research into different aspects of the Ripper. Others are interested in the socio-political side, and the Whitechapel Society reflects that. At the moment we are endeavouring to set up a permanent memorial to the victims in Whitechapel. We are negotiating with Christchurch, Spitalfields.

"About two hundred thousand people go on Ripper walking tours every year. The summer months will see about two or three different tours every night. They promote interest and they're very good for tourism, they're very good financially for the Borough of Tower Hamlets. They don't tend to like them very much though – the local authority could take a better view of the borough's history."

The Whitechapel Society also conducts its own walking tours, continuing the tradition that began at the time of the Ripper theme pub and has earned the disdain of the self-righteous ever since. Beadle himself conducts Ripper tours, as does the society's secretary, Sue Parry. "No disrespect to the others, but these are what I call proper historical tours in which we do all the murders – not just a few," he says with a quiet sense of pride.

As for the enduring fascination with the identity of the elusive Ripper, Frogg Moody admits, "If we do find out there are going to be a lot of disappointed researchers and Whitechapel Society attendees. It's 'Hunt the Ripper', that's the crux of it, it's the world's greatest whodunnit."

The original ripperologist, Colin Wilson, says that he attributes our abiding obsession to "the love of a mystery – if we knew the answer beyond all doubt we'd lose interest."

"I believe the case will never be solved," concurs Jon Ogan in his emphatic manner. "That, I guess, is the reason why most people are drawn to it!"

With their highly specialised hobby, ripperologists have all – as the song almost says – created their 'own personal Jack the Ripper'; individual hobbyhorses which may well be vaporised if the true identity of the Whitechapel murderer were ever known.

As for any conjecture as to that identity, it's perhaps best left at this point to Bobby Wayman, former licensee of the Jack the Ripper pub: "It was probably the potman who worked in the Ten Bells!"

As it transpires, he may not be that far wrong...

Cutthroat Conspiracies and Royal Rippers

"But now all is silent around the good old home;
They all have left me in sorrow here to roam,
But while life does remain, in memoriam I'll retain
This small violet I pluck'd from Mother's grave."

'Only a Violet from Mother's Grave' by Will H. Fox,
as sung by Mary Kelly on the night before her death

"I pity your condition . . ."

Mrs Maxwell, the wife of the lodging house deputy at Dorset Street, can see that Mary has the horrors of drink upon her. Here at the corner, where Dorset Street is met by the tiny residential enclave of Miller's Court, the poor young thing shakes like a leaf and looks sick as a dog.

Mrs Maxwell says to try a hair of the dog that bit her. But Mary has already tried to take another drink and retched it straight back up, like a cat vomiting a furball.

The woman places a kindly hand upon Mary's, who puts on a brave face and swallows her panic. Mary gives a pallid half-smile and shuffles away.

Her shawled shoulders carry the same weight of burden as women twice her 25 years, but her fading prettiness does not yet reek of corruption. The corpuscular veins in her nose and cheeks remain largely unbroken. But such bodily deterioration belongs surely to the future, whether in several years or mere hours from now . . .

***

Mary Jane Kelly is a popular girl around the pubs and backstreets of Commercial Road. But she is detached by time and distance from anything that might previously have been called 'home'. Her early childhood in Ireland, in the town of Limerick, is little but a blur to her. Much clearer is her time in Wales, where she grew from a girl into womanhood, and where the ghosts of a previous life lay buried.

Sweet young Mary, married to a coalminer at 18; widowed by the time she was 21, when her man died in a pit explosion. Supported herself as a prostitute on the streets of Cardiff and the old docks around Tiger Bay, before falling into a period of consumption and malnutrition, the working girl's lot, and entering the workhouse infirmary.

When Mary came to London she was too worldly-wise to believe the streets were paved with gold, yet she'd gone in search of the hope that had long since vanished from her life. She'd later tell her friends, when drinking in the Ten Bells, that she'd worked in a high-class bawdy house up west, and that all her clients were proper gentlemen. There had been gifts, and horse-drawn carriages, and visits to Paris. Some might say she was living the life of a fairytale princess rather than a whore, and that her wonderful stories were little but a fancy.

All anyone can really know is that, when Mary crossed town from the West to the East End, she was as in need of salvation as any of them. She'd found it at first, too. Her Roman Catholic faith had led her to find a place among the nuns at the Providence Row Convent and Night Refuse, Spitalfields. Just a hundred yards away from the carousing at the Ten Bells.

Mary would scrub floors and clean bedpans, and try to conduct herself with the humility that, as the sisters frequently reminded her, her saviour had shown when sent to suffer upon this earth. Such meek acceptance of her place in the world was the only path to true piety, so she'd been told with irritating regularity when she'd gone on to work for the family of Providence Row's lawyer. Until she'd polished one too many floors and emptied one pan too many, and escaped her humble station to slip off back into the night, never to return.

Now Mary has left the Sisters of Mercy and joined the Sisters of Joy, selling themselves for brief, transient moments of elation on the streets. For this sweet young woman, this Mary Jane, is a popular girl around here . . .

***

Still in her last fading bloom of youth, Mary feels privileged to be able to conduct her carnal liaisons behind four walls. She has not yet fallen so far that she has to embrace strangers who shoot their muck into her up against some rickety fence, nor to trawl the streets in the early hours of the morning looking for fourpence for a bed.

But the phantom of fear is always there at the back of her eyes; when the manic delirium of drink is upon her – the curse of too much, or too little – she knows that destitution and despair are but a thimbleful of gin away, and that awaking one morning to find her looks and her charm all gone will send poor Mary off to the knacker's yard.

But for now, she has her looks; she has her room, she has her security. All that she now lacks, in her little hidey-hole at number 13, Miller's Court is her man. For Joe Barnett has gone away just this last week, though he can't stay away long enough for her to feel the break is permanent. He's been good to her, considering he's lost his job as a Billingsgate fish porter this last summer gone, and is now just ducking and diving in any way he can to survive.

But poor old Joe can never bear to think of the other men. Her Joe, her strong man, was too much of a little boy to accept the compelling maxim of needs must when the Devil drives. He still brings her money when he can, but they no longer cohabit and he doesn't have his key – not that either of them do, since they lost the key to the room when they'd both been out on the drink together.

She'd been forced to break the window of her room that same night, and it has remained like it ever since. Now, bolstered with a few stiff drinks and with a gentleman to take care of her on this early morning of Friday 9 November, the day of the Lord Mayor's Show, she reaches her hand through the splintered pane to pull the door off its automatic spring lock.

Here, inside this rectangular cubby-hole, all will be secure for a little while at least. Once they have finished their business Mary will feel drunk enough, will feel safe enough, to sink into the sheets and sleep in his presence. For she's seen so many like him that nothing he can do will hold any surprises.

They come and go these fellows, all different and all the same. This one is so like all the others that she feels she's made his acquaintance before, though her memory is no longer reliable enough for her to truly know.

All she knows now is that she can enjoy a few hours' oblivion in this tiny space, where time ceases to pass whilst the chaos of the outside world passes by her broken window . . .

***

At the 2008 Museum of London lectures, a member of the audience observed how, after the fifth canonical murder, "the public outrage seems to ramp up again because that actually takes place in [Mary's] home, which is another level of outrage over the general sensibility."

Alexandra Warwick, the lecturer to whom the observation was addressed, concurred: "It is, I think, because it's domestic space. It becomes a public space, that's the problem with it, because we like to think that the inside of our body is like the inside of a house: that nobody's going to fiddle about with it, nobody's going to enter without permission. And that absolute opening up of her body in the domestic space is one of the reasons why it becomes more outrageous."

***

Mary snaps back to consciousness in a trice, as if suddenly awakened by the return of delirium tremens. It takes a moment for her to realise that the air denied to her lungs is being squeezed from her throat by one iron-handed grip.

"Who are you? Who are you sir, that you should do this to me!"

When the residents of Miller's Court are later roused by word of this most extreme of atrocities, only one witness will admit to hearing the word, "Murder!" cried out around the early pre-dawn. As far as we can know, Mary never spoke further. But we can imagine the questions and accusations, the cries and implorations, that ran through her mind.

"WHO ARE YOU, SIR?!" Her question remains eternally unanswered, but it still cries out to us from the ether.

The chemise that she wears to bed is peeled back and sinking into her skin, as the blood from her throat wound soaks every fibre of her physical being. The outrage has been committed, but the butchery has just begun. As Mary sinks into the bed and into extinction, he is atop her, carving into her as if he wishes to divide her soul from the marrow of her bones.

Mary no longer perceives the distance between herself and the surrounding objects, the distinction that places her as a sentient living being, as something apart from the wooden bedside table that sits aside her. Mary Jane Kelly's name will find immortality of a sort, but her mortal form is now ripped asunder. The person that was Mary has already ceased to exist.

The outlines of plumpness and pulchritude that delineated her still unspoiled body are torn open. Mary is dead, but her organic workings continue their functions until the moment they're wrenched from their fleshly shell. Her intestines sluice the alcoholic liquids and to try to digest the little food that she's eaten, even as they're pulled out of the crude incision in her belly.

Mary unfolds. The centre is dragged out of her human form as surely as the viscera is drawn from her guts. The wet upper bowels and the digestive tubes slop noisily down upon the bedside table. But his assault on the feminine form is not over. For this place is not like any of the others. It is closed off from the streets, hermetically sealed. In this place time no longer exists, and it is here that he can finally achieve what his growing tensions have urged him to do all these last long weeks.

To remake the female form according his to own destructive rage. To become an omnipotent god in a universe of chaos.

Her breasts, full but slender though already feeling the weight of gravity, are objects of both desire and disgust to him. He demonstrates his wrath, slicing through the soft flesh and the mammalian tissue, groping, pulling, tearing until they are nothing more but fat and gristle oozing from deep wounds.

He pants softly, ecstatically, as the curved flesh and nipple that house one breast are peeled back and flung over her lifeless shoulder. The deep furrow in her belly becomes like a gaping menstrual quim, opening to his touch as he releases the womb and its attendant organs into the dark dawn.

But still he cannot stop.

The blade comes down. And down. And down. It cannot stab enough times – into her face, her arms, her throat – to truly obliterate her in the way that he truly needs to. He simultaneously needs to own, to possess, and yet to destroy every last atom of that which he desires.

This time there is no hesitation and no half-measures. He pushes his knife upwards into the gristle of her nose and pulls it away. He slashes and incises inexactly, with growing mania, but the work is properly done. Her lips, eyelids and ears are mere fleshly tatters. The human identity is stripped bloodily from her face.

If this is a woman – if this is a human being – then femininity and humanity are endless reservoirs of organic life. It fills the room, as he continues to tear her internal being out in the open. Her flesh and fatty tissue are peeled open like a gaudily budding flower. Her inner workings are laid open to the eye. Her womb and kidneys are tossed and discarded over the top of her splayed right arm, just missing her head.

In a final triumphant exploration of her form, he cuts the stilled heart free from its aortae and scoops the wetly glistening prize into his bag. This is the last symbolic remnant of her humanity, and it will belong forever more to him . . .

***

It is not known exactly when Mary Kelly died. Reports of final sightings vary too greatly, and suggestions as to when the mutilations took place range from pathologist Dr Bond's estimated 2:00am to 8:00am, as suggested by the woman who believed she saw Mary taking an early drink with the man who must have been her killer. (London's licensing laws then seem to have been more liberal even than today's culture of supposedly 24-hour drinking. The rigid opening hours that characterised Britain up to the late 1980s would not be introduced until World War 1.)

All that can be known is that, although domiciled in her own room, Mary was still as in thrall to booze as the other women and had drank away most of her rent money. It was when an attendant named Bowyer came to try to collect her rent arrears – a number of weeks' worth running into shillings, then a not inconsiderable sum – sometime after ten that her appalling end was discovered.

At 10:45am, Bowyer glimpsed the organic wreckage that was once Mary Jane Kelly through the broken window. The police were called immediately, but a concern about why the room should be locked from the inside – a misunderstanding relating to the missing key – and a sensible reluctance to contaminate any evidence meant that police didn't actually force entry until 1:30pm.

Reputedly, all of the officers who attended that day were traumatised by what they were forced to survey. Some would refuse to speak about it; others tried to banish all recollection of the image from their mind.

Forensic photography was then in its infancy; its testimony to the obliteration of Mary Jane Kelly, to the way in which her body was distributed all over her private living space, is one of the earliest and most infernal examples of this technical art form. Among the supporting photographs, shots of the remains of female clothing, burning in the grate, showed that the killer had also destroyed some of Mary's few last remaining possessions. As there did not seem to have been any evidentiary value to what was burned, Inspector Abberline surmised that the murderer was trying to create light in which to view his own handiwork, in the early morning darkness.

"It's always interested me that it's one of the few photographs that you get of domestic interiors in the slums," Alexandra Warwick remarked more than a century later, "the pictures of the East End are almost all outside, they're in the streets. You see very few insides. It's very striking, that domestic detail: the kettle and its melted spout; the rag in the window."

"[Daniel] Farson was the first to publish the photos of the victims," remarks ripperologist Bill Beadle, "or certainly the first in Britain. It gave me a considerable shock, I can tell you. I don't think I've ever seen a sight quite as bad as Mary Kelly. When I was doing a Ripper Walk, I said to the walkers that the photograph of Mary Kelly defines the word 'hideous'."

In the 1970s, as we shall soon discover, an elaborate and popular theory as to what lay behind the Ripper murders would link the crimes for the first time in the public consciousness with the late-19th/early-20th century painter, Walter Sickert. Sickert, whose figurative art was an almost ghostly form of Impressionism, was certainly interested in the subject of sexual homicide. In latter-day theorising, some significance would be attributed to his painting *Jack the Ripper's Bedroom*, a stylistically gloomy 1908 work that depicts his lodgings at 6 Mornington Crescent, Camden Town; it was a far cry from the East End, but also bore one of the numerous verbal traditions that said the Ripper (in this case supposedly a veterinary student) had once lived there. More supposedly significant is *The Camden Town Murder*, a 1910 depiction of a brooding male form with a naked female on the bed beside him. (The crime which inspired Sickert actually took place in 1907, almost two decades after the Whitechapel murders.)

It's been suggested more than once that the supine nude on the bed may represent Mary Kelly. However, its intact and unbroken appearance is light years away. If more apposite parallels are sought, we need look no further than Farson's old friend and Soho acolyte Francis Bacon; noted for his imaginative distortions of the human form, the neo-expressionist's 1962 triptych *Three Studies for a Crucifixion* features the disturbing central image of a mutilated human being on a bed.

As a homosexual with a sense of aesthetic grotesquery, Bacon's work was often (though not exclusively) fixated on exaggerations of the male form, though the sexes could often appear androgynous. As a reputed participant at rent-boy orgies with the sadistic gangster Kray and Dan Farson, it can be safely surmised that his more extreme works are suffused with the imagery of blood and semen.

So it was with Mary Kelly's remains, allegedly according to Abberline. Though never substantiated, one of the many rumours of the time claimed the detective inspector believed he'd detected seminal fluid among Mary's faeces. As she'd already been disembowelled, then it must in fact have been a case of a highly-excited murderer ejaculating over her remains, rather than anything as conventional as anal sex.

***

On 12 November 1888, the public inquest on Mary Kelly was closed after a single day, the Metropolitan Police now viewing the role of the press as singularly antagonistic. Sir Charles Warren had already resigned as Commissioner of the Met on 9 November, though it was kept quiet till the following week. He was sick of attacks on his command and his force by the armchair theorists of the press and public, all convinced that, if only their pet theory had been followed, the Ripper would have been caught by now. It's believed that his resignation's occurrence at the same time as the discovery of Mary's remains is purely coincidental.

On Monday 19 November, crowds thronged the streets of the East End, mainly comprising local women, to watch Mary's escort by horse-drawn hearse from St Leonard's Church, Shoreditch, to her final resting place. In death the fallen sinner had returned to the Catholic flock. Her funeral was paid for out of local donations, but her grave – at St Patrick's Cemetery in the Essex town of Leytonstone – was left anonymous, with no headstone to mark her passing.

(Mary was buried in a pauper's grave, with several other corpses buried atop her in the years that followed. In 1986, an eccentric local ripperologist named John Morrison – Leytonstone having long since been assimilated into the London Borough of Waltham Forest – made the heartfelt gesture of a headed gravestone for Mary. He also produced an extraordinary amateur Xeroxed publication called *Jimmy Kelly's Year of the Ripper Murders 1888* – which hypothesised that the Ripper was one James Kelly, Joe Barnett's rival in love. It seems to be a variation on the theory that Barnett himself had some domestic motive for committing serial murder – see Chapter Thirteen.)

For all the sympathy that the lonesome ends of 'unfortunate women' like Mary elicited from the middle and upper classes, there was still disdain for poor women who resorted to prostitution. Indeed, the laissez-faire conservatism of the time held a generalised contempt for the poor, who were seen as architects of their own misery. (This is arguably true of chronic alcoholics or of clinical drug addicts in general. But it leaves aside the question of whether the drug of choice is being used to escape a miserable level of existence, before the drug itself becomes the problem.)

There was also a strong vein of radicalism in the late Victorian era which saw the Whitechapel murders as emblematic of what were perceived as pre-revolutionary times. On 30 September, the first victim of the 'double event', Liz Stride, had been murdered close to the International Working Men's Club, where Essex-born utopian socialist William Morris had given a lecture two nights previously.

"And it's interesting," remarked Professor Christopher Frayling at his 2008 Museum of London lecture. "A lot of the socialist writers of that period wrote about Jack the Ripper: Morris did, Bernard Shaw did, and they treated him as a sort of terrorist who was drawing attention to slum conditions. Which in a ghastly way completely ignores the victims."

On 24 September, *The Star* had run George Bernard Shaw's now famous polemical letter, headed, 'Blood Money to Whitechapel'. In it, the social activist and philosophical playwright made the ironic observation of the Ripper as a great social reformer, the only man who could focus the concern of the wealthy upon the East End: "Whilst we conventional Social Democrats were wasting our time on education, agitation, and organisation, some independent genius has taken the matter in hand, and by simply murdering and disembowelling four women [this number was – and remains – debatable], converted the proprietary press to an inept sort of communism."

"It's a horrible thing to say because it makes it so callous," protests Frayling. "Stead had been writing about [urban deprivation], there had been plays about it and there had been books about it, and no one took a blind bit of notice. And so Shaw said that it took a man killing women of the street to draw the West End's attention to the horrors of living in the East End."

"It's a very flippant remark," agrees Bill Beadle, "and I said in one of my earlier books that the problem with Shaw is that he is a socialist who cares endlessly about the poor from a West End apartment. But even so," he demurs, "he did get it right in a sense. I'm not sure about his view that if a duchess had been murdered and mutilated then the murderer would have undoubtedly been caught – he was sowing the seeds of about a hundred years in which the police were generally regarded as bumbling idiots, and that's quite the opposite, it's just that they didn't, in the end, get a result.

"But Shaw did make a lot of sense when he spoke about the social conditions and drawing attention to them. It was accidental, but I and most of the people in the Whitechapel Society do believe that in the long term there was a beneficial spin-off – almost imperceptibly, things did change in the East End of London."

Shaw's letter – whilst seeming to subscribe to the terrorist's ethos of the ends justifying the means – can also be seen as political satire of a particularly vicious kind, akin to Jonathan Swift's 1729 'A Modest Proposal', in which the author suggests that the starving Irish cannibalise their children. Despite the brutally flippant tone of Shaw's polemic, the series of murders did coincide with an increase in philanthropic focus on London's slums. As *Ripper and the East End* exhibition curator Julia Hoffbrand notes, "Even Queen Victoria telegraphed her Prime Minister saying, 'Can't anything be done to improve the conditions in the East End?' – especially for the women. Because these murders and the reporting of them really threw the spotlight on the terrible conditions there."

Not that this would necessarily have pleased Shaw, who saw philanthropy (as opposed to his desired state socialism) as merely a pious indulgence of the rich. One less affluent benefactor was orphaned children's benefactor Dr Thomas Barnardo. He had opened his first East

End shelter for destitute boys in 1867. As a local activist, he was one of those who identified the corpse of Long Liz Stride – who he recognised by sight – at the mortuary in early October 1888. Unsurprisingly perhaps – given the tidal wave of contemporary theories that Inspector Abberline complained he was drowning in – the kindly Dr Barnardo briefly became a suspect for the Whitechapel murders himself.

The murders became not just a stick with which to beat the police, or their political masters, but also began to take on the character of an international incident. The foreign media took a keen interest not just in the Ripper crimes but also in the deprived East End environment in which they occurred. It evinced a certain Anglophobic *Schadenfreude*, a guilty delight that the most powerful nation on earth also harboured the world's vilest criminal and some of its foulest slums. The American press took particular delight in reporting the embarrassment of its erstwhile political masters. "All day long Whitechapel has been wild with excitement," reported *The New York Times* the day after Annie Chapman's murder. "The four murders have been committed within a gunshot of each other, but the detectives have no clue. The London police and detective force is probably the stupidest in the world."

For their part, many patriotic Englishmen clung to the conviction that such bestial atrocities could never have been perpetrated by an English hand. Theories of foreign Rippers proliferated, often with racist overtones. *Referee* columnist George R. Sims appears to have believed that the Vassili theory (see Chapter Five) was particularly plausible because of the suspect's nationality, hailing from a state that had been Britain's principal rival on the international stage over the preceding decades. "The 'Russian' theory of the atrocities is worth thinking-out," he opined in his column of 2 December 1888. "The Russians are a sensitive and excitable race, and mental exaltation is not only very common, but it usually borders on insanity. We all have seen how political fanaticism will drive a Nihilist to the commission of murder; but it is not so generally known that religious fervour drives some sects to the most horrible self-mutilation. The Russians are very apt to rush into extremes, and they seem to have an idea that social and eternal salvation can only be obtained by means most repugnant to civilised and well-balanced minds. It is therefore not impossible that the man Vassili, who, about sixteen years ago, murdered a number of women in Paris, and who is reported to have been released from a lunatic asylum last January, may again have thought it his duty to work out the eternal salvation of the wretched East-end women."

Another theory that didn't come to light until several years after Sims' death in 1922 certainly fits such a view of the Russians as volatile and conspiratorial. According to this Russian Ripper hypothesis, the perpetrator was the mysterious Dr Alexander Pedachenko, "the greatest and boldest of all Russian criminal lunatics". Pedachenko had been recruited and despatched to London by Ochrana, the Russian Secret Service, in order to either destabilise the government by making fools of the police, or to discredit Russian radicals then enjoying sanctuary in London. Pedachenko attempted this by murdering prostitutes, aided and abetted by two accomplices. This theory was later championed by the pioneering (and controversial) ripperologist Donald McCormick. As is often the case with McCormick's Ripper theories, crucial documentation appears elusive at best, suggesting to the cynical that it may only have ever existed in the author's fertile imagination. Add the supposed written testimony of the infamous 'mad monk' Grigori Rasputin as evidence for the theory – supposedly seen by the theory's originator, sensational journalist William Le Queux, and quoted in his 1923 book *Things I Know about Kings, Celebrities and Crooks* – and you have all of the elements for a lurid spy thriller, but none for a credible criminal investigation.

There's nothing implausible about secret service agencies planting terrorist cells in rival nations to destabilise their governments. However, whilst such agencies are not above sponsoring acts of extreme violence, it stretches credibility to believe that any sane spymaster would believe much might be achieved by murdering part-time prostitutes. Ochrana surely cannot have hoped to bring the British Empire to its knees by paralysing the East End vice trade.

Despite this, some of the figures at the centre of the Scotland Yard investigation are reputed to have believed that political conspiracy was behind the Ripper crimes. In *The Rise of Scotland Yard* (1956), author Douglas G. Browne wrote, "Sir Melville Macnaghten appears to identify the Ripper with the leader of a plot to assassinate Mr Balfour at the Irish Office." Arthur Balfour MP was known as 'Bloody Balfour' for his ruthless suppression of the Home Rule movement in Ireland, which made him a prime target for the Fenian terrorists who unsuccessfully plotted his assassination in 1888. But if he ever held the opinion that Jack the Ripper was a Fenian terrorist then Macnaghten does not appear to have kept it for long, as no such suggestion appears among the famous Macnaghten memoranda. Unlike Le Queux, however Browne is generally recognised as a reputable source, and so some ripperologists have speculated that he had some authentic basis for his statement – perhaps the Home Office files consulted for his book and now missing – leaving the Fenian Ripper theory as just one more tantalising blind alley.

***

All of the above theories were a product of their particular period of history. More recently, the pervasive idea of Mary Kelly as the ultimate victim in a web of conspiracy extending from the lowest echelons of society to 'the highest in the land' was the result of a number of fragmentary events that took place throughout the 1960s and 1970s.

In August 1960, after the publication of his short series 'My Search for Jack the Ripper' in the London *Evening Standard*, original ripperologist Colin Wilson was contacted by a prominent medical consultant named Dr Thomas Stowell. Over lunch, Stowell cited the seductive idea of the Ripper as a deviant member of the aristocracy – specifically Queen Victoria's grandson, Prince Albert Victor Christian Edward ('Prince Eddy'), the Duke of Clarence. By his own account, Wilson was entertained by the hypothesis but not convinced; it was too contradictory of his own research which suggested that genteel, pampered lifestyles had yet to produce a sexual murderer. (As previously stated, this theory seems to fall down when related to murderous despots like Caligula.)

"He didn't actually reveal Stowell's theory," notes Bill Beadle, "Stowell revealed it himself, but unfortunately Stowell died soon afterwards and his son burnt his papers, so there's something of a gap there." Immediately prior to Stowell's death, he had published an article in the November 1970 issue of *The Criminologist* entitled 'Jack the Ripper – A Solution?' Stowell refrained from naming his royal suspect, but the implications were fairly direct. It caused an apparently unexpected sensation and led directly to the 'Jack the Ripper revival' of the 1970s, which has maintained the Ripper as a shadowy component of popular culture ever since. Wilson believes that the huge wave of media interest in Stowell's hypothesis led to the doctor's death in the same month as the article's publication.

But in fact the idea of the Ripper as a member of the Royal Family had already entered the cultural currency. In 1967, an English translation of French writer Philippe Jullian's 1962 book *Edward [VII] and the Edwardians* described what an apparently contemporary rumour from the time of the murders of Prince Eddy as the Ripper. Interestingly, this seems to stem from his arrest in a raid on a brothel which is strongly inferred to have been a nest of rent boys. (Other accounts of the young duke's affairs strongly dispute suggestions of homosexuality.)

"There is from the very first murder a deeply conflicted discourse that identifies [the Ripper] as 'the other' and as the same," described Alexandra Warwick at her lecture. "'The other', unsurprisingly, depends upon the perspective; for the West Enders, it was obvious that the murderer came from London's serious poor, already regarded as being utterly different from themselves; for the people of Whitechapel, he had to be a Jewish immigrant, or a wealthy gentleman, preying on their women. The perception of sameness comes from the anxiety of people about what is among them, with the murderer's ability to appear and disappear so easily suggesting that he was, perhaps, one of their own."

In his essay 'On the Origins of the Royal Conspiracy Theory', ripperologist Stewart Evans notes that the first indirect linking in print of the Duke of Clarence and the Ripper crimes harks back to 1935, when a series of newspaper articles following the death of a London hospital consultant, Dr Thomas Dutton, both claimed him as a friend of the late Prince (who died in 1892, purportedly during a flu epidemic) and inferred that he knew the identity of the Ripper.

Subsequent to the Stowell-Wilson meeting of the early 1960s, the theory seems to have been absorbed into the personal beliefs of others connected with these two men. Four years prior to the publication of the controversial Stowell article, *Criminologist* editor Nigel Morland teased with hints of privileged knowledge in a monograph written for academic publishers Tallis Press in Oxford. The following is culled from the closing passages of *An Outline of Sexual Criminology*, published in June 1966:

"Despite the many books on the subject, and those with an inside (or inspirational) 'knowledge' of the Ripper's identity, there is much to suggest that he was a man of most excellent standing and background whose parents appear to have been of German extraction [i.e. the House of Hanover, from whom the British royal family are directly descended] . . . The reticence which surrounded him has been vouchsafed to the writer from an impeccable source and suggests that the police at the time were engaged in attempting to *prevent* any further murders during the height of the outbreak, and that to arrest the man concerned was the last thing desired for obvious reasons; the same source also suggests that the Ripper died in a nursing-home near Ascot in 1892. An influenza epidemic was raging at the time, and this was used to 'cover' the demise of the Ripper . . ."

With the benefit of hindsight, Morland's inferences seem obvious, even heavy-handed. He would be chiefly responsible for propagating the Royal Ripper theory and, in an introduction to the US-published book *Prince Jack* by Frank Spiering, recalled a meeting as a young man with the aging and retired Fred Abberline, former detective inspector on the Whitechapel case – who purportedly told him the Yard had known the Ripper was "one of the highest in the land". Strangely, however, like Stowell, once the theory took hold then Morland began to backtrack. (His own 1979 *Criminologist* article, 'Jack the Ripper: The Final Word', performs a volte-face and claims no evidence for the 'Prince Jack' theory.)

In his Museum of London at Docklands lecture, Professor Clive Bloom noted how, in pop-culture terms, "By the 1960s [the Ripper] is dressed as a gentleman should be, in the evening wear of cloak and top hat. He is now the symbol of predatory aristocracy, and that is how he must remain, wrapped in the mystery of money and opulence, slumming in the East End. At least a decade before Stephen Knight's *Jack the Ripper: The Final Solution*, in 1976, there was no possibility of undoing the powerful mixture of royal connivance and Masonic intrigue that Knight seems to have purloined in his work."

Bloom's case in question to is the 1965 film *A Study in Terror*, taken from a post-Conan Doyle Sherlock Holmes mystery by Ellery Queen in which the Baker Street detective pursues an aristocratic Ripper. He might just as easily have put forward Baker-Berman's 1959 *Jack the Ripper*, which pushed a similar scenario a full year before the Wilson-Stowell meeting.

"For the Ripper had found his most powerful ally in the monarchy," continues Bloom. "No longer a marginal or deranged basket-case, he is now at the heart of the Establishment, and if Walter Sickert and the Duke of Clarence could be dragged in, so much the better for the story . . . People ceased to trust authority from the 1970s onwards, and Jack reflected this trend. For the most part the Establishment played the part of the villain, while the working class throughout remained exploited and put upon. How then could Jack be one of the working class?"

As Bloom infers, all these elements would coalesce in the 1970s bestseller *Jack the Ripper: The Final Solution*, by former *East London Advertiser* reporter Stephen Knight. The final catalyst for Knight's epochal conspiracy theory was the 1973 screening of an innovative BBC1 drama-documentary series. *Jack the Ripper* was co-written by Elwyn Jones, creator of the popular BBC cop shows *Z-Cars* and *Softly*,

Softly. Utilising his bluff British police characters Barlow and Watt as narrative anchors, the series took a historical sojourn back to 1880s Whitechapel via dramatic reconstructions, with the latter-day 'tecs examining the clues from a modern perspective.

Each 50-minute episode of the six-part series examined the known suspects in the case – principally M. J. Druitt, Aaron Kosminski and Michael Ostrog, the three contemporary men in the frame according to the Macnaghten memoranda. The series also brought a newly evolving theory into play when, in the final episode aired on Friday 17 August 1973, it granted one Joseph Sickert his place on the national stage.

Sickert, then a white-bearded man in his late forties who appeared older, claimed to be both the illegitimate grandson of Prince Eddy, Duke of Clarence, and the son of the artist Walter Sickert, painter of *Jack the Ripper's Bedroom*. (Neither claim was ever substantiated up to the death of Joseph Sickert, himself an artist.) To lend matters even more of a bizarre twist, he explained that his mother had been born of a clandestine affair between Clarence and one Annie Crook, an artist's model for Sickert; Annie was not only a commoner but a Catholic to boot, creating a possible constitutional scandal. Reacting like all repressive establishments under threat, the agents of British royalty had Annie committed to a mental asylum where she would die; after Eddy passed (some theorists claim he succumbed to syphilis, not the flu), Sickert, his formerly trusted confidant, rescued the child of the liaison, Alice Crook. His guardianship of her would lead to a sexual relationship, which in turn bore their bastard son.

More pertinent to the point of the TV series, the hushed-up scandal was said to have put an Establishment conspiracy into murderous momentum. It was not so straightforward as to suggest, as Stowell had done, that Albert Victor himself was the Ripper, but its suggestion of decadence and corruption among 'the highest in the land' was enough to leave seasoned cops Barlow and Watt raising their furrowed brows. But there again, they were only actors . . .

As Alexandra Warwick explains: "The contradiction between the ordinary and the extraordinary continues in the contemporary popular imagination . . . Jack the Ripper must have been exceptional, covering up an exceptional circumstance – such as senior Freemasons commissioning the killings to disguise the existence of a child born from the secret marriage between Queen Victoria's grandson and a Catholic shop-girl . . ."

Such was the basis of Stephen Knight's much-disputed but explosive historical case study: royal physician Sir William Gull and a coachman named John Netley were killing prostitutes to cover up the secret knowledge that Clarence had married Annie Crook. As a veteran medical man and Freemason, Gull had both the anatomical skill and the insider's knowledge to mutilate the victims' bodies according to secret Masonic rites; Netley, as a thuggish lackey of the establishment, would do anything in order to advance himself up the greasy social pole. (The irony of Freemasons – with their subversion of Roman Catholic ritual – committing murder to protect the royal heads of the Anglican faith from papal contamination is little remarked upon.)

"Stephen Knight's famous book, *Jack the Ripper: The Final Solution*, as a written work, is the best book ever on the Ripper murders," is ripperologist Bill Beadle's more than fair summation. "As a factual enquiry into the Ripper murders, it's a fraud from beginning to end."

As with many who grew up in the 1970s, as a boy the current writer found Knight's all-pervasive conspiracy theory as intoxicating as the TV show which inspired it. If spokespersons for Buckingham Palace elected to say very little about the accusations against their forebears, or to curtly deride them, well, *they would, wouldn't they?*

On closer inspection, over the years certain key aspects of the accusations haven't born scrutiny. Evidence for the existence of an Annie Crook has been painstakingly pieced together by ripperologists; she certainly seems to have spent some time in an asylum, and to have led a life of sadness and hardship before dying in the 1920s. But there was no suggestion that she was a Catholic – in fact records list her at one point as an Anglican Protestant.

"Stephen died sadly very young, about thirty-three," recalls Beadle, "when he succumbed to brain cancer. He'd written a very imaginative novel called *Requiem at Rogano*, about a serial killer who goes back in time. At the time of his death he was actually becoming a good crime historian, he wrote a book with Bernard Taylor on a series of crimes. Unfortunately, because of his illness, Stephen could only do two of them: Tony Mancini and the pitchfork murder of Charles Walton, but those two chapters are exceptionally good." Mancini was a petty thief acquitted of the 'Brighton trunk murder'; Walton was gorily murdered in the Warwickshire countryside in 1945, in a case with suggestions of black magic ritual.

Long before Knight's death in 1985, Joseph Sickert had publicly retracted his claims as a hoax. (He perversely restated them after Knight died. Research has shown that they had some basis among his family folklore, though details appeared to have been altered.) But claims that Gull et al were leaving false clues to the Whitechapel murders would segue into Knight's final book, *The Brotherhood*, an 'exposé' of Freemasonry, suggesting that the author knew he was weaving an intricate web of fiction.

It seems that Knight, in his ambition to rise from his status as local newspaper reporter to become a bestselling author, hit upon the classic journalistic formula which still holds true today: conduct intensive authentic research in order to support an imaginative hypothesis that nobody can either prove or disprove.

For all the derision now heaped on Knight's theorising, Frogg Moody of the Whitechapel Society is hesitant to dismiss him: "He did help to forward Ripper studies, because he found one or two things that nobody even knew existed. A lot of the stuff that the BBC researchers found out at the time, which came out in the book *The Ripper File*, was important but it's gone missing. So the only reference we've got to it is in their book." It certainly seems to be the case that the BBC researchers and Knight all had access to the police files before they were released to the Public Records Office at Kew in the mid-1980s, and before much of the original material was stolen.

"I can tell you that a friend of mine, an ex-girlfriend's brother, was working at a psychiatric hospital in Derbyshire as a nurse," elaborates Moody, "and one day this guy turned up to give a talk on some form of psychiatry and alluded to the Ripper murders. He actually had the pictures of the Ripper victims – not just one or two, he had quite a few of them. I said to my friend, 'How many are you talking about?' because we've obviously got certain autopsy pictures. He said, 'Quite a lot,' so they obviously went missing from the files and he was using them to illustrate his talk."

"*Jack the Ripper: The Final Solution* is the most profitable Ripper book ever written," acknowledges Beadle. "I think it's still in print today, and it started a little cottage industry all by itself." But as to its supposedly factual basis: "Sir William Gull was actually a poor old man who was seventy-two years old and had a stroke two years earlier. It's ridiculous." And the theory's originator? "Basically Joseph Sickert was a nutcase," laughs Beadle. "I met him once and he didn't do anything to dispel my feeling that he was as nutty as a fruitcake."

But the Sickert theory would persist and grow in stature, until it occupied a unique position in popular culture that straddled factual research and fiction. The conspiratorial hypothesis was that Mary Kelly, as the last and youngest of the canonical victims, had gone to ground in the East End after having been Alice Crook's nursemaid. Taking to prostitution to support herself, her lubricated loose tongue informed some older working girls of the royal scandal. And so the four destitute women – Polly Nichols, Annie Chapman, Liz Stride, Katie Eddowes – became blackmailers of the Establishment, which would cut its bloody swathe through the East End before finally butchering poor Mary.

Alan Moore and Eddie Campbell's remarkable graphic novel, *From Hell*, would make great play of the hypothesis in a fictional context, adapting Knight's framework into an occult study of the late Victorian era. It also provided the image of Sir William Gull as a clinical sadist, presenting the mutilations as something more than arcane Masonic ritual. So, how do today's criminological professionals view him as a suspect?

"You're back into the mythology of someone like Hannibal Lecter," opines forensic psychologist Laurence Alison. "You've got someone who is a well-to-do, financially-secure individual, has got an education, got a decent job: doesn't happen. You don't get serial murderers who are in a position of authority. [In modern terms], unless there's any serious suggestion that Gull was a sex offender he should be very low on the priority list."

Knight himself described the Sickert hypothesis in his book as, "the most arrant, if entertaining, nonsense ever spun about Jack the Ripper, with the possible exception of the suggestion that the murderer was an escaped gorilla." But then, of course, Knight utilised his impressive research and powers of persuasion to bolster Sickert's claims, leading a whole generation of nascent ripperologists to the conclusion that there was something very rotten in the state of the United Kingdom.

"Watergate had just happened and everyone was fascinated by conspiracy," expounds investigative psychologist Jon Ogan, "which really fuelled the Whitechapel conspiracy. It would be interesting to do a psychological study on people believing in all this, to find out whether they believe in control from without or within. It's likely to be 'without' for people who believe in that kind of stuff. Maybe that's what people subconsciously want to believe – that these poor, disenfranchised women held so much sway. Parts of the case have been proven to be absolute rubbish. People now tend to write books that say the conspiracy bit was crap – but have Gull on his own doing it, or Sickert on his own doing it."

There are now two generations of vaguely disinterested people who assume – without ever having made to recourse to Stephen Knight, *From*

Hell, or even any of the Ripper movies – that the Ripper murders had something to do with the British monarchy. As Professor Christopher Frayling describes of the filming of his 1988 documentary, *Shadow of the Ripper*:

"I did an interview with three prostitutes in Spitalfields, which we had to do in silhouette. And although this isn't in the programme, a most extraordinary thing happened: I was talking to them about how vulnerable they felt, how dangerous it was, a couple of them actually worked on the street and had all sorts of horrible things happen because they were at their most vulnerable – so when the camera stopped running I said, 'Okay, I shouldn't ask you this, but what sort of person, from your experience, do you think the Whitechapel murderer was?'

"And one of them said: 'Prince Charles.' And I thought: 'From your *experience?*' We didn't include that. She'd been reading too many books about Jack the Ripper!"

As inferred by Jon Ogan, there is a psychological need fulfilled by conspiracy theories. It overcomes the obvious difficulties that some people have in believing in chaotic ripples created by random violence, when major figures on the world stage like JFK can been killed by one malcontent loner, or Princess Diana's fatal car crash is caused by a driver mixing drink with prescription drugs.

This principle seems to work conversely in the Ripper case – in which diseased, drink-sodden, old-before-their-time whores are dignified by grandiose theories that they somehow had the inside dirt on the royal family. The sad truth is that the extent of these girls' power ran to being able to find a local man to fuck up against a wall for their lodging money.

Chapter IX

'Central Casting Seeks Ripper Victims:
Only Those with Own Teeth Need Apply'

February 1927. As the lights go down, an elderly man takes off his coat near the back of the auditorium. He removes his Homburg to reveal a bald head, framed by iron grey hair on his temples, then sits down slowly – his bones evidently not as young as they once were – neatly placing his hat and coat upon his lap. He has a heavy, unfashionable moustache and strong features; his eyes are fixed upon the blank screen in front of him. Most of his fellow picture-goers haven't bothered to doff their headgear – it isn't that sort of cinema – and he is surrounded by a sea of flat caps, grimy bonnets and broad-brimmed black hats that indicate a large number of Jewish patrons among the lively audience. The pianist in the corner hammers the keys heavily, vainly attempting to make his selection of popular tunes audible over the cacophony of cockney banter echoing around the room as children caterwaul, men curse and women explode with laughter.

The man considered going to one of the opulent picture palaces that have sprung up all over London over the past few years – huge halls decorated to resemble Egyptian temples or Persian pleasure gardens, where ladies take tea and gentlemen watch the film in silent appreciation. But somehow it seemed right to visit the Rivoli on Whitechapel Road on this occasion. He remembers when it was the Jewish Theatre, where locals came to see plays performed in Yiddish until it burnt down in 1879, then the Wonderland, and a boxing ring, before the new fad for moving pictures saw it reborn. The penny gaffs of yesteryear have all but gone, jolly rat-holes driven out of existence by a new generation's appetite for the dazzling electric worlds conjured by a whirring projector.

The first presentation has begun, and the pianist changes his tempo to match the scenes on the screen. The audience are even more boisterous – drunken voices shout derisory commentaries to the action. It's a British film, and East End audiences don't warm to domestic dramas featuring awkward actors posing as aristocrats against flimsily-constructed drawing-room sets.

The man is here for the main feature. It's entitled The Lodger. *He read the novel some years before, in his laboured fashion – he wasn't a practised reader – and so he knows that the villain is called 'the Avenger'. He likes that. It seems rather more satisfying than the crude, hackneyed name that was emblazoned over every newspaper all those years ago. Yes, 'the Avenger' is better by far than 'Jack the Ripper'.*

The man had also pored over the newspaper previews of the film in some detail. The fellow in charge is a young chap named Alfred Hitchcock, who wasn't even born in 1888. It stars a popular actor named Ivor Novello, who makes the ladies swoon. He finds himself hoping that the women in the audience will somehow see him *in the irresistible star of the show. He shifts in his seat slightly, as the thought raises the remnants of feelings not fully extinguished by his advanced age.*

*Finally, the first film ends to hoots of derision from the audience, and after a brief interlude the main feature begins. The opening title looms onto the screen – *The Lodger: A Story of the London Fog* – emblazoned with the ominous silhouette of a figure in a hat and coat behind it. The man cannot shake the troubling thought that there was no fog on those cold, clear nights 40 years ago.*

A pretty girl's face dominates the screen in a rictus of terror. The audience begins to settle down, hungry for the horrors to come. She is pretty, fresh-faced and young – not like the haggard creatures he struggles to picture from so long ago – as are all the actresses that parade pertly across the screen. Young, lovely, golden-haired, but wrong . . .

The auditorium becomes quieter still as the camera finally alights upon Novello, some 15 minutes into the presentation, his languid eyes staring from above a scarf that swathes his face. Some of the men in the audience begin to shout and hoot – the actor is a little effeminate for their tastes, but stern looks from their womenfolk soon silence them. They've come to see their matinee idol, and won't be cheated of the price of their tickets.

As the drama unfolds, a strange emptiness begins to overtake the man. He isn't sure quite what he expected to feel when he brooded in anticipation over the film. Some glimmer of that intoxicating blend of fury and lust that emerged from the pit of his belly to consume him, all those years ago? Certainly not this curious hollowness . . .

When it becomes clear that Ivor Novello is not *the Avenger, it doesn't help. Nor does it help when he realises that the character of the Avenger matters little to Mr Hitchcock. Sitting alone as the lights go up, and the last of the other patrons file out noisily into Whitechapel Road, he tries to pin down the feeling that consumes him. It is a sense of losing something, of a dim realisation of memories draining away. Of his past, his history, being taken from him and drifting into the distance . . .*

***

The above is, of course, a flight of fancy. The majority of theories insist that the perpetrator of the Whitechapel atrocities died shortly thereafter, or had his career cut short in some other fashion that would preclude the killer from becoming a cinemagoer in the 1920s. It isn't, however, impossible that the Ripper was still living in London when *The Lodger* was first screened in 1927, though he would have been getting on in years: at least in his late sixties, if the crimes had been committed as early as his late twenties. (Most of the varying sightings of the victims with clients suggest men in their early thirties to early forties.) It remains intriguing to know what the Ripper might have made of his big screen presence, as the film industry slowly pulled Jack into focus, creating much of the modern mythology that surrounds the crimes.

Hitchcock's *Story of the London Fog* was only the first of several cinematic adaptations of Marie Belloc Lowndes' 1913 novel of that name. There have been four *Lodger*s to date, of varying levels of fidelity to the source material, alongside a number of films that borrow heavily. The story – which developed from a dinner-party anecdote into a magazine story, then into a popular novel – evolved yet further as it became the first standard cinematic blueprint for the Whitechapel murders. In the process, the gap between the real crimes and the popular face of the Ripper yawned ever wider.

In the first instance, the Ripper was renamed the Avenger in the transition to the printed page. By the time *The Lodger* had expanded into a full-length novel it had also been cut loose from its chronological setting to become a contemporary thriller. The first version of 'The Lodger' had been published in *McClure's Magazine* in 1911, and it's difficult to imagine a popular magazine of the day repeating the appalling details of the Ripper crimes any more than a studio of the 1920s would even hint at the psychosexual undertones on the big screen.

But still, violent spectacle as entertainment was not as much of a taboo as some suppose. Public hangings had only been abandoned in Britain in 1868, partly because they were evidently enjoyed as entertainment, much to the disgust of Victorian authors such as Charles Dickens and William Makepeace Thackeray. In the Paris of 1897, the Grand Guignol theatre had been founded, specialising in short plays depicting graphic scenes of torture and mayhem, frequently seasoned with sexual themes. "At one performance, six people passed out when an actress, whose eyeball was just gouged out, re-entered the stage, revealing a gooey, blood-encrusted hole in her skull," writes Mel Gordon in his book *Grand Guignol: Theatre of Fear and Terror*. "Backstage, the actors themselves calculated their success according to the evening's faintings. During one play that ended with a realistic blood transfusion, a record was set: fifteen playgoers had lost consciousness. Between sketches, the cobble-stoned alley outside the theatre was frequented by hyperventilating couples and vomiting individuals."

Far from being an underground operation catering to a ghoulish niche audience, the Grand Guignol thrived as a Parisian institution, attracting not just local regulars but curious tourists and eminent attendees in evening dress, including aristocrats and even royalty. It was such a success that a number of foreign versions were launched, including the London Grand Guignol which debuted in 1920. Its star was the celebrated stage actress Sybil Thorndike, discovered in 1908 by George Bernard Shaw (the dramatist who made the acidic satirical observation of the Ripper as a social reformer 20 years before). Ms Thorndike was butchered, tormented and mutilated on a regular basis on the stage of the Little Theatre, just off the Strand. The unwelcome attentions of the theatre censors at the Lord Chamberlain's Department – who took a dim view of such activities and frequently cut or banned some of their more extreme productions – finally proved too frustrating, and London's Grand Guignol took its final curtain call in 1922.

Even after the attentions of the Lord Chamberlain, the Little Theatre showcased graphic violence then unimaginable on the big screen. As an intriguing afterword, in 1948, *The Times* reviewed a play entitled *Murder Most Foul* by Claude Pirkis that, like the Grand Guignol productions, consisted of a series of plays or sketches. The reviewer refers to it as "a grand guignol bill, and two of the three pieces are horribly up to standard . . . Oddly enough, it is the piece remotely connected with an actual crime that tells least on the stage. Mr. Pirkis's proffered solution to the mystery of Jack the Ripper is as good as any other guess, but it lacks the essentially theatrical colour of the other plays."

The Times theatre critic wasn't the only one inspired to put pen to paper by the production of *Murder Most Foul*, which coincided with the 60th anniversary of the Whitechapel murders. One correspondent sent his views to the manager of the theatre at which the play was being performed in a couple of letters, and didn't share the critic's satisfaction with the playwright's solution to the Ripper enigma. The fact that he also signed off, "Yours truly, Jack the Ripper," prompted the shaken manager to forward the letters to Scotland Yard. The authorities don't appear to have taken them too seriously, but a reporter for *Reynolds News* got wind of the letters and, sensing a story, decided to investigate.

'Jack' wasn't impressed by Pirkis' suggestion that the Ripper was a physician: "What a hope," he wrote. "Horse doctor more like." He further confided that he was 84 years of age (which would have made him 24 in 1888) and was much amused whenever he read accounts of his activities, adding that he'd like to pay a visit to the theatre in person, but, "perhaps it wouldn't be wise." In his second letter, our self-styled octogenarian Ripper boasted of the crimes of his youth, adding, "I done another two after, one in 1912 and one in 1916."

The reporter took one of the letters to compare it with the handwriting on the 'Dear Boss' letter sent to the Central News Agency on 27 September 1888 – the communication that first coined the 'trade name' Jack the Ripper. He concluded that there were striking similarities in both the phraseology and handwriting of the 1948 and 1888 'Ripper' letters, and that the differences might easily be accounted for by the passage of 60 years – though he stopped short of conclusively declaring them the work of the same hand.

Of course, the other problem with the letters sent to the theatre manager is that, even if we were sure that they were definitely written by the author of the 'Dear Boss' letter, we can't be sure *that* was the work of the same hand that butchered the East End prostitutes in 1888. Police later poured cold water on any such suggestions, dismissing the letter as a hoax. In which case, Claude Pirkis' play may at best have merely inspired an obnoxious 19th-century hoaxer to try his hand again. For all of which, the episode still gives a thread of plausibility to the fancy of the Ripper at a picture-house that opened our chapter.

Murder Most Foul borrowed its solution from the 1929 Leonard Matters book *The Mystery of Jack the Ripper*, which had been reissued in 1948. It identifies the killer as the pseudonymous Dr Stanley, an eminent surgeon driven to vengeful insanity after his son contracted syphilis from a London streetwalker. Whatever the merits or demerits of Matters' theory, his was the first serious full-length study of the crimes, reigniting interest in the case that appears to have been rapidly dwindling since the 1890s. Marie Belloc Lowndes and Alfred Hitchcock may well have chosen to sideline the Ripper in their respective 1913 and 1927 *Lodger*s not for fear of rekindling painful memories, but because, prior to 1929, the British public appear to have largely lost interest in 'Saucy Jack'.

In his 2008 lecture on cinematic representations of the crimes, 'Jack the Ripper: A Legacy in Pictures', Professor Clive Bloom attributed the resurgence of interest to the publication of Matters' book:

"There was a lot of interest at the time in the master criminals and what we'd now call psychopaths, the homicidal people in this period. It was post-[*The Mystery of Jack the Ripper*] that people started getting interested . . . This book came out, fascinated people; there was already an interest from the First World War really, if you think of [the fictional] Dr Fu Manchu and all these people lurking around the East End. And then by the 1920s they were already doing Fu Manchu coach tours around the East End. You could actually hire a charabanc and you'd go around and have someone on the deck, pointing out the opium den, or, 'That's where Fu Manchu did this or that.' This is a fascination with everybody who's *not* in the East End, that's the point. It's not a fascination for East Enders."

In both the original novel and Hitchcock's subsequent cinematic version, the murders in *The Lodger* largely serve to provide a dramatic backdrop to the theme suggested by the title. At a time when the economic climate and custom encouraged many to welcome strangers under their roofs as paying guests, the story plays upon the natural anxieties provoked by such a situation, that the man you've invited under your roof might prove to be a monster. The identity of that monster – Ripper or Avenger – is perhaps less important than the scenario itself. Recalling the immediate reaction to the expanded version of *The Lodger*, first serialised in the *Daily Telegraph*, Marie Lowndes wrote that she "began receiving letters from all parts of the world, from people who kept lodgings or had kept lodgings".

Effective horror fictions often – albeit unconsciously – touch upon common concerns of the day in order to achieve their impact. An analogy might be made with *The Texas Chain Saw Massacre* (1974), which exploited contemporary fears about the perils of picking up strange hitchhikers to establish its unsettling opening. Again, fears about sharing private space with a potential maniac fuel a saga of paranoia, which pits the importance of maintaining social convention against the looming possibility of bloody transgression.

Alfred Hitchcock's 1927 *Lodger* follows his source material in exploiting common concerns about entertaining strangers, though links to the atrocities of 1888 are hazy at best. Indeed the murders seem almost incidental, details with which to carefully ratchet up the tension in an early example of the techniques of cinematic suspense that would become the young director's trademark. He was also, perhaps hampered by the leading man that the studio selected as the suspicious lodger. The Welsh actor Ivor Novello was a dapper, dark-eyed matinee idol, difficult to portray as a plausible Ripper. This could have been used to the film's advantage – playing with audience expectations by suggesting that a romantic lead like Novello could be a killer – but studio bosses, protective of their star's image, would brook no such ambivalence. "They wouldn't let Novello even be considered as a villain," Hitch later observed. "The publicity angle carried the day, and we had to change the script to show that without a doubt he was innocent."

Hitchcock's *Lodger* concentrates on manipulating audience sympathies by emphasising the title character's status as a wronged man, unjustly persecuted for crimes he hasn't committed, a common theme in the director's work. In his penultimate film, *Frenzy* (1972), the hero is mistakenly identified as a sex killer known as the Necktie Murderer. Hitchcock makes his trademark cameo in the film's opening minutes, where a victim of the Necktie Murderer washing up on the riverbank inspires a couple standing next to him in the crowd to discuss Jack the Ripper. "He used to carve 'em up," observes the man. "He sent a bird's kidney to Scotland Yard once, wrapped in a bit of violet writing paper . . . or was it a bit of her liver?" (*Frenzy* was inspired by the 1950s/60s case of the Thames Towpath Murderer – a.k.a. Jack the Stripper. See Chapter Twelve.)

Whilst *The Lodger* was Hitchcock's third feature, he preferred to see it as his first. It features his first personal cameo alongside flashes of the directorial genius that would later make him an iconic Hollywood figure. In *English Gothic* Jonathan Rigby hails the film as "visually dazzling", though Denis Meikle dismisses it as "deeply flawed" in *Jack The Ripper: the Murders and the Movies*, critical of the emphasis of style over content. It's difficult to appreciate silent cinema today, at least in the way in which it was intended to be enjoyed – a patina of quaint charm tends to obscure its original intent – but contemporary audiences and critics were highly impressed, hailing it as a landmark in British cinema.

Hitchcock's first triumph owed much to the apprenticeship he'd recently served in Germany, where he'd worked for Berlin's celebrated UFA Studio under the legendary auteurs F. W. Murnau and Fritz Lang. In *Jack the Ripper: The Murders and the Movies*, Denis Meikle suggests that Hitchcock's *The Lodger* borrows heavily from the style of *Nosferatu*, the unofficial 1922 expressionist adaptation of *Dracula*. If interest in Jack the

Ripper had dwindled in his old London stalking grounds, a morbid fascination with the East End atrocities of 1888 appears to have endured in early 20th-century Berlin.

One might even suggest that the Ripper's troubled spirit found a new home in the German capital. The horrors of World War 1 had a devastating impact on Europe, but none more so than on the losing side. The vast loss of life was compounded by national humiliation and devastating economic ruin, which in the long term would lead to the rise of the Nazi party. In the short term it led to a sense of grim desperation and wild abandon that expressed itself in a storm of self-destructive excess centred on Berlin. Germany's Weimar Republic – between the end of World War 1 in 1918 and Adolf Hitler's appointment as Chancellor in 1933 – has become synonymous with decadence, an era when Berlin became a modern Babylon awash with sex and drugs, to an edgy cabaret soundtrack. It was a dark golden age for both crime and the arts, which interbred in this frenzied, febrile atmosphere.

The American actress Louise Brooks visited Berlin in 1929 to play Lulu, one of the Ripper's most famous fictional conquests, where, she observed, "sex was the business of the town . . . At the Eden Hotel where I lived the cafe bar was lined with the better priced trollops," Brooks recalled in her memoir *Lulu in Hollywood*. "The economy girls walked the street outside. On the corner stood the girls in boots advertising flagellation. Actors' agents pimped for the ladies in luxury apartments in the Bavarian Quarter. Racetrack touts at the Hoppegarten arranged orgies for groups of sportsmen. The night club Eldorado displayed an enticing line of homosexuals dressed as women. At the Maly there was a choice of feminine or collar-and-tie lesbians. Collective lust roared unashamed at the theatre. In the revue *Chocolate Kiddies*, when Josephine Baker appeared naked except for a girdle of bananas, it was precisely as Lulu's stage entrance was described. 'They rage there as in a menagerie when the meat appears at the cage.'"

Dadaist artist George Grosz's queasily-stylised, satirical depictions of squalor and degradation in 1920s Berlin made him one of the era's foremost visual chroniclers. He had himself photographed as Jack the Ripper, menacing his future wife with a knife. "What was it that drove Grosz to open the boundaries between art and life – first to depict killers on his canvases, then, to impersonate them in photographs?" asks Maria Tatar in *Lustmord*. (The term *lustmord* – lust murder – is still in use today, originating with Krafft-Ebing's 1886 *Psychopathia Sexualis*.) " . . . Was this part of the same syndrome that led Frank Wedekind to enact on stage the role of Jack the Ripper in a play that he had written and that had starred his wife as Jack's victim? Or that motivated Otto Dix to paint a self-portrait entitled *Sex Murderer* and to smear it with his red handprints – just as if he wanted to be caught red-handed? That real-life murderers and their victims have a habit of turning up in plays and novels or making appearances in paintings and films even as artists construct their own identities as murderous assailants suggests a strange bond between murder and art, one to which Thomas de Quincey referred in his meditations 'On Murder Considered as One of the Fine Arts' (1827).'

Of course, as the English essayist de Quincey suggests, an artistic fascination with violent crime is far from confined to Germany, nor did interest in the Ripper wholly expire in Edwardian England. Walter Sickert, whilst born in Germany in 1860, had become a leading light among English Impressionist painters. Sickert was intrigued by the grim and grimy reality of urban life, particularly crime. In 1908, he painted a scene where a desolate-looking man sits on a bed next to a supine naked female figure, her face turned away, entitling it *What Shall We Do for the Rent?* Sickert subsequently retitled this and three other nudes in sequence as *The Camden Town Murder*, in reference to a notorious crime of the previous year. On 11 September 1907, a part-time prostitute named Emily Dimmock took a client back to her Camden flat; they had sex, then he slit her throat, calmly washing off the blood in her basin before disappearing. The story caused a prurient press sensation and it's likely that Sickert saw an opportunity to promote his work by associating it with the case.

His *Jack the Ripper's Bedroom*, from around the same time, depicts an ominous, claustrophobic room with a dark shape at the window. His elderly landlady had told him of a consumptive young veterinary student she suspected of being the Ripper; his secretive manner and tendency to walk the streets at night, combined with an eagerness to get the morning papers and his burning of a suit of clothes, had all aroused her suspicions. The writer Sir Osbert Sitwell later recalled that the eccentric artist became somewhat preoccupied by the Whitechapel murders. Some have also speculated that this is the story Marie Lowndes heard – perhaps at second-hand – at a dinner party, inspiring *The Lodger*.

"The Ripper broods over modernity," observed Professor Bloom in his lecture. "His crimes represent a new aesthetic, the aesthetic of the ugly, to be found in the work of the surrealists and Dada, influenced by the explorations of Freud. The beautiful in art was already out of date in the 1880s, when the Belgian symbolists came to London. Whistler was howled down by Ruskin and the public, and a new aesthetic of dispensation was abroad, and the decay and decadence perceived to follow the Ripper was in accord with the rise of magic, Satanism, absinthe and reincarnation that marked the end of the century. The Ripper is a figure of the modernist canon, when the desolate cosmos seems all there is after Auschwitz and Hiroshima, when an empty universe is obsessed with its own destruction or abjection. As a cultural icon, the Ripper is just as much at home in the work of modernist composer Alban Berg, when he appears in the third act of the opera *Lulu*, as on the sleeve of Screaming Lord Sutch's 1972 rock album *The Hands of the Ripper*. He fascinates us still in an age of voyeurism and existential angst, where slippage, the subversive and borderline take central stage."

Berg's opera *Lulu* – which he was still perfecting when he died in 1935 – is one version of Jack's most important manifestation in Weimar culture. It was based upon the Frank Wedekind play of the same name, produced and often performed in two parts – *Erdgeist* ('Earth-Spirit' – 1895) and *Die Büchse der Pandora* ('Pandora's Box' – 1904), which Wedekind continued to revise until his death in 1918, resulting in a number of versions. The plays were also adapted for the screen, with at least a dozen adaptations of various descriptions beginning with a 1917 Hungarian film version starring Emil Jannings, though this *Lulu* lacks the Ripper. Subsequent adaptations would redress the omission, most notably the classic 1929 German version, *Pandora's Box*, directed by G. W. Pabst, and starring the devastatingly alluring Louise Brooks. "Lulu is not a real character," Wedekind once explained, "but the personification of primitive sexuality who inspires evil unaware. She plays a purely passive role."

In every version of the Wedekind play Lulu is the ultimate femme fatale, the original sex bomb causing devastation wherever she goes. In most versions, after a life of luxury Lulu is finally reduced to earning her living selling her body on the streets of London, where she finally meets her match. "It is in the worn and filthy garments of the streetwalker that she feels passion for the first time comes to life so that she may die," wrote Louise Brooks of her most famous role. "When she picks up Jack the Ripper on the foggy London street and he tells her he has no money to pay her, she says, 'Never mind, I like you.' It is Christmas Eve and she is about to receive the gift which has been her dream since childhood. Death by a sexual maniac."

Jack, like Lulu, is an elemental force, as much a slave to his essential nature as his victim. In a disturbing sense, the brutal climax is the closest to a love scene to be found in this decadent exploration of desire. In addition to subsequent screen versions of the Wedekind plays, the Berg opera is also performed live surprisingly frequently for such a difficult modern piece, with a version staged at London's Royal Opera House at time of writing. "Rising in society and then slinking through its seamy underbelly, is Lulu a liberated woman or the ultimate victim?" ponder the programme notes.

Voluptuous Panic, Mel Gordon's peerless analysis of Weimar Berlin decadence, features a photograph from a "Comic cabaret 'Jack the Ripper' scene", dated 1926, reminiscent of George Grosz's 'self-portrait' as the Ripper. In this case the female 'victim' is practically naked and giggling at her knife-wielding assailant. As Gordon illustrates, *lustmord* bubbled fiercely beneath the surface in Berlin's uniquely perverse and creative cultural melting pot. Jack the Ripper also became something of a cult figure at a time Londoners were mostly grateful to allow the grisly episode to sink into obscurity.

"The social boundary between vicious criminal behaviour and unconventional sex became increasingly blurred during the Weimar era," writes Gordon. 'For one, German courts gave voice to public defenders and criminologists who believed that domestic and street violence, underworld pursuits, and outlaw activity in general were deeply rooted in implacable hormonal imbalances. Some psychologists maintained that all crime, from kleptomania to strangulation, was a form of sexual discharge. The puzzle of how and why the criminal mind functioned differently and required hypererotic and illicit sources of gratification intrigued not only Germany's academicians and social scientists but permeated the pages, canvases, and screens of Weimar's popular culture."

German cinema first visited the Ripper legend in the 1924 film *Das Wachsfigurenkabinett* (*Waxworks*), a classic example of the atmospheric style of filmmaking that inspired Hitchcock's *The Lodger*. It's a compilation of three tales wrapped in the story of a young poet commissioned to provide stories to accompany exhibits in a wax museum. The film has a distinguished cast and crew that reads like a 'who's who' of Expressionistic filmmaking. Expressionism as a loose fine art/theatrical/cinematic style emphasised emotional states – particularly *disturbed* emotional states – over realism, with Alban Berg's opera *Lulu* as a classic example.

Like Hitchcock's *The Lodger*, *Waxworks* is a tentative early contribution to Ripper cinema. It confuses the penny-dreadful figure of Spring-Heeled Jack and the Whitechapel Ripper, the plot dividing into a series of stories dreamt by its poet protagonist, inspired by the tableaux he has been employed to caption. The first is a medieval Arabic fantasy featuring the despotic caliph Harun Al-Rashid (Emil Jannings), the second a darker tale about the tyranny of Ivan the Terrible (Conrad Veidt), concluded by a brief sequence where the poet is menaced by the murderous Jack (Werner Krauss) against an expressionistic landscape, before waking up after imagining he has been stabbed. An enchanting oddity, whilst it's frequently cited in horror film texts *Waxworks* doesn't fit easily into any specific genre.

The position of Jack the Ripper on the generic map is an interesting one, occupying a twilight zone between the thriller and the full-blooded horror film. German Expressionistic filmmakers, fleeing the rise of the Third Reich, would play a pivotal role in establishing the style and tone of Hollywood's first wave of gothic horror. At one end of the scale, however, thriller films would menace their audiences with wholly realistic threats, whilst in the improbable, implausible and finally impossible territory of gothic horror the dead would rise from their tombs and people would be possessed by demonic forces. (Such phenomena are, of course, the bedrock of the world's great religions.) Whilst most films inspired by authentic true-crime cases remain firmly in the realms of the thriller, many of those emanating from 1888 London stubbornly occupy the horror canon. Few other cases share the dubious distinction of crimes that transcend newspaper headlines to become mythic – perhaps only that of the 'Wisconsin Ghoul', Ed Gein, and Charles Manson's 'Family' of killer hippies.

In this light, the wax museum seems an apt stalking ground for the archetypal Saucy Jack. Alongside the menacing house guest of *The Lodger*, and the primal force of sexual aggression that extinguishes Lulu's flame of feminine sexuality, a third category of Ripper emerges in the animated waxwork. Wax museums are curious places. The very term 'museum' – as opposed to gallery or show – underlines the grey area that waxworks occupy between exploitation and education. Devotees of wax museums can attest that there is something curious about these inanimate zoos of captured simulacra, which seem to move in the corner of your eye when you're on your own. If that room is a Chamber of Horrors, complete with Jack the Ripper, then such ambivalently pleasing chills are intensified manifold.

It's a classic case of what the Ripper's contemporary Sigmund Freud defined as *Das Unheimliche* – 'The Uncanny' – in his influential 1909 essay of that title. The simultaneous feeling of revulsion and attraction towards something that seems both familiar and profoundly wrong, it was coined as a concept by the psychologist Ernst Jentsch in his 1906 essay 'On the Psychology of the Uncanny': "In telling a story one of the most successful devices for easily creating uncanny effects is to leave the reader in uncertainty whether a particular figure in the story is a human being or an automaton and to do it in such a way that his attention is not focused directly upon his uncertainty . . ." Such a device has been employed in countless horror films, but particularly in those concerning wax museums and the inhabitants of the ominous 'Separate Room' ...

The 'Separate Room' was the term employed by Madame Tussaud's wax museum for their figures of infamous criminals and scenes of bloodshed, before *Punch* magazine coined the term 'Chamber of Horrors' in 1846. The magazine was actually criticising the museum's special display of royal court dresses during a year of famine and dire want among the poor, but the term stuck as a description for their collection of villains and executions.

The roots of the Chamber of Horrors lie in the French Revolution, when the original Madame Tussaud began taking death masks of the victims of the guillotine, later used to fashion tableaux of those that died during the Terror. Whilst the making of death masks has now been largely abandoned as a funeral practice, the link between the figures displayed in the Chamber of Horrors and the real people depicted endured when her travelling museum found a permanent home in London in 1835. In addition to working from life wherever possible, Tussaud's went to considerable effort and expense to obtain authentic artefacts relating to the cases they featured – from clothes actually worn by the accused to furniture or even structural elements from the scene of the crime, which would go on display alongside the completed figure.

Such attention to detail and concern for veracity not only strengthened the claims of Madame Tussaud's to represent a museum rather than a ghoulish freak show, but also lent the Chamber of Horrors a strange, almost totemic quality – the visitor walking among the exhibits would almost literally be rubbing shoulders with killers.

The attraction was a huge success, drawing visitors as eminent as the Duke of Wellington and Queen Victoria, and the introduction of a notable new criminal to the collection was like an opening night, with queues curling out of the building to catch a chilling glance of the Chamber's newest inmate. Not everybody was a fan. William Makepeace Thackeray fretted over the addition to the Chamber of effigies of Frederick and Maria Manning, sent to the gallows in 1849 for the murder and robbery of an elderly friend of theirs. "Should such indecent additions continue to be made to this exhibition the 'horrors' of the collection will surely predominate," the author fretted. "It is painful to reflect that although there are noble and worthy characters really deserving of being immortalised in wax, these would have no chance in the scale of attention with thrice-dyed villains."

It's an argument that echoes to this day relating to the depiction of violence in the media. Does it inspire criminality, as some contend, or act as a cathartic safety valve? The Victorian public continued to vote with their feet and, after Madame Tussaud died in 1850, her sons Francis and Joseph expanded the Chamber of Horrors the following year to cater for the popularity of exhibits like the Mannings, displayed alongside an effigy of their victim and a scale model of the room in which he was murdered. In an attempt to stave off criticism, the Tussauds assured visitors that "so far from the exhibition of the likenesses of criminals creating a desire to imitate them, experience teaches that it has a direct tendency to the contrary." Reliably confirming or contesting such claims has challenged generations of criminologists, psychologists and sociologists.

John George Haigh, the Acid-bath Murderer, visited Madame Tussaud's Chamber of Horrors on the day before his arrest in 1949. Haigh subsequently became a popular exhibit, bequeathing a suit of clothes to Tussaud's for the display. Peter Sutcliffe, the Yorkshire Ripper, is reported to have been a boyhood regular at the waxworks in Blackpool, particularly favouring a macabre anatomical display. If a visit to the Chamber of Horrors was really the first step on the road to Hell, you would expect a queue to the scaffold to mirror those that formed outside Madame Tussaud's when a new horror was due to be unveiled. But no such symmetry has ever been observed.

Despite this, Madame Tussaud's descendents continued to endeavour to defend the propriety of their Chamber of Horrors. In the 1870s, her grandson Joseph made a valiant effort to rename it the Chamber of Comparative Physiognomy. Physiognomy – the ancient art of determining character according to facial characteristics – was popular in the day, and if Joseph Tussaud might have legitimately claimed some scientific value to his exhibits in attempting to identify a distinctive criminal 'look'. To make such a claim plausible, the models had to be as close to their inspiration as humanly possible.

For this reason also, Tussaud's could claim with a certain high-mindedness that they had never featured an effigy of Jack the Ripper. How can you create the likeness of somebody who's never been identified?

But this claim is only partially true. Three figures have occupied the Chamber of Horrors who have been put forward as credible Ripper suspects: George Chapman was executed in 1903 for poisoning three women (though only convicted of one murder), and popular rumours suggests he was posthumously accused by Inspector Frederick Abberline of being the Ripper. When Dr Thomas Neill Cream, the madcap globetrotting abortionist and poisoner, was finally hanged in London in 1892, his last words are reputed to have been, "I am Jack the . . ." The fraudster and conman Frederick Bailey Deeming was executed in Australia for the 1891 murder of two wives and four children who he'd killed in England earlier that year; many also suspected him of the Ripper crimes. In addition to this unlovely trio, the Chamber of Horrors may just possibly have displayed an effigy of the woman who poisoned Saucy Jack: Florence Maybrick, who was convicted of murdering her husband James in 1889, after a highly controversial trial. (Equally controversial is *The Diary of Jack the Ripper*, published in 1993 and purportedly exposing its alleged author, James Maybrick, as the Ripper.)

Madame Tussaud's could at least claim to be a cut above the opportunistic travelling waxworks that set up in Whitechapel Road in the autumn of 1888, exhibiting a crude figure as one of Jack's victims. It's a distinction they enjoyed for a century, until in 1988 Tussaud's commemorated the centenary of the Ripper crimes with a new tableau in their newly revamped Chamber of Horrors, the first major update of the exhibition since 1884.

Pauline Chapman describes the display in her book *Madame Tussaud's Chamber of Horrors* as "a reconstruction of a dark, narrow cobbled Victorian street, a sinister alley where the effigy of prostitute Mary Kelly, last victim of Jack the Ripper, leans waiting for custom at the door of her sordid room. In a dim passage the body of Catherine Eddowes lies bloody and mutilated by the invisible Ripper, while patrons drinking in the Ten Bells are disturbed by the sound of screams and running feet."

The new display's opening received some unwelcome attention, when members of the radical feminist group Women Against Violence Against Women picketed the queue outside. It was the same group who'd campaigned vigorously against pornography and horror videos in the wake of the Yorkshire Ripper murders of 1975-80. (Tussaud's had decided against creating a waxwork of the perpetrator, Peter Sutcliffe.)

Despite never actually displaying a figure of Jack the Ripper, the connection between Madame Tussaud's and the Ripper is longstanding.

When the *Reynolds News* reporter wanted to find a sample of the Ripper's writing to compare with the letters inspired by the production of *Murder Most Foul* in 1948, he naturally went to Tussaud's, who held a copy of the facsimile issued by the police in 1888. The climactic scene in Marie Belloc Lowndes' *The Lodger* was originally set in Madame Tussaud's, though later versions dispensed with the setting. "The presence of those curious, still figures, suggesting death in life, seemed to surprise and affright him," Belloc Lowndes wrote of her killer, the Avenger. Jack the Ripper's elusive 1915 big screen debut, *Farmer Spudd and His Missus Take a Trip to Town* (a 'hayseed' comedy which frustratingly only appears in Ripper filmographies), was filmed partially at Tussaud's. Such a haunted environment – full of figures that are hybrids of truth and fiction – is peculiarly appropriate for a figure like Saucy Jack, who has evolved into a macabre amalgam of fact and folklore.

There are numerous examples of Jack invading the media via the wax museum. In 1963, the legendary American fantasy TV series *The Twilight Zone* decided to explore the Ripper legend in an episode entitled 'The New Exhibit', where the five most notorious waxen inhabitants of the Chamber of Horrors appear to be coming to murderous life, inevitably led by the Whitechapel Ripper. In a more irreverent two-part story from goofy spy-spoof series *Get Smart*, entitled 'House of Max', the show's bumbling heroes are on the trail of Jack the Ripper in London. The murderers turn out to be waxworks, animated by the owner of a local Chamber of Horrors.

The 1973 film *Terror in the Wax Museum* includes a prominent place for a waxwork of Jack the Ripper in a story that resembles a warmed-over plot from an old *Scooby Doo* cartoon, performed by some of horror cinema's B-list. A film entitled *Waxwork* debuted on the Ripper centenary in the US; like its German namesake, it used the conceit of a wax museum to stage a series of macabre vignettes, though in this case Ripper aficionados would have to wait four years for a sequel, *Waxwork II: Lost in Time*, for Jack to enjoy any screen time.

Coincidentally, that same year the specialist UK computer game company Horrorsoft released *Waxworks*, perhaps the first major Ripper manifestation in the medium. *Waxworks* has a very similar plot to its cinematic namesakes, whereby players enter different classic horror scenarios via a wax museum; one of these is Victorian London, where the protagonist must confront the Ripper himself. Jack's journey from a waxen Chamber of Horrors cliché to a computer game character – like his transformation from a Victorian London music-hall bogeyman to a Weimar Berlin artistic archetype – illustrates the myth's versatility. But it was inevitably Hollywood that would prove most influential in establishing the version of history's most distinguished sadist that dominates modern folklore . . .

X

'I Rave; and I Rape and I Rip and I Rend' – The Occult Ripper

It is just after lunch on a bleak, damp December day at the Brighton municipal crematorium in 1947. A strange crowd of around a dozen mourners have assembled to commemorate the passing of the gentleman the press once dubbed 'the Wickedest Man in the World'; huddled in the cold, sterile chapel, their bohemian demeanour strikes a colourful contrast.

At a quarter-to-three, the sound of heavy footfall on the gravel outside heralds the arrival of the deceased. The doors swing open and the coffin is set down upon the rollers that represent the very last leg of the journey into infinity. An elderly, dignified man makes his way to the front of the chapel, and places two books upon the lectern. He clears his throat, and then begins to read from the first in a commanding, sonorous tone. Several of the mourners clearly recognise the verse as by the Beast himself – "I rave; and I rape and I rip and I rend, Everlasting, world without end!" – some even respond with cries of "Io Pan!"

The readings last some 20 minutes – poetic imprecations to a forgotten god – a surreal episode surely without precedent and unlikely to be repeated in such a drab environment. As the coffin slides towards the furnace, a pretty young girl darts forward and casts a bouquet of roses onto its wooden lid, saying something that nobody can quite catch in a husky German accent. The unorthodox congregation file out, witnessed by a small press contingent already trying to wring one last line of sinister scandal. Finally, as if on cue, the heavens open with shards of lightning and hammering rain as the smoke rises from the chimney of the Brighton crematorium. Is this the thunderous applause of forsaken deities or a final rumble of divine disapproval?

***

Convention has it that the demise of such men of mystery – and the inimitable Aleister Crowley surely deserves such an epithet – should be appended with an observation to the effect that he took his secrets with him to the grave. But Crowley, the self-styled Great Beast, was anything but reticent. The sheer volume of books, essays, correspondence and other written ephemera he penned during his long career prove a daunting challenge to any casual researcher. In the face of this, it's easy to forgive those who prefer the majority verdict that the Edwardian occultist was simply a charlatan and compulsive liar, and leave it at that. In their impressively comprehensive *Jack the Ripper A-Z*, authors Begg, Fido and Skinner dismissively define Crowley as an "alleged theorist" in a brief entry. This is perhaps a little disingenuous. He may have been an unsavoury and fanciful, even mendacious, character, but in the realms of ripperology this rather comes with the territory.

Inconvenient evidence is often overlooked when it contradicts a pet theory; crucial documents that underpin some of the more outlandish hypotheses have a habit of 'disappearing'. And documents aren't the only things that disappear in connection with the Whitechapel crimes, according to some accounts.

Aleister Crowley was certainly more than an 'alleged' theorist, in that he put his ideas down on paper on more than one occasion. The Beast took up the thread with characteristic bombast in his autobiographical *Confessions of Aleister Crowley* (1929), casting his mind back to the time when "London was agog with the exploits of Jack the Ripper. One theory of the motive of the murderer was that he was performing an Operation to obtain the Supreme Black Magical Power. The seven [sic] women had to be killed so that their seven bodies formed a 'Calvary Cross of seven points' with its head to the west. The theory was that the killing of the third or fourth, I forget which, the murderer acquired the power of invisibility, and this was confirmed by the fact that in one case a policeman heard the shrieks of the dying woman and reached her before life was extinct, yet she lay in a *cul-de-sac*, with no possible exit save the street; and the policeman saw no sign of the assassin, though he was patrolling outside, expressly on the look-out."

Human sacrifice, Calvary crosses and invisible assassins – it's irresistible stuff for anybody looking for a sensationally lurid solution to one of history's most grotesque mysteries. It's also hardly likely to add much to the credibility of any ripperologist who endorses it. But Crowley is the joker in the ripperology pack – a wild card who many feel inherently damages the credentials of any theory he's associated with. Yet the elements he brings to the mix – of forbidden blood rites and strange sex ceremonies – has proven too heady a witch's brew for some to resist, though it inevitably makes for a very murky concoction.

Nigel Cawthorne's overheated true-crime paperback, *Satanic Murders*, deals with pre-20th century "murder, madness and mayhem" in a chapter entitled 'From Early Satanism to Jack the Ripper'. With circumspection not always evident in his study, Cawthorne describes Jack as "a killer who performed ritual murders which seem to have had some occult overtones . . . Interestingly, if you plot the five murders on a map, they mark out the points of a pentagram, the five-pointed star."

It doesn't take the keenest of investigators to notice certain discrepancies between our two occult theories even at this early stage. The number of victims has dwindled from seven to five, whilst the mystical shape they are fashioning on the map of the East End using murder sites has morphed from a 'Calvary Cross' to a pentagram. In the book *Jack the Ripper's Black Magic Rituals* by theorist Ivor Edwards, the mystical symbol being outlined becomes the *vesica piscis* – two overlapping circles, forming a pointed oval – with significance in Christian, Masonic and New Age lore. It all seems a little reminiscent of the constellations made by joining stars in the night sky – spurious patterns only evident to those actively looking for them. Is it really plausible for a murderer to wander the streets of London by night, carefully selecting his victims by geographical location to abide by some obscure occult formula?

Answering such a question requires not only investigating whether there is any precedent for such rites, but also looking into the character of occultists past and present. Though he claimed to have the crucial items of evidence in his possession, Crowley's black magic theory was almost certainly second-hand, repeating rumour from cronies and rivals within the gossipy occult community. Comic-book writer and occultist Alan Moore gives Crowley a walk-on part in his acclaimed graphic novel *From Hell*. A teenaged Beast bumps into Detective Inspector Abberline outside the mortuary where the autopsy is being carried out on a Ripper victim, and tells him he's read that a man is killing ladies to make himself "magic and invisible". In the novel's extensive notes, Moore remarks, "Crowley moved with his mother to London in 1887 when he was thirteen. Given that in later life he showed more than a passing interest in the Whitechapel murders, it seemed possible that he may have been drawn to them as a spectator during his childhood."

Moore's novel, whilst far from the only Jack the Ripper book with a strong occult slant, is arguably the only one to successfully weave such a mystical element into the very fabric of its text. Writing *From Hell* was something of a revelation to its author. "One word balloon in *From Hell* completely hijacked my life," he revealed to *The Guardian* in 2002. "A character says something like, 'The one place gods inarguably exist is in the human mind.' After I wrote that, I realised I'd accidentally made a true statement, and now I'd have to rearrange my entire life around it. The only thing that seemed to really be appropriate was to become a magician."

Whatever one may make of Mr Moore's unusual career path, *From Hell* remains among the most compelling investigations of the Ripper crimes, occupying a curious space between fact and fiction by virtue of largely abandoning the obvious task of identifying the killer (though a suspect is put in the frame) in favour of trying to get to the bottom of what the Whitechapel murders actually *mean*. Peeling back the layers of reality, searching for patterns and congruities in apparently random events and ultimately manipulating them to your own ends is one workable definition of magic. (In the occult as opposed to the music-hall sense – Crowley distinguishes the former with an extra 'k'.)

This is what Moore does in *From Hell*, an oblique approach we must endeavour to employ, if not embrace, in our search for the occult Ripper. Rhyme takes precedence over reason. Numbers, colours and letters can be twisted to propel perilous leaps of logic – as can shapes, in the theories which give the locations of the Whitechapel murders special geometric significance. It is a world where nothing is ever a coincidence, and curious minor details are often indicative of profound hidden developments. This is the same sort of thinking involved in conspiracy theories, and there is considerable overlap between occult theories and those involving shadowy Ripper conspiracies.

Whilst Aleister Crowley's tender years in 1888 mean he has yet to be put in the frame as a potential Ripper suspect – even the Great Beast wasn't *that* precocious – there are some curious parallels worth exploring briefly. Both Jack and the Beast were tabloid sensations. Whilst the Ripper suckled the infant tabloid press in the 1880s, in the 1920s Crowley presided over British yellow journalism's coming of age. The Beast was arguably the first consummate tabloid villain, "a man we'd like to hang", "king of depravity", and most famously "the wickedest man in the world", according to *John Bull* magazine, among his most determined detractors. (In a 2006 readers' poll, *BBC History Magazine* declared Jack the Ripper the worst Briton of the last 1,000 years.)

In his *Confessions*, Crowley makes brief reference to the Ripper when discussing his own growing media notoriety, noting, "I enjoy the joke thoroughly. I can't believe that anything can hurt me. It would hurt my pride to admit it, I suppose. When a newspaper prints three columns, identifying me with Jack the Ripper, it never occurs to me that anyone in his senses would believe such rubbish." Perhaps.

Crowley was the archetypal attention-seeker. The credo of the magus is often cited as, "To know, to will, to dare, and to keep silent," but he was seldom backward in coming forward. While his favoured identity was that of an English country squire, complete with tweed plus-fours and a pipe, he also adopted the persona of a Scottish laird, a Russian count or a Persian Prince, all clad in regalia to match. If he could not be admired then the Beast was quite happy to be the centre of attention for altogether less reputable reasons, and wasn't above shock tactics.

Was the Ripper a compulsive exhibitionist? If any of the letters were authentic, then it would seem so. Perhaps this offers an alternative motive for the crimes: most of the victim's bodies – particularly that of Annie Chapman, with legs akimbo – appear to have been arranged by way of display to shock whoever came upon them. Might the mutilations simply have been the most effective way of creating the most disturbing tableaux, an egomaniacal atrocity to feed a pathological pleasure in outrage for its own sake? Were the murders committed for the benefit of the 'audience'?

Such speculation takes us a little too far from our central enquiry, though it is fair to say that developing a sinister mystique is practically a part of the black magician's job description. Perhaps the most insightful sketch of Crowley's personality comes from the celebrated writer William Somerset Maugham. Maugham never fell under the Beast's spell, but found him compelling enough to use him as the inspiration for Oliver Haddo, the title character in his 1908 novel *The Magician*. Crowley's reaction was typically ambivalent. Initially he was outraged, describing Maugham's portrayal as "malignant" (Crowley's contrasts between his infamy and Jack the Ripper's were triggered by its publication), but thought the book accurate enough to accuse its author of plagiarising his private papers in order to write it. In retrospect, he concluded, "*The Magician* was, in fact, an appreciation of my genius such as I had never dreamed of inspiring."

"Though Aleister Crowley served, as I have said, as the model for Oliver Haddo, it is by no means a portrait of him," Maugham insisted nearly fifty years later. "I have made my character more striking in appearance, more sinister and more ruthless than Crowley ever was. I gave him magical powers that Crowley, though he claimed them, certainly never possessed."

So what was Crowley really like in the author's estimation? "I took an immediate dislike to him, but he interested and amused me," he wrote in *A Fragment of Autobiography*. "He was a fake, but not entirely a fake." That phrase – "a fake, but not entirely a fake" – is one worth remembering, as it echoes down the rogues' gallery of black magicians.

Maugham's last observation reflects something that bedevils the casual Crowley scholar and lifetime devotee alike. "If the reader happens to have passed his life in the study of what is nauseatingly known as 'occult science', he would, if he were sufficiently intelligent, grasp one fact firmly; that is, that the persons sufficiently eminent in this matter who have become known as teachers, are bound to have possessed in overflowing measure the sense of irony and bitter humour," wrote Crowley in his 1947 essay on Jack the Ripper. "This greatest treasure in their characters is their only guarantee against going mad, and the way they exercise it is notably by writing with their tongues in their cheeks, or making fools of their followers."

In his controversial 1991 book *Blasphemous Rumours*, broadcaster and journalist Andrew Boyd attempted to promote the Christian conspiracy theory that a secret international satanic cult exists, dedicated to ritualised murder and sexual abuse of children. He borrows a chapter title from Aleister Crowley's *Magick in Theory and Practice* – 'Of the Bloody Sacrifice' (the full title is originally suffixed by 'and Matters Cognate') – writing that "perhaps the most notorious and celebrated advocate of human sacrifice in modern times was the British father of modern occultism, Aleister Crowley."

"It is necessary for us to consider carefully the problems connected with the bloody sacrifice, for this question is indeed traditionally important in Magick," Crowley writes in the opening of his own chapter on the topic. "Nigh all ancient Magick revolves around this matter."

The passage that really seals the deal as far as Boyd is concerned is the following, which certainly appears to imply that the Great Beast advocated human sacrifice: "For the highest spiritual working one must accordingly choose that victim which contains the greatest and purest force. A male child of perfect innocence and high intelligence is the most satisfactory and suitable victim."

From the point of view of the Ripper crimes, it's worth pointing out that the victims – female, mainly middle-aged, and hardly of "perfect innocence and high intelligence" – could hardly have been further from

Crowley's description of the ideal sacrificial candidate. Crowley also added a strange footnote – referring to himself in the third person by his magical name – commenting, "It appears from the magical records of Frater Perdurabo that he made this particular sacrifice on an average of about 150 times every year between 1912 and 1928." Is the Beast writing with his tongue in his cheek in the hope of making fools of his followers – or perhaps his Christian critics? By his own calculations, Crowley had sacrificed some 2,400 children, which surely tests the credibility of the most outlandish conspiracy theory.

More sympathetic commentators explain that Crowley often used deliberately provocative analogies and euphemisms in his work, perhaps to underline how Christian morality is far more comfortable with violence than sex. In this case, apparently the Beast was referring to ritual masturbation, something he felt sure could not be mentioned in print for fear of prosecution. If a foetus is a human being prior to birth, then why not prior to conception? – in which case spilling your seed is a form of human sacrifice (as well as the sin of Onan, as described in the Old Testament).

Suffice it to say, there is little if any evidence to suggest Aleister Crowley ever indulged in human sacrifice in any authentic sense, and his theories in that department appear in direct contradiction of the Whitechapel murders of 1888. Of course, those theories were first set down on paper decades later, so perhaps the Ripper was following occult doctrines elucidated by the Beast's predecessors. On 1 December 1888, a correspondent for the *Pall Mall Gazette* made just such a suggestion in a front page story entitled, 'The Whitechapel Demon's Nationality: and Why He Committed the Murders'.

Identifying himself mysteriously as 'One Who Thinks He Knows', the author bases his theory on the enigmatic, apparently anti-Semitic graffiti, found after the murder of Catherine Eddowes chalked on a wall in Goulston Street. He speculates that the eccentric spelling of 'Jews' points to a French culprit, following a risible line of reasoning:

Frenchmen are "notoriously the worst linguists in the world", allowing for a grammatical problem with his theory, while he eliminates a French-speaking Swiss or Belgian Ripper on the basis that "the idiosyncrasy of both those nationalities is adverse to this class of crime." Furthermore, "in France, the murdering of prostitutes has long been practised, and has been considered to be almost peculiarly a French crime." Unsurprisingly, few subsequent ripperologists have paid much attention to this 'Jacques le Ripper' theory as to the killer's identity. The writer's speculations on the motive, however, have aroused substantial subsequent interest.

"Now, in one of the books by the great modern occultist who wrote under the *nom de plume* of 'Eliphaz Levy', *Le Dogme et Rituel de la Haute Magie*, we find the most elaborate directions for working magical spells of all kinds," notes the *Pall Mall*'s correspondent. "The second volume has a chapter on Necromancy, or black magic, which the author justly denounces as a profanation. Black magic employs the agencies of evil spirits and demons, instead of the beneficent spirits directed by the adepts of *la haute magie*. At the same time he gives the clearest and fullest details of the necessary steps for evocation by this means, and it is in the list of substances prescribed as absolutely necessary to success that we find the link which joins modern French necromancy with the quest of the East-end murderer. These substances are in themselves horrible, and difficult to procure. They can only be obtained by means of the most appalling crimes, of which murder and mutilation of the dead are the least heinous. Among them are strips of the skin of a suicide, nails from a murderer's gallows, candles made from human fat, the head of a black cat which has been fed 40 days on human flesh, the horns of a goat which has been made the instrument of an infamous capital crime, and a preparation made from a certain portion of the body of a *harlot*. This last point is insisted upon as essential and it was this extra-ordinary fact that first drew my attention to the possible connection of the murderer with the black art."

Our author then proceeds to explain the Ripper's true motive. Here we find perhaps the first instance of the idea of the murders being committed in specific locations, determined by the desire to plot a mystical symbol across the map of London using the bodies of his victims. "Did the murderer, then, designing to offer the mystic number of seven human sacrifices in the form of a cross – a form which he intended to profane – deliberately pick out beforehand on a map the places in which he would offer them to his infernal deity of murder?" he challenges. "If not, surely these six *coincidences* are the most marvellous event of our time."

In order to make his cross fit, he is obliged to include at least one murder seldom ascribed to the Ripper whilst discounting another, widely recognised as Jack's final atrocity. In light of this, it's tempting to regard his black magic theories in a similar light to his Francophobe twaddle.

But some have taken the theorist, one Dr Roslyn D'Onston Stephenson, in deadly earnest. He was christened Robert D'Onston

Stephenson in 1841, and some believe the titles of doctor and major he affected were fraudulent. Assumed names – it is tempting to say 'stage names' – are a common feature among occultists, and Stephenson was at least a dabbler in the black arts.

According to some theorists he was more than that. Some insist that Stephenson was in fact the Ripper himself, his article in the *Pall Mall Gazette* written to gloat over his crimes whilst throwing police off the scent. It is almost certainly Stephenson that Crowley is referring to in his Ripper revelations, and Stephenson who Ivor Edwards identifies as behind *Jack the Ripper's Black Magic Rituals*. His most dogged accuser is the ripperologist Melvin Harris. D'Onston had a colourful past before he became a freelance journalist, according to Harri, "he had panned for gold in the United States, witnessed devil worship in the Cameroon and hunted for the authentic rope trick in India. For a while he even courted danger as a surgeon–major with Garibaldi's army." Having said that, Harris admits, "D'Onston's newspaper writings are packed with deception; biographically, they are of limited use and his tales of magic in Europe, Asia and Africa are just too exaggerated to be true." So was he another case of 'a fake, but not entirely a fake'?

More pertinently, was Stephenson actually boasting about the crimes? Harris establishes that his suspect was in the vicinity at the time, though convalescing at the London Hospital on Whitechapel Road. Stephenson was suffering from neurasthenia, a very 19th-century complaint whereby the sufferer's nerves come under such pressure as to render them a physical invalid. It was a popular diagnosis among Bohemian artists, as it implied an excess of sensitivity, and some saw it as illustrating the thin line between genius and madness. In Stephenson's case it seems likely that his chronic alcoholism was exacerbated by the toxic preparations he took in order to try and control the side effects of his heavy drinking.

Critics of Stephenson as a suspect suggest it unlikely that an invalid was capable of the Whitechapel murders. The Ripper crimes unsurprisingly fascinated both the inmates and staff of the London Hospital. Dr Morgan Davies, in particular, took such an animated interest and exhibited such an intimate knowledge of the murders, according to Stephenson, that he just had to be the culprit.

Stephenson insisted that Dr Davies had revealed via a bizarre recreation of the crime that the final victim was sodomised, a detail not generally known (and disputed by many), and duly reported his suspicions to the police. The victim was Mary Kelly, who he later ruled out in his article, whilst Dr Davies doesn't appear to have been French. At this stage, the occult aspects of the murders don't seem to have occurred to Stephenson.

Inspector Roots, the police officer who took Stephenson's statement when he reported his suspicions on Boxing Day 1888, said he'd known Stephenson for 20 years, describing him as "a travelled man of education and ability, a doctor of medicine of Paris and New York: a major of the Italian army". Clearly Roots accepted many of Stephenson's colourful claims about his past, but doesn't appear to have taken his accusations against Dr Davies as seriously.

Nor do the police appear to have been unduly impressed when a man had presented himself at the station two days before and identified Stephenson – who Roots describes as "perpetually fuddled" – as Jack the Ripper. This was an unlikely amateur detective named George Marsh, who had formed a drunken pact with Stephenson to share the proceeds if they successfully captured the Ripper, before falling out with his former drinking buddy.

The episode appeared to be descending into farce. Melvin Harris is adamant that Stephenson was only ever playing the fool in order to throw people off the scent, presenting the journalist W. T. Stead as a character witness who believed that Stephenson was more just a plausible fantasist. It was Stead who commissioned Stephenson's Ripper article for the *Pall Mall Gazette*, and according to Stephenson it was Stead who furnished him with the dubious insider information about the sodomy of Jack's final victim.

"He has been known to me for many years," wrote Stead, introducing some of Stephenson's journalism in an 1896 edition of the *Borderland* quarterly. "He is one of the most remarkable men I ever met. For more than a year I was under the impression that he was the veritable Jack the Ripper; an impression which I believed was shared by the police, who at least once had him under arrest; although, as he completely satisfied them, they liberated him without bringing him to court."

Stead is justly celebrated for his 1885 campaign against child prostitution in the *Pall Mall Gazette*, an example of the New Journalism at its crusading best. Whilst he often acted with the best of motives, Stead was also a shameless sensationalist – surely the only reason for publishing Stephenson's madcap speculations on the Ripper crimes in 1888. His biographical note on Stephenson sounds more like the promotional blarney of a seasoned showman than a serious accusation. Would a man like Stead – willing to go to gaol for his principles over the issue of child prostitution – really have employed somebody he seriously believed to have been butchering London streetwalkers?

Harris's principal source, however, was neither Stead nor Crowley ("whose concern for the truth was minimal," according to Harris), but a colourful Italian occultist named Vittoria Cremers – or at least her recollections as recorded by the journalist Bernard O'Donnell in 1930. In 1888, Cremers made her way to England; there she threw herself into the burgeoning Theosophy movement – the forerunner to the New Age which attempted a synthesis of diverse, primarily Oriental, mystical traditions – taking an active role in the publication of the movement's journal, *Lucifer*.

Theosophy was founded in 1875 by Helena Blavatsky, a robust Russian medium who claimed to receive communications from the spirit world. Her heady blend of exotic Eastern ideas, spiritualism – a growing trend throughout the late-1800s – and occult science proved a popular recipe, and Theosophy attracted numerous fashionable converts. Among these was the authoress Mabel Collins, who became attracted to the movement in 1881 but was later expelled by its leader.

Collins had read a number of articles on the occult in the *Pall Mall Gazette*, signed 'RD', which much impressed her. W. T. Stead had commissioned Roslyn D'Onston Stephenson to write more of the same, this time in an attempt to cash in on H. Rider Haggard's hugely successful fantasy-adventure novel *She*, purporting to expose the shocking magical practices of the Dark Continent. Mabel Collins began to exchange letters with the *Pall Mall Gazette*'s occult correspondent, who she was convinced was a great magician, and the two appear to have became lovers. Vittoria Cremers was not impressed at the new arrival, who she clearly regarded as a rival. Despite this, Stephenson contributed an article on African magic to *Lucifer* in 1890, and the trio set up in business together as the Pompadour Cosmetique Company.

The venture was not a success. According to Cremers, the relationship between Stephenson and Collins also began to sour. Mabel became increasingly convinced that her lover was not only an occult authority, but a black magician and the man responsible for the Ripper crimes. Threats of blackmail began to fly between the increasingly acrimonious parties. It was in this volatile situation that, whilst searching Stephenson's belongings for some incriminating love letters she says he planned to use against Collins, Cremers claims she found some bloodstained neckties. Initially she was baffled as to their significance, until Stephenson later confided in her secrets about the Ripper murders. He said that the killer, a surgeon of his acquaintance, had escaped the crime scenes with the body parts he had taken as trophies from his victims, concealed beneath his tie. Cremers immediately concluded that Mabel's suspicions were justified, and that the terrifying man she had shared a house with had actually been making a confession.

This is the basis of the most popular theory of Jack the Ripper as a black magician, the story later repeated by Crowley – who claimed to have had possession of the incriminating ties – and reported periodically in the press in various forms. Whilst Melvin Harris seems convinced that his case is watertight, however, it clearly wouldn't convince a court of law. Cremers makes for an unreliable witness at best, her testimony as quoted by Harris reading with all of the breathlessness of a penny dreadful. The Italian dowager would have been in her 70s when she allegedly recalled the story of some four decades previously to O'Donnell, whose unpublished manuscript we must also take on trust.

During that time, neither she nor Mabel Collins appear to have felt the need to inform the authorities of their fascinating secret (though the fact that Crowley was aware of it suggests somebody was gossiping along those lines). Collins and Cremers parted company shortly after the events the latter describes, a separation she appears to have blamed on Stephenson – giving ample motive for a woman scorned to spread wicked rumours.

The closer you get to the occult milieu, the more it becomes a world of smoke and mirrors, of slander and backbiting, of assumed names and miraculous claims. Establishing anything concrete in such an environment can prove frustratingly difficult, and the details of Roslyn D'Onston Stephenson's career remain the subject of debate among ripperologists. The idea of him fleeing the streets of the East End in 1888 with a freshly excised uterus lodged neatly behind his necktie, to smuggle it back to his hospital bed, does seem fairly ludicrous.

But what if the over-imaginative journalist had stumbled upon the truth in the long hours spent convalescing and pondering on the Ripper? Might Jack the Ripper have been killing to some kind of occult agenda? It's perhaps possible that Stephenson made the assumption that the killer was French because of the Eliphas Levi (note the correct spelling) connection – though, as he himself observes, an English anthology of Levi's occult texts had recently been published. So did this book contain instructions for rites that might have inspired a mystically-minded Ripper?

Levi was certainly a highly influential occult authority, whose reputation had grown since he died in poverty in 1875. The Theosophical Society, founded that same year, incorporated many of his doctrines into their sprawling cosmology, whilst the Great Beast Crowley claimed to have been his reincarnation (sharing a date of birth with the French occultist's year of death).

The Golden Dawn, the occult order in which Crowley served his occult apprenticeship, had also been founded in 1888, the year of the Ripper murders. It drew heavily from Levi's scholarship, and would go on to become one of the most influential occult organisations of the modern world, boasting an impressive list of influential and fashionable Victorians who hoped to become enlightened by initiation into its mysteries.

One of the Order's founders was one Dr William Wynn Westcott, who was also a London coroner. A man with medical knowledge, who founded his occult order in the year of the Ripper crimes – could it be mere coincidence? One commentator doesn't think so. Journalist Christopher Smith has concocted a theory he calls 'Jack the Ripper: The Alembic Connection', which has Westcott presiding over the churchyard sacrifice of the Ripper victims before his hooded Golden Dawn minions dump their bodies in the backstreets of the East End. It's an implausible theory for numerous reasons – more a gothic flight of fancy than informed criminological speculation – but even though the Golden Dawn may be wholly blameless, might not another organisation or individual have committed the Ripper crimes with satanic intent?

"Witchcraft, properly so called, that is, ceremonial operation with intent to bewitch, acts only on the operator, and serves to fix and confirm his will, by formulating it with persistence and travail, the two conditions which make volition efficacious," Eliphas Levi writes in *Dogme et Ritual de la Haute Magie*, the 1855 text Stephenson name-checked in his Ripper article. "The more difficult or horrible the operation, the greater is its power, because it acts more strongly on the imagination and confirms effort in direct ratio of resistance. This explains the bizarre nature and even atrocious character of the operations in Black Magic, as practised by the ancients and in the middle ages, the diabolical masses, administration of sacraments to reptiles, effusions of blood, human sacrifices and other monstrosities, which are the very essence and reality of Goetia or Nigromancy. Such are the practices which from all time have brought down upon sorcerers the just repression of the laws. Black Magic is really only a graduated combination of sacrileges and murders designed for the permanent perversion of a human will and for the realisation in a living man of the hideous phantom of the demon."

It all sounds very ominous, if rather vague – a suggestion that committing atrocities allows the black magician to unleash some demonic inner force. This certainly could fit with a potential profile of an occult Ripper, but one phrase that doesn't invite such an interpretation is "formulating [the rite] with persistence and travail, the two conditions which make volition efficacious" – most of the Ripper murders were committed in a matter of minutes, the longest crime taking a few hours at most. The occult rites Levi describes are the product of weeks of meticulous preparation, conducted for obvious reasons in secluded spots where the magician was unlikely to be disturbed. The idea of a black magician choosing the streets of Whitechapel, teeming with life day and night, as the venue for his human sacrifice is highly implausible.

The concept of drawing a vast occult symbol using dead bodies is also worth disposing of at this point. Harris insists that in order to see Stephenson's 'cross' one must "mark the sites of the murders on an ordnance survey map of the period (not the usually inaccurate sketch maps)". Even accepting this, arcane black magicians would not have had access to ordnance survey maps – or accurate maps of any description – and there is no obvious occult precedent for drawing crosses, *vesica piscis* or any other giant mystical insignia across the landscape using corpses. Levi makes no mention of it, and if Jack the Ripper was attempting such a bizarre operation, he was almost certainly dancing to the beat of his own drum. So just what was involved in the blood sacrifices of authentic occult tradition?

"Most of the processes in the textbooks involve the killing of an animal, usually a young goat, at some stage in the operations," writes Richard Cavendish in his chapter on 'The Sacrifice and the Summoning' in *The Black Arts* (published in 1967, and still perhaps the best popular text on the subject). 'In the older grimoires this is done long before the ceremony itself begins and the animal's skin is used to make parchment . . . In the later grimoires the sacrifice tends to be more closely associated with the ceremony itself and in modern rituals the victim is sometimes slaughtered at the height of the ceremony. This is done to increase the supply of force in the circle. In occult theory a living creature is a storehouse of energy, and when it is killed most of that energy is liberated . . . The animal should be young, healthy and virgin, so that its supply of force has been dissipated as little as possible."

To return to Whitechapel in the autumn of 1888, the Ripper's victims were anything but 'young, healthy and virgin'. Journalist Arthur Doisy, who covered the case for *The Star*, had become convinced that Jack was a black magician when he "heard of the bright farthings and burnt matches which he said might have formed the 'flaming points' of a magical figure called a 'pentacle' at each angle of which such points were found" at the murder sites. But his accounts of strategically-placed matches and candle stubs are not borne out by more reliable testimony.

Most importantly, at the risk of stating the obvious, the Ripper's victims were human and Cavendish makes clear that the authentic texts are all but unanimous in prescribing animal sacrifice in their black magic rites. So, is there no evidence of human sacrifice in the history of black magic?

"It would obviously be more effective to sacrifice a human being because of the far greater psychological 'kick' involved," concedes Cavendish in *The Black Arts*. "Eliphas Levi said that when the grimoires talk about killing a kid they really mean a human child. Although this is highly unlikely, there is a tradition that the most effective sacrifice to demons is the murder of a human being. In 1465, a jury in Norfolk found that John Caus and Robert Hikkes had summoned up a spirit and promised to sacrifice a Christian to it if it led them to buried treasure. The spirit did and they found more than 100 shillings, but they cheated the spirit by baptising a cock with a Christian name and burning it. In 1841, treasure-hunters in Italy murdered a boy as a sacrifice to a demon which they believed would find buried treasure for them."

Cavendish raises a couple of valuable points here, the first of which contradicts Eliphas Levi. The esteemed Professor of Transcendental Magic may have been revered by occultists in the Victorian and Edwardian eras, but as a reliable source on authentic occult tradition, he leaves a lot to be desired. "One doesn't go to Levi for a scholarly interpretation of notoriously difficult texts," writes Gary Lachman in *The Dedalus Book of the Occult*. "One reads him for the sheer fun and romance of his books . . . Levi is never dull. His pages may be riddled with howlers, but you want to turn them, and the reader invariably gets value for money."

Another fake, but not entirely a fake? Like Crowley, Levi liked to pepper the stew, which was ultimately why his books proved so popular and influential. The other point raised by Cavendish that strikes a chord is his mention of buried treasure. Many an aspirant student of the black arts must have been disappointed by how grasping the authors of the original grimoires appear to have been. Finding buried treasure was the medieval and renaissance equivalent of winning the lottery – a life-changing stroke of luck that *might just* happen – and the history of sorcery is depressingly replete with stories of magicians claiming to know how to fashion charms for locating hidden gold.

A popular example is the 'hand of glory'. Consisting of the severed hand of an executed criminal cupping a candle made from human fat, it was supposed to be able to find treasure and unlock doors. A variant on the theme came to prominence during the Ripper murders, via an Austrian scholar named Dr Bloch who'd made a study of local superstitions:

"A Vienna Correspondent calls attention, in connection with the Whitechapel murders, to a strange superstition among German thieves, which survives in some quarters even to the present day," according to *The Echo* on 9 October 1888. "In various German criminal codes of the seventeenth and eighteenth centuries, as also in statutes of a more recent date, punishments are prescribed for the mutilation of female corpses, with the object of making from the uterus and other organs the so-called *Diebslichter* or *Schlafslichter*, respectively 'thieves' candles' or 'soporific candles'. According to an old superstition, still rife in various parts of Germany, the light from such candles will throw those upon whom it falls into the deepest slumbers, and they may, consequently, become a valuable instrument to the thieving profession. Hence their name. At one time there was a regular manufactory of such candles. That this superstition has survived amongst German thieves to the present day was proved by a case tried at Biala, in Galicia, as recently as 1875. In this the body of a woman had been found mutilated in precisely the same way as were the victims of the Whitechapel murderer."

This, of course, proves nothing, and nothing came of Dr Bloch's suggestion. But the fact remains that his theory has a far sturdier basis in authentic lore than anything suggested by Roslyn D'Onston Stephenson in his article. Might Jack the Ripper have been a thief – possibly a German immigrant – acquiring ingredients for a folkloric tool of the trade? It seems highly improbable, but no more improbable than somebody stalking the streets of London trying to draw occult symbols across the map with corpses, female genitalia wedged snugly beneath their necktie. Yet the latter makes for a more satisfying story somehow, and the theories that make for good copy survive by a sensationalist process of natural selection.

In 1992, FBI Special Agent Kenneth Lanning wrote a report on the satanic crime wave that was supposedly threatening American society, a conspiracy theory later dubbed the 'Satanic Panic' by sociologists. In his conclusion, Lanning referenced the Ripper crimes: "On a recent television program commemorating the one hundredth anniversary of Jack the Ripper, almost fifty per cent of the viewing audience who called the polling telephone numbers indicated that they thought the murders were committed as part of a conspiracy involving the British royal family. The five experts on the programme, however, unanimously agreed the crimes were the work of one disorganised but lucky individual who was diagnosed as a paranoid schizophrenic. In many ways, the murders of Jack the Ripper are similar to those allegedly committed by Satanists today . . .'

What Lanning is saying is not that the Ripper crimes resembled the murders that some Christian conspiracy theorists and tabloid journalists claim were perpetrated by elusive cultists, but that the public is inclined to believe the story they find most exciting and memorable, however improbable.

There certainly were Satanists around at the time he wrote the report. In 1966, the San Franciscan sorcerer Anton LaVey had created something of a media sensation by founding a Church of Satan, which, like the Golden Dawn, attracted a number of celebrity adherents. In 1969, his *Satanic Bible* was published, which, like Crowley's *Magick in Theory and Practice*, features a chapter on sacrifice. Provocatively entitled 'On the Choice of a Human Sacrifice', it pours scorn on previous sorcerers for even advocating animal sacrifice, suggesting the use of sexual rites as a more efficacious alternative and condemning criminality of all kinds. The only human sacrifice LaVey does condone is that directed at those who make themselves targets by virtue of their antisocial behaviour, conducted by use of magical curses.

According to LaVey, he launched just such a curse on the hated hippie movement in 1969, resulting in the infamous Manson massacres that irrevocably tarnished the flower-power generation. Almost twenty years later, a group of his most influential disciples from among the fringe and counterculture movements staged an event to commemorate the curse with a combination of avant-garde film and music performance, deliberately designed to resemble a cross between a black magic rite and a fascist rally.

It also fell on the near-centenary of the murder of Martha Tabram, and was dubbed 8/8/88 in recognition of the date of its performance and the supposed mystical significance of the number eight. "8/8/88 was a recapitulation of a destruction ritual that Anton LaVey performed on

August 8, 1969," organiser Boyd Rice told *Fifth Path* magazine in 1992. "We did it nineteen years later, to the day and hour . . . the event was a complete success. It was sold out, and the line to get in was stretched around the block. Magically, it was a perfect success. It set the stage for a lot of things which have happened since, and a lot more things yet to happen."

Charles Manson is a criminal who has attained a mythic status to rival that of Jack the Ripper, and, while he was the focus of the 8/8/88, those in attendance may well have had Saucy Jack on their minds. Boyd Rice is best known as a pioneer of avant-garde 'industrial' music and a cultural agent provocateur, and has been branded a fascist by critics – a charge he refutes. Rice dedicated *Easy Listening for Iron Youth*, the 1991 compilation album of his work under the title NON, to a series of history's most notorious figures, including Jack the Ripper. The sleeve includes a quote from LaVey: "There is a demon in man that should be exercised, not exorcised."

Another principal 8/8/88 organiser accused of fascist sympathies is the author and occultist Nikolas Schreck, who later married LaVey's daughter Zeena. In 1989, Schreck and Zeena released an album entitled *The Fiery Summons* as part of the band Radio Werewolf. The album features the track 'From Hell', in which Schreck reads from some of the original letters Jack the Ripper allegedly sent in 1888 over a sinister musical background.

The album's liner notes include "a word of caution", identifying the recording as "sonic magic . . . The very act of hearing this music serves as an initiation into the lycanthropic mysteries," promises Schreck. "This particular exercise is intended to awaken the dormant regions of the human mind, thus stimulating a process of resurgent atavism. This process has previously been understood as lycanthropy and indeed this is a ritual to unleash the beast in man . . ."

Whatever one may make of this, there have thus far been no reported cases of *The Fiery Summons* influencing any regrettable incidents. There is also something in what Schreck says: medieval and renaissance accounts of werewolf trials are usually insistent that the accused does not change shape, but merely attains the bestial behaviour and murderous appetites of a predator. (See Chapter Five.) The Ripper crimes occurred at a time when psychiatry was eclipsing superstitious explanations of human behaviour, turning the werewolf back into a man, in a manner of speaking.

Some still prefer to see the Ripper through a magical lens. In *From Hell*, Alan Moore provides some of the most convincing occult analysis of the crimes. It doesn't involve identifying the Ripper as a black magician – though there are strong elements of that in Moore's Ripper, Dr William Gull – so much as scrutinising the events to highlight strange synchronicities and patterns.

Just as Crowley claims to have been the magical progeny of Eliphas Levi, Moore links the Ripper murders with the conception of Adolf Hitler (the crimes precede Hitler's birth by around six months – the same formula Crowley employs to prove his link with Levi). As Moore explained to *Rue Morgue* magazine in 2001, "so many of the movements in technology and other fields in the 1880s had contained the seeds of the twentieth century . . . That was when the machine gun was invented, when the motor car was invented; it was when the French moved into Indochina, which would lead to the Vietnam war; it was the West's first clash with contemporary Islam; the Mitchelson-Morley experiments proved that the ether didn't exist, which led to Einstein's theories, which led to Hiroshima . . ."

The interviewer, Gary Butler, pressed Moore on whether he shared any of the viewpoints of the mystically-minded Ripper he had created. "Yeah, obviously," he confessed. "Though I tried to psychically channel William Gull where possible . . . But it seems to me that perhaps in bygone times, archaic ways of thinking were actually much richer than our modern mindset. Rationalism has given us so much, but it has taken away as well . . . In the renaissance everything has correspondence with everything else – everything becomes a fairly rich tapestry. Compare that to a world in which symbols don't mean anything anymore, people don't connect them up, and a fact is a fact. There is a certain barrenness there in our modern mindset."

In other words, an occult approach to Jack the Ripper is unlikely to identify the perpetrator. But you might learn something far more interesting . . .

Chapter XI

Ripping the Silver Screen

Whilst Weimar Berlin witnessed the nativity of celluloid horror, the genre was christened in Hollywood, California. The catalyst for this was the surprise success of two 1931 films – *Dracula* and *Frankenstein* – which made stars of the actors Bela Lugosi and Boris Karloff and saved the studio responsible, Universal, from bankruptcy during the lean years of the Great Depression. The Gothic chillers that followed were henceforth known as 'horror pictures'. As already suggested, celluloid interpretations of the Ripper story largely found themselves corralled into this genre ghetto, though Universal fought shy of invoking the spirit of Saucy Jack.

They did, however, visit his stalking ground, and just as Universal's set dressers created eerie, heavily expressionistic versions of Transylvania and Germany, so they conjured celluloid versions of Victorian London's threatening backstreets. (Many of the most talented filmmakers of Weimar Berlin fled to the US when Hitler came to power, and were influential in creating the distinctive look of golden-age Hollywood Gothic.)

Whilst the Ripper himself never emerged from the billowing fog fabricated on Universal's backlots, according to Professor Clive Bloom Jack haunted the sets in all but name. In his 2008 Docklands lecture 'Jack the Ripper: A Legacy in Pictures', Professor Bloom suggested that *The Werewolf of London*, starring Henry Hull, is a spin on the Ripper myth.

"This world is not empty, it is teeming with life, but that life has gone to the bad," he says of the generic London setting of this film and others like it. "It is a world of diseased skin and cracked and toothless smiles. Its inhabitants are forever coming out of the boozer . . . *The Werewolf of London* was made in 1935, it's the first werewolf movie, and in it, it has Mrs Moncaster and Mrs Whack, who are two completely gin-soaked idiots, and in fact at one point one of them actually socks the other one to get rid of her.

"And they're in the East End pub just before the werewolf – a.k.a. Jack the Ripper, actually – goes trotting around the streets to try and kill people. And of course they invite him into their homes, they always do. The common part of them is nasty, but quite amusing. One thing that Mrs Whack and Mrs Moncaster do is remind us that the world of Jack the Ripper is the world of the music hall too . . . The inhabitants are forever coming out of the boozer drunk, arm in arm, or out of the pawnshop, or hanging around street corners, smoking in the shadows, up to no good. Ragged children lurk in dirty and torn clothes. Inebriated women look for their rent and stroll in cheap feather boas and red petticoats, saying, with a wink, 'Sixpence, guv'nor?' or, 'Cheers, duck!' For this world has its own patois. Sailors skulk and whores half-heartedly solicit until Jack catches their fated eye. It is a world full of stereotypes." What Professor Bloom is suggesting is that the atmosphere and setting are at least as important in Ripper films as the characters or story – for little else about the film is truly suggestive of the Whitechapel murders.

Whilst *The Werewolf of London* may have been the first major werewolf movie it wasn't the very first, preceded by at least four celluloid treatments of the myth, the first of which – a lost short film entitled *The Werewolf* – was made by Universal back in 1913. Critics in 1935 still appear to have regarded the story as old hat. "At least two contemporary critiques considered *Werewolf of London* a familiar yarn," observes Jonathan Rigby in *American Gothic*, "the *New York Times* opining that 'the central idea has been used before' and Britain's *Monthly Film Bulletin* calling it 'another story on the werewolf legend'. Given the paucity, and obscurity, of previous werewolf subjects . . . it's reasonable to assume that these critics were alluding to the Jekyll and Hyde motif. The two themes are obviously connected and the film shows every sign of wanting to pick up some of the lustre contained in Paramount's *Dr Jekyll and Mr Hyde*." Henry Hull's werewolf is also substantially less hirsute than better-known versions, and perhaps the only lycanthrope to pause, before heading out on a night of mayhem, in order to put on his hat and scarf.

There are links between the Ripper case and the werewolf myth, which are examined in greater detail in Chapters Five and Ten. For now, suffice to say that, if *The Werewolf of London* is a Jack the Ripper film, then so too are the numerous screen interpretations of Robert Louis Stevenson's *The Strange Case of Dr Jekyll and Mr Hyde*. All of the familiar clichés of nocturnal Victorian London, which Professor Bloom identifies as archetypes of Ripper cinema, were first established in Hollywood in *Jekyll and Hyde* pictures. There are well in excess of 100 such adaptations of

Stevenson's novella, making a survey of them all impossible, though it is worth noting that – bar an obscure Danish version of 1910 – early versions draw heavily from the 1887 Thomas Russell Sullivan stage adaptation. It was this play that the actor Richard Mansfield was performing in London in 1888 – the performance so powerful that some fanciful souls supposed Mansfield himself might be the Ripper. (The role helped make his career, though the actor felt it prudent to temporarily remove it from his repertoire.)

The Sullivan script also influenced the first truly cinematic version of the story, still regarded by many as the classic big screen adaptation and the one Rigby supposes inspired *The Werewolf of London*. It was in turn inspired by the success of Universal's horror pictures, being released on the New Year's Eve of 1931. Directed with startling verve by Rouben Mamoulian and starring Fredric March, his Jekyll is a humanitarian physician driven to unleash his primitive instincts by a restless libido. Hyde is a simian sexual sadist, his torture of the prostitute Ivy Pearson still disturbing to the modern eye. The innovative Hyde makeup suggests the transformation as one of devolution, touching upon scientific theories that touched a raw nerve then, and – sad to say – still do today. The implication is that, rather than creatures created perfect by God then tainted by our own weakness, we are apes civilised by progress, always at risk of sliding back into our former bestial selves. Jekyll's devolution was also social – from a respectable 'Doctor' to a proletarian 'Mister', Hyde's brutality implicitly linked with his descent into working-class vulgarity.

Leaving aside any supposed 'factual' sightings of the Ripper for now, a parallel path of social mobility can also be observed in imaginary depictions of Jack. Whilst a few early theorists favoured a well-to-do culprit, illustrations in the popular press suggested a humbler candidate. Access to Jekyll's wardrobe ensured that Hyde took to the foggy London streets attired in a top hat and opera cape – which cinema would eventually establish as standard-issue uniform for its Rippers – but he invariably looks ill at ease in such finery, a parvenu at best.

In 1932, Ivor Novello revisited the role of *The Lodger*, which Denis Meikle regards as superior to the silent version filmed under Alfred Hitchcock. This time Novello is accused of being 'the Bosnian Murderer', though, despite adopting an Eastern European accent, the audience knows that their hero is still far too 'nice' to actually be the killer. The Ripper's ascent up the social ladder would be a gradual one, from popular assumptions that he must be a crass commoner to modern cultural convictions that only a well-spoken gent could feasibly fit the frame. In class terms, it's a kind of Jekyll and Hyde transformation in reverse.

The definitive version of Marie Belloc Lowndes' novel was filmed in America in 1943. This *Lodger* returned the action to 1888 and, for the first time, put the spotlight fully on the killer – who wasn't an Avenger or Bosnian Murderer, but Jack the Ripper.

"I'd refer to the novel now and again I suppose," reflected the film's screenwriter, Barré Lyndon. "One thing I did was to go over to the Huntington Library and look into the newspaper reports in the London *Times* of that particular period. The reports are very restrained, but it's all there." A strong cast and solid production value, combine with powerful direction from John Brahm and a mesmeric performance from Laird Cregar to create a film that is not only the first full-fledged Jack the Ripper picture, but also, according to many connoisseurs, the best.

Brahm exhibited his background in German Expressionist cinema with claustrophobic urban web of suspense and shadow from which the corpulent Cregar, playing the tormented Mr Slade, looms. Cregar had an unusual acting background, playing the doomed English aesthete Oscar Wilde on the stage and menacing heavies in Hollywood *noir* thrillers, and he brings a bit of both seemingly contradictory approaches to his Ripper, successfully combining weighty menace with a curious undertone of queasy pathos.

Professor Bloom emphasised the role of the generic setting at the opening to his 2008 lecture: "An East End of the mind is the scene of terror, and nothing must detract from that effect," he described, indicating how the growing gap between the cinematic Whitechapel and the authentic scenes of the Ripper crimes could only add to the myth's potency. "Everything must be mysterious, half-glimpsed, half-acknowledged. It is endless night in the East End of the mind. This is why the fictional East End is rarely, if ever, shot on location, because this world has to be isolated and contained. Its alleys and cobbled byways are the equivalent of the labyrinths of the mind. Endlessly uncoiling and endlessly confined in a circumscribed place, therefore it has to take place basically on a lot. The East End has to be recreated in filmland as a set that is airless, claustrophobic, without escape . . . There is no sky, nothing to indicate an outside world. Water may lap by the banks of the Thames, yet it is oily, going nowhere." Jonathan Rigby gives a more prosaic assessment of *The Lodger*, describing the film's first murder as "an opening scene that set the fog-laden example by which all Ripper films would be judged".

By that measure, the 1953 US film *Man in the Attic* falls somewhat short. A fairly faithful remake of the 1944 *Lodger*, the reptilian Hollywood villain Jack Palance takes the role of the menacing Mr Slade. Palance is one of those performers who always give value for money, though in *Man in the Attic* he struggles to overcome modest production values which never quite transport the viewer to Victorian Whitechapel. A series of fumbled period details conspire against any aspirations to authenticity, not least the hairstyles of Palance's Ripper and the Scotland Yard Inspector, played by Byron Palmer, which could only have been the Brylcreemed products of a 1950s barber. (Criminologist viewers may be more upset by the use of fingerprinting in *Man in the Attic*, though it was far from the first fictional treatment of the Ripper to commit this chronological offence.)

The film's female lead, Irish actress Constance Smith, was no stranger to sinister house guests, having appeared in the 1949 British production *Room to Let*. As its name suggests, this is yet another spin on the *Lodger* story, where an elderly couple begin to suspect that the mysterious man renting their spare room might be concealing a deadly secret. The tenant in question, Dr Fell – played by the funereal Valentine Dyall – does indeed turn out to be Jack the Ripper, recently escaped from a lunatic asylum. While the parallels with *The Lodger* are obvious, the film's immediate source was a BBC radio play by Margery Allingham. (Dyall was best known for his radio work, introducing BBC radio's horror plays as 'the Man in Black'.) Perhaps unsurprisingly – as Allingham was primarily a mystery author, creator of the gentleman sleuth Albert Campion – *Room to Let* hinged on a classic locked door mystery. Whilst not without its charms, *Room to Let* isn't a major film by any estimation, and its chief significance lies in its status as one of the first excursions into the macabre by the struggling, low-budget British studio, Hammer Films.

By the end of the decade Hammer would become a household name, synonymous with Gothic-horror period pieces. Like Universal nearly thirty years before, the studio first discovered the commercial potential of goosebumps courtesy of adaptations of the Frankenstein and Dracula stories, whose successes in 1957 and 1958 made stars of their lead players, Peter Cushing and Christopher Lee. Early British cinema had been hamstrung by the tendency of unimaginative directors to simply park a camera in front of a popular stage show and film it. Hammer successfully assembled a team of talented professionals – art directors, costume designers and set dressers, as well as actors and directors – capable of translating the best of Britain's rich theatrical heritage to the dynamic medium of film.

Hammer's output became iconic – an inimitable Gothic fairytale world of elegance and evil set in the once-upon-a-time of the 1800s. The Ripper, meanwhile, first saw his name in lights courtesy of a British film in 1959. *Jack the Ripper* wasn't a Hammer film, but a production by a rival studio eager to emulate Hammer's success. In *Jack the Ripper: The Murders and the Movies*, Denis Meikle suggests that the 1926 *Lodger* had overtones of *Nosferatu* due to director Alfred Hitchcock's innovative use of expressionism's shadow-bound visual style, and that Ivor Novello's performance in the 1932 version was resonant of Bela Lugosi's iconic role in *Dracula*. If so, then the 1959 *Jack the Ripper* takes us into similar territory to Hammer's *Dracula*, which saw Christopher Lee don the cape of the Prince of Darkness the previous year.

"Think of the Ripper running through the streets of Whitechapel, cape billowing behind him, and it's difficult not to think of Dracula," observes Maitland McDonagh in an article on Jack's screen career for horror magazine *The Dark Side*. The 1959 *Jack the Ripper* helped establish the regulation Ripper uniform – top hat and opera cape – that has stayed with us ever since, and is all but interchangeable with the clichéd Count Dracula costume to be found in any good fancy dress outfitters. (Neither Lugosi nor Lee favoured headgear for their interpretations of the Count, but John Carradine's 1940s Dracula donned a topper, as did Gary Oldman for *Bram Stoker's Dracula* in 1992.)

Professor Clive Bloom opines that the cinematic Jack the Ripper has most in common with Hammer's version of Baron Victor Frankenstein, brought to life by the remarkable Peter Cushing as a wiry, driven monomaniac, both imperious aristocrat and cold-blooded surgeon. By this time, the imagined links between the Ripper and both the medical profession and the upper classes are now all but indelible:

"In *The Curse of Frankenstein*, we have an increasingly obsessed Victor," Bloom observes of Cushing's debut performance as Frankenstein, "armed with medical bag and knife, and dressed in a top hat and cloak in a peculiar contemporary costume which we call Victoriana, so beloved of Hammer, who goes out at night on secret missions to retrieve body parts of the dead – in order to build his schizoid double, who turns monstrous because of the substitution of a mad brain. Both Victor and the monster are mad – but Victor, locked in his laboratory and driven by the passions that will sacrifice the women of his household, is the maddest of all."

Jack the Ripper represents something of a halfway house between the rich new strain of Gothic and the cold leftovers of more traditional British horror cinema. Its scriptwriter, Jimmy Sangster, had also written Hammer's first Frankenstein and Dracula pictures and would go on to pen a number of the studio's classic horror movies of the 1960s. "I was always frightened that the facts would get in the way of the story," Sangster later observed, constructing a ghoulish Gothic whodunit centred round the Mercy Hospital for Women. His principal source is evidently the Leonard Matters book, *The Mystery of Jack the Ripper*, and there is never any real doubt that the Ripper is a doctor, the only question being which one.

In a sign of the Ripper's escalating social status, whilst not yet a count (or indeed a prince) Jack turns out to be the hospital's eminent director, played by Ewen Solon, who is crushed by a lift in the film's gruesome climax. It's the sequence that sticks in most viewers' memories, as the black and white film briefly shifts to colour in order to show the killer's blood bubbling up through the floor to full effect.

It's a gimmick that underlines *Jack the Ripper*'s transitional status, as Hammer had distinguished their entries into Gothic territory by finding the budget to film their bloody fables entirely in Eastmancolor. The lurid results dismayed Hammer's prissy British critics, just as *Jack the Ripper* upset a Tennessee censor objecting to the sight of "heads and hands amputated on screen". By way of contrast, French critics lauded the film as "one of the greatest Anglo Saxon horror films", "a perfect manual of sexual perversion" showcasing "delirious sexuality".

Watching the film now, it's difficult to see what either the Americans or the French were getting so steamed up about, as the amputations and perversion they describe are conspicuous by their absence. (It is possible that a more explicit version of *Jack the Ripper* exists, as alternative versions of films were sometimes issued for distribution in overseas markets more tolerant of celluloid flesh and blood.) The same is true of Hammer films which, while routinely reviled as sadistic exercises in excess in their day, now seldom qualify for more than a '12' certificate on DVD.

"Historical veracity (and the fact the killer is ultimately unmasked and apprehended) aside, *Jack the Ripper* did more to entrench the myth in the popular mind than anything before or since," concludes Meikle. It took Hammer over two decades to get around to revisiting the Ripper after they'd had a *Room to Let* in 1949. When they did, they wisely sidestepped issues of historical veracity. The studio's 1970s output was long routinely dismissed by horror aficionados as a series of desperate attempts to update their Gothic formula in the face of flagging ticket sales. Only recently have genre enthusiasts begun to re-evaluate Hammer's final years as a film studio and give credit to a number of these late productions as bold and offbeat exercises in Gothic cinema. Their two Ripper films are excellent examples: *Hands of the Ripper* and *Dr Jekyll and Sister Hyde* were both made and debuted in 1971. They are, however, worlds apart – the former bathed in grisly pathos, the latter an irresistible wallow in ghoulish camp.

Dr Jekyll and Sister Hyde reputedly began as a casual dinner party joke by screenwriter Brian Clemens. He is perhaps best known as the co-creator of *The Avengers*, the classic British TV series that gave the secret agent genre a stylishly surreal, kinky 1960s spin. (*The Avengers* aired a Ripper-inspired episode entitled 'Fog' in 1969, though by this time Clemens was only involved as co-producer and the show was past its best.) By the time his *Sister Hyde* gag had expanded into a script, Clemens had anachronistically incorporated not just a gender-bending Jekyll, but Burke and Hare, the Edinburgh bodysnatchers of the 1820s, and of course Jack the Ripper.

Jekyll, played by Ralph Bates – then being groomed as a new horror icon by Hammer – develops an elixir of life, which also transforms him into the luscious but immoral Hyde, a scarlet woman brought to life by the smouldering Martine Beswick. The elixir requires female hormones, which ultimately leads to Jekyll and his feminine alter ego prowling the streets of London, looking for unwilling donors. Though it's never quite spelled out, the implication is that these are obtained by genital mutilation – hence the Ripper angle.

Dr Jekyll and Sister Hyde demonstrates that both Hammer's trademark lush period Gothic and the clichés of Ripper cinema were already sufficiently well established to be ripe for affectionate parody. The film is very much of its time, having fun with sexual role reversals – particularly pertinent at a time guys with long hair and chicks in jeans were troubling traditionalists. Director Roy Ward Baker and his stars largely play it straight, allowing their dark fable's ironic gallows humour to speak for itself.

Despite Hammer's tried and tested expertise at evoking period atmosphere, it's difficult to know where to start with a shameless Gothic burlesque like *Dr Jekyll and Sister Hyde* in terms looking for realism. For all that, *Dr Jekyll and Sister Hyde* is still a horror movie rooted in one of history's grisliest episodes. Ripper film expert Denis Meikle is quick to bring movies to task for careless historical inaccuracies; yet, in the scene featuring the film's most disturbing murder, where Bates takes a knife to a streetwalker, Meikle confesses to being struck by "its uncanny resemblance to the killing of Mary Jane Kelly. The room is bare but for a bed and chair, the former sited in approximation of Kelly's own. At some time during the early hours of 9 November 1888, a 'blazing' fire was lit in number 13. Kelly was slaughtered on her own small bed. Whether by accident or design, Baker comes nearer than any director before or since to a real sense of the Miller's Court murder, not only through his staging of the action but through filming it in the flickering firelight and against an eerie blue-green glow from studio lamps, which plays on a deeper level to intimate the presence of death. Taken in isolation, this episode ranks as one of the high points in Ripper cinema."

The Hands of the Ripper is something of a misnomer – its French title, *Daughter of the Ripper*, gives a much better idea of the theme. Jack himself appears only briefly in the Whitechapel prologue, where his infant daughter witnesses him killing her mother. He is garbed in the standard issue cloak and top hat, with a facial disfigurement suggesting syphilis. It implies both the prevailing current theory of the day as to the Ripper's motive, and the 'sins of the father' theme of the film, which suggests that the pox is not the only hereditary curse that can pass down a tainted bloodline.

We rejoin the story in the Edwardian era, as the pioneering Freudian psychiatrist Dr John Pritchard (ably played by Eric Porter) attempts to cure Jack's grown daughter, the deceptively fragile Anna (Angharad Rees) of the homicidal blackouts that come on when certain triggers spark memories of her childhood trauma.

It is an exceptionally gory film by Hammer's standards, with a number of imaginatively bloody set pieces that prefigure the creative approach to murder that characterise the slasher flicks of subsequent decades. Whilst 'under the influence', the Ripper's daughter despatches her victims with a shard of glass, a fistful of hatpins into the eye socket and even pinions one lady to a door with a poker. The fact that the victims are largely innocents, trying to help the afflicted Anna, gives *Hands of the Ripper* something of the pathos of a werewolf picture, where a killer is doomed to destroy everything in his path, benign or otherwise.

One of the central themes of the film is a conflict between science and the supernatural. Dr Pritchard's single-minded efforts to cure Anna with psychoanalysis are ultimately doomed, and play a pivotal part in the unfolding tragedy, as does spiritualism, with two scenes featuring séances – only one of which appears to be fraudulent. Indeed, by the end of the film the viewer is left with the powerful impression that Anna's problem may indeed be a form of demonic possession, beyond the power of conventional science and medicine to address. The Ripper crimes occurred in the midst of a spiritualist revival, with several mediums attempting to involve themselves in the search for the killer. By 1971, London was at the tail-end of another fad for unorthodox spirituality in the shape of the hippie mysticism that prefaced the birth of the 'New Age'. (It's interesting to note that, in the 21st century, psychiatry and belief in the supernatural are no longer necessarily adversarial, with Freudian theories finding a sympathetic hearing among New Age therapists who believe the roots of their clients' problems lie in repressed infant trauma.)

Hands of the Ripper would prove to be one of Hammer's last horror movies, as the studio struggled to compete with increasingly graphic contemporary shockers from both Hollywood and the Continent that made the British studio's period Gothic look dated and stuffy. As early as 1960, the Hollywood ex-pat Alfred Hitchcock – who'd cut his teeth on *The Lodger* many years earlier – had suggested a disturbing new psychosexual direction for the killer thriller in *Psycho*. This time Hitch wasn't under studio pressure and his improbable suspect, personably played by Anthony Perkins as mild-mannered misfit Norman Bates, does turn out to be the culprit.

Previous celluloid Rippers had already visited similar psychological territory. Jack Palance's Ripper shared Norman's unhealthy mother obsession in *Man in the Attic*, whilst Laird Cregar's *Lodger* was a performance at least as psychologically suggestive as Perkins' unbalanced hotelier. Psychology aside, what shocked many viewers was the casual modernity of the Hitchcock masterpiece. (Censors were particularly concerned at a flushing toilet.)

Ripper movies had successfully distanced the viewer from the horror with generations of London fog. *Psycho* opened a floodgate for films that brought the knife of the homicidal maniac worryingly close to home. But it would take time for the 'stalk-and-slash' flick to evolve into the cliché of 1980s straight-to-video horror, each step taking the concept further from Whitechapel as the mysterious Ripper devolved into a motiveless slasher.

"'Jack' was the monster of the nineteenth century – there's lots of 'Jack monsters' in the nineteenth century," says Professor Clive Bloom. "They soon became the homicidal maniacs of the 1930s, 40s and 50s, the psychopath of the 60s and 70s, and the serial killer of the late twentieth century. He changes his nomenclature every decade, giving rise to both

Norman Bates with his mother fixation and Hannibal Lecter with his taste for human flesh. And this is where the Ripper has given us both the type and the genre beyond the immediate surroundings of his crimes. He's provided a script which killers and filmmakers have followed ever since. The lone, psychologically-deranged killer becomes the symbol for existential fear and self-loathing."

Alan Moore, creator of the acclaimed graphic novel *From Hell* (originally serialised 1991-6), also recognises an archetype established in Victorian Whitechapel that has echoed down cinema aisles for decades. "It's the thread running away from the murders, the lives that are affected by it, the way that those murders grew out of human history – particularly, English history," he told *Rue Morgue* magazine in an interview to coincide with the 2001 release of the big screen adaptation of *From Hell*. "And it somehow became part of the western mindset. We have that shadowy figure lurking in the back somewhere, and it manifests itself in all of our slasher films, all of our *Halloween* and *Friday the 13th* and Freddy Krueger movies: the idea of someone in the shadows with something sharp. It's a very persuasive concept, and I think that it was first called to our attention in the autumn of 1888."

A gradual relaxation in film censorship led to the rise of low-budget films that employed lurid sensationalism and explicit sex and violence in order to sell tickets. Human nature being what it is, early examples of such films can be found as far back in the history of film as you care to look, but exploitation cinema enjoyed something of a golden age in the late 1970s. Stalk-and-slash films, with their formulaic blend of nubile flesh and flamboyant death scenes, are classic examples of the form. More creative bargain basement moviemakers have come up with an impressive range of celluloid sleaze, sadism and unalloyed strangeness in their efforts to convince curious viewers to part with their cash. Enthusiasts maintain that exploitation films are almost invariably more entertaining than bland Hollywood product, and at their best represent the wild maverick cousin of the worthy arthouse fodder beloved of the serious cineaste.

As a case rich with carnage and twisted sexuality, the Ripper was ripe for cinematic exploitation. The fact that many exploitation pictures hail from less familiar film territories also adds a welcome dash of exoticism to the mix. The missing link between *Psycho* and slasher staples like the infamous *Halloween* and *Friday the 13th* film franchises is the *giallo* genre. At the same time as Italian filmmakers gave the Hollywood Western a new lease of life with their grittily nihilistic Spaghetti Westerns of the 1960s and 70s, Italy's film studios were giving the classic thriller a similar amoral makeover. Taking their name from the Italian for 'yellow' (the signature colour of the covers of the country's pulp crime paperbacks) and starting in the 1960s, *giallo* movies are typically triumphs of visual style over substance. Creative camerawork and suspenseful editing – punctuated by explicit sex and violence – make up for frequent deficiencies in dialogue and plotting, as black-gloved stalkers menace scantily-clad models in chic locales. *Giallo* is the stuff cults are made of, with the Roman director Dario Argento as the genre's most celebrated exponent.

Horror devotees may adore *giallo* thrillers, but many cinephile Ripperologists remain more resistant to their Latin charms. A typical borderline case is *Blade of the Ripper* (1970), a contemporary serial killer flick set in Vienna with a typically-labyrinthine plot enlivened by kinky sex and stylised violence. Its director, Sergio Martino, is a cult figure among *giallo* fans, as is its charismatic star the French sex kitten Edwige Fenech, and the film is highly regarded by Euro-horror aficionados. The Ripper connection, however, is tenuous – *Blade of the Ripper* was merely a more commercial title than the original (and more appropriate) *The Strange Vice of Mrs Wardh*. "Boring and confusing" is the damning verdict of the excellent *Hollywood Ripper* online guide, evidently not in awe of Signor Martino's reputation as an auteur in certain quarters. (Martino's *giallo* was to be remade in Turkey as *Aska susayanlar seks ve cinayet* (1972), the salacious translation being *Thirsty for Love, Sex and Murder*.)

Another borderline case – oft condemned, but not on account of boredom – is the 1981 film *The New York Ripper*. Among the most infamous horror movies ever made, it was banned in numerous territories. Sleazy, violently misanthropic and sadistically misogynistic, it was written and directed by controversial Roman cult director Lucio Fulci, best known for his surrealistically gruesome zombie films. Links to the crimes of 1888 are once again tenuous in this noxious contemporary thriller, where a sexual psychopath carves his way through the slimy underbelly of NYC, whilst disconcertingly quacking like a duck. Yet there is no denying that Fulci's fierce, mean-spirited movie thrusts the central theme of sexual brutality – frequently glossed over by Ripper films and ripperologists alike – violently into the audience's face.

It's arguable that Fulci's use of the term 'Ripper' had more to do with finding a catchy title than anything else. A large part of the exploitation filmmaker's art lay in coming up with an eyecatching name for the picture, and a suitably lurid advertising campaign to match. Many low-rent commercial studios (including Hammer) frequently designed posters before a page of script had been typed. In these circumstances, films often hit the screens bearing little, if any resemblance, to the panoply of prurient delights and gut-wrenching horrors promised on the promotional material.

Some opportunist distributors choose titles to try to piggyback off the success of high-budget blockbusters (some refer to such cash-ins as 'mockbusters'), while it isn't uncommon to release exploitation movies with several different titles in order to test the water. A classic example of such shenanigans is the 1981 film *The Ripper of Notre Dame*, which features neither Saucy Jack nor hunchbacks. The title is one of a dozen employed for a film made some seven years before, most of which are indicative of the original intent to cash in on the success of *The Exorcist*. If nothing else, the plot – which features a priest driven to murder by his conviction that women are evil, and misplaced homicidal piety – features one of the motives long posited for the Ripper crimes.

The Ripper of Notre Dame generally delivers in terms of tawdry sex and violence (though the extent to which it delivers varies according to which version you happen to view). It is directed and co-written by its male lead, Spanish workaholic Jess Franco, perhaps the archetypal exploitation filmmaker. Ignored by the mainstream, reviled by many regular horror fans as a morally-bankrupt purveyor of slapdash smut, he nevertheless has devotees who maintain that his voluminous back catalogue demonstrates a uniquely lurid vision.

It was perhaps inevitable that Franco would focus his inimitable zoom lens on Victorian Whitechapel, which he did in the 1976 German film *Jack the Ripper*. It's among his more polished work – though, considering the unseemly haste with which he works, this is relative and not necessarily a virtue. *Jack the Ripper* offers a ramshackle rollercoaster ride through the myth aimed at jaded thrillseekers, careering between hirsute pudenda and explicit evisceration, loosely bolted together with the haphazard plotting and absurd dialogue beloved of Franco fans. The title role of the Ripper as a mad doctor (perhaps redolent of suspect Dr Tumblety – see Chapter Thirteen) is taken by the late Klaus Kinski, who adds an unpredictable charge of kinetic mania to any scene he steals. In *Jack the Ripper*, however, he appears to lose interest in the whole business occasionally, a feeling sometimes shared by less enthusiastic viewers.

Franco's fellow Spanish horror legend, Paul Naschy, encountered *Jack the Mangler of London* three years earlier. The burly, multi-talented Naschy is best known for his performances as Waldemar the Werewolf, inspired by a childhood love of Universal horror pictures. Despite scenes of crowd-pleasing nudity from his actresses and sprays of crimson plasma from his effects artists, the consequent air of naïvely contagious enthusiasm lend many of Naschy's Gothic melodramas a certain disarming, almost childlike charm.

The Mangler of London represents his first horror role without his trademark wolfman suit, and he seems somewhat at sea in this cheesy killer thriller. He plays a crippled acrobat stumbling through a sketchily-realised version of London's red light district in Soho, littered with unconvincing disembodied human remains, searching for the maniac who mangled his missus. "Hilarious" is the backhanded endorsement *Rue Morgue* gives *The Mangler* in their retrospective roundup of Ripper films, whilst the *Hollywood Ripper* site at least credits it as the first "gore-orientated" film to feature a Ripper copycat killer in a modern setting, a plot device employed by several subsequent flicks without shelling out on expensive period sets and costumes.

Notable examples include the overrated Abel Ferrara's *Fear City* (1984), retitled *The Ripper* for largely commercial reasons, the much derided *Night Ripper* (1986) and *Jack's Back* (1988), which Denis Meikle cites as a textbook example of a crude attempt to shoehorn a Ripper angle into an otherwise unremarkable thriller, doubtless encouraged by the centenary of the Whitechapel murders.

More amusing are those movies that at least attempt to bring Jack back in a real rather than rhetorical sense, employing quasi-supernatural MacGuffins. In *Terror at London Bridge* (1985), the titular edifice is relocated to Arizona, complete with a cursed stone that contains the spirit of Jack the Ripper and a heroic nemesis in the form of David Hasselhoff. The same year Jack returned courtesy of a cursed ring in *The Ripper*. This production benefits from a brief cameo from Tom Savini in the title role – the sultan of splatter, courtesy of his pioneering gore effects on George Romero's seminal zombie flicks – though this is one highlight in a film that otherwise labours under a paucity of budget and ideas.

Far more noteworthy is *Time after Time* (1979), which employs a science-fiction plot device to relocate its Ripper and boasts far healthier production values. The mystery of why Saucy Jack disappeared after his 1888 murder spree is answered by the suggestion that he jumped into a time machine and relocated to 20th-century San Francisco. The owner and inventor of the machine, author H. G. Wells – played by Malcolm McDowell – sets off in hot pursuit. The Ripper was originally intended to be Robert Louis Stevenson, author of *The Strange Case of Dr Jekyll and Mr Hyde*, but this extra literary conceit was abandoned in favour of a straight adventure romp. The only serious point made is that Jack – played by David Warner – revels in the modern era, believing the world has finally embraced his moral standards.

Rolling Stone Mick Jagger was originally intended to play the Ripper, which might have added an intriguing generational conflict undertone to the tale. Jagger and his longhaired contemporaries were once described as the heralds of society going to hell in a handcart, but in this context, it won't wash. There may be much wrong with the modern day, but the Whitechapel murders highlight how deplorable conditions were for many of our 19th-century ancestors. We may have more serial killers stalking the streets of modern Britain and America, but we have considerably fewer people dying of malnutrition.

In the 1970s, Swedish cinema meant sex, so it's perhaps appropriate that Scandinavia's contribution to the Ripper canon should come in the form of a softcore romp entitled *What the Swedish Butler Saw*. Released in 1976, Jack plays little part in this above-average sex comedy of the era, enlivened by its Victorian setting and being shot in 3D. Intriguingly, it appears to have been inspired by an anonymous 1908 novel entitled *A Man with a Maid*. Olympia Press, the legendary Parisian erotica publisher who later reissued it, describe the novel as the story of Jack, a Victorian gentleman, who plots sweet revenge on the fiancée who jilts him, not to mention her maid, a close friend, and his rival's mother-in-law. Setting up residence in the 'Snuggery', once the soundproof 'mad room' of an insane asylum, he subjects Alice and the rest of his female company to bondage and orgiastic sexuality, dealing out both pleasure and pain in exacting revenge. The film is considerably tamer than this synopsis of its source material might suggest.

Recent years have witnessed a growth of interest in oriental cinema among horror fans, and Western enthusiasts coined the term 'J-horror' for Japanese genre films. But by no means all of Japanese genre cinema is as comparatively restrained, as witnessed by 'pink cinema' with its combination of softcore sex and sadism. The Ripper would take his place in pink cinema courtesy of the 1976 movie *Assault! Jack the Ripper* – which, in terms of content, owes more to the case of Richard Speck, the spree killer who murdered eight nurses in a Chicago hostel in 1966.

One might hope that *Assault! Jack the Ripper* would offer the last word on the obsessive sexual aspects of the crimes, but there are always other angles to exploit. Like many exploitation pictures, *Edge of Sanity* (1989) drew on funding from several different nationalities as a Franco-Hungarian-British-American co-production. The film itself is similarly chimeric – a hybrid of period Gothic, kinky soft porn and MTV-style visual overload which many critics found difficult to swallow. Casting Anthony Perkins as the Ripper lends some post-*Psycho* gravitas, largely dispelled by putting Gérard Kikoïne in the director's chair, a Frenchman principally known for his porn CV who served his apprenticeship with Jess Franco. Another take on the Jekyll and Hyde/Jack the Ripper axis, many critics condemned the film as a tasteless exercise in Reagan-era excess that sways dementedly between its Victorian setting and tawdry 1980s chic. Others embraced it for identical reasons.

Edge of Sanity was made at the height of the crack cocaine epidemic, and it's entirely in keeping with the film's overripe 80s ethos that Jekyll makes the transition to the Ripper via a crack-pipe. The drugs angle has been arguably under-explored in the Ripper mythos. Gin-consumption was regarded as a plague among England's urban poor by the 1880s, with strong parallels in attitudes towards the American crack epidemic of a century later. (There are also broad parallels between popular attitudes towards syphilis and AIDS – the virus that killed Anthony Perkins in 1992 – that cross the century.)

We know that most, if not all, of Jack the Ripper's victims were alcoholics. But in true Jekyll and Hyde style, did the Ripper himself partake of the demon drink in order to unleash the beast within? "Alcohol and drug abuse among sociopaths predictably increases with age, and many serial murders are fuelled by artificial stimulants," notes Michael Newton in *Serial Slaughter*, before cataloguing a series of killers with habits that appear to have contributed to their crimes.

One of the Victorian era's most famous fictional drug addicts employed narcotics not to inspire crimes but to solve them. Sherlock Holmes' cocaine addiction is described by his friend Dr Watson as his "only vice". As already noted, Holmes became involved in the Ripper case only after the death of his creator Arthur Conan Doyle. The relationship served to steer Jack's cinematic career away from the ghetto of exploitation cinema, back towards the more reputable territory of the whodunit.

Their first cinematic encounter came in 1965's *A Study in Terror*. A British movie, it was an ill-fated attempt to launch a new Sherlock Holmes franchise, which somewhat compromises its status as a satisfactory exploration of the Ripper crimes. There is something of the Jekyll and Hyde split personality about *A Study in Terror*, a film that is too dark to work as an action-adventure yarn but never quite has the courage to immerse itself wholly in that darkness, the presence of the fictional Holmes always standing between us and the authentic horrors suggested.

Some suggest that the degrading influence on *A Study in Terror* came not from some mysterious potion, but its co-producer, Herman Cohen, a brash American with scant respect for the typical cinemagoer. (Cohen lobbied against the title, insisting horror fans would never watch a film with the word 'study' in its billing.)

For all that, the production values are high, with some solid performances from a strong British cast, and the film tries to ground its plot in historical fact by identifying the victims by name. This ultimately underlines the perils of trying to root a film too firmly in reality when history stubbornly refuses to fit the 'beginning, middle, end' structure of the conventional storyline. The order and pacing of the murders are altered to accommodate the dramatic requirements of the story, and there were other compromises too. One common to most if not all Ripper flicks is the posthumous makeover of the wasted, desperate streetwalkers to add a little glamour and solicit audience sympathy. In *A Study in Terror*, for example, the role of the wretched, pudding-faced brunette Annie Chapman is taken by the archetypal buxom blonde 'dolly bird', Barbara Windsor.

The other major compromise comes with the identification of the Ripper. By the 1960s, Jack's ascent up the social ladder was well underway. The original ending had Holmes confronting a depraved aristocratic Ripper in a climactic fire; according to Denis Meikle, the co-producer crassly changed the emphasis of the climax to fit his own prejudices. "The original had intended the fault-line to run with the British aristocracy, cosseted in regal splendour while the poor lay destitute on the streets," Meikle writes in *Jack the Ripper: The Murders and the Movies*. "After Herman Cohen had fallen for the lure of ermine, the aristocracy – barring one demented exception – was given a clean bill of health, with the prostitute and her protector becoming the villain of the piece."

Clearly, Jack the Ripper was not immune to the tenor of the times. *Murder by Decree* revisited the Jack-versus-Holmes story in 1979, once again examining the crimes in light of Victorian class conflict. Despite being another film that unabashedly blends fact and fiction, *Murder by Decree* is widely regarded as running neck-and-neck with the Laird Cregar *Lodger* as the most effective cinematic depiction of the Ripper crimes. It was expertly helmed by Canadian director Bob Clark (also responsible for the classic 1974 slasher film *Black Christmas*) and features a stellar cast, led by Christopher Plummer as Holmes and James Mason as Dr Watson. It's also heavily influenced by Stephen Knight's 1976 bestseller, *Jack the Ripper: The Final Solution*, which posits the Ripper crimes as the work of a Masonic conspiracy committed to protect the good name of the Crown. While many now contend that Knight's conclusions are no more non-fiction that Arthur Conan Doyle's Sherlock Holmes stories, it does provide a solid framework upon which to hang this descent into Gothic Victoriana.

Plummer is an unusually sensitive, even sentimental Sherlock, whose conflict with the Establishment even makes him something of a socialist crusader. Like *A Study in Terror*, however, *Murder by Decree* stops short of finishing on a revolutionary note, preferring to have Holmes become complicit in the government cover-up rather than expose it. According to the assessment of the *Aurum Film Encylopedia: Horror*, "the credit for the stunningly filmed picture must got to the director and cameraman whose combined efforts create genuinely eerie surreal sequences and transform the city of London into a disturbing space, in which every dark recess and alleyway exudes a sense of corruption and menace that culminates in the hallucinatory dockside confrontation with the Ripper. If the film-makers had been able to muster more political courage their movie could have been a very powerful masterpiece."

The centenary of the crimes begged commemoration, which it received in spades in the shape of a lavish UK TV movie which aired in the autumn of 1988. The political pendulum appears to have swung to the right again in this *Jack the Ripper*, which may have had something to do with its star, Michael Caine, then one of the biggest British names in Hollywood and a staunch conservative. He plays Detective Inspector Abberline in a version of the story that is unusual in presenting the police – frequently depicted as bumbling flatfoots – as competent or even heroic figures.

"If Sherlock Holmes had evinced socialist tendencies in *Murder by Decree*, the protagonists of *Jack the Ripper*, on the other hand, were true blue literally and politically," according to Denis Meikle. "The Metropolitan Police are Custer's Seventh, standing firm in the face of a Sioux nation determined to run them down." This reactionary spin seems a little much for Meikle, who, whilst conceding that it offers period detail aplenty and some powerful moments – particularly the murder of Catherine Eddowes – accuses the film of being "pitched at a puerile level".

An interesting example comes in the foregrounding of the actor Richard Mansfield (Armand Assante). The psychic Robert Lees suggests that Caine's Abberline might benefit by witnessing Mansfield's performance in *Dr Jekyll and Mr Hyde*, specifically the play's transformation scene. It's a remarkable episode but a somewhat disingenuous red herring. The transformation is clearly achieved using special effects, undermining much of the careful effort to make this *Jack the Ripper* the last word on the case. In promising to offer a definitive solution the film inevitably falls short as inaccuracies creep in. The IMDB site catalogues several such, from the excised kidney being examined by the wrong character to a police sergeant wearing an anachronistic hat. Perhaps most telling is the criticism, "Catharine Eddowes and Mary Kelly are wearing glamorous clothing and look middle-class, when in fact they were down-at-heel unfortunates."

"*Jack the Ripper* has a surface veneer of truth and authenticity," writes Meikle. "It appears to have gone to tremendous lengths to recreate the scene of the crimes (and in the case of the crime-scenes themselves, it succeeds) but underneath, all is trickery and sleight-of-hand: everything about the film is as histrionically overblown and distorted as the fake Richard Mansfield's latex mask."

By way of contrast, Canada's *Rue Morgue* magazine describes it as "finely crafted", whilst the *Hollywood Ripper* site eulogises its centenary treatment for "attention to significant detail about the crimes and their impact on society", its excellence only marred by its speculative finale. If nothing else, these wildly differing assessments highlight the way in which the political undertones of the case – crucial in making it a sensation in 1888 – hadn't lost their relevance a century later.

The Ripper's cinematic career in the 90s included a number of offbeat appearances. In 1994 he is one of a quintet of imaginary friends – all murderers recalled from a childhood visit to a Chamber of Horrors – who advises a young girl on how to deal with troublesome friends and family in the underrated 1994 British black comedy *Deadly Advice*. *Ripper Man* (1996) is a rather more frenetic affair, where Mike Norris – son of noted martial artist Chuck – follows in his father's footsteps and employs his ass-kicking skills on a man who fancies himself the reincarnation of Jack the Ripper. *The Ripper* (1997) heats over the ridiculous theory that the Duke of Clarence was the killer, and is chiefly notable for its cheap Anglophobic tone. It is, however, worth restating that foreign interest in the Ripper crimes has had overtones of anti-English sentiment ever since the crimes were reported by the international press in 1888. Just as there were many Londoners who couldn't believe a monster like Jack could possibly be an Englishman, many foreigners revelled in the thought of the uptight, arrogant Brits producing such an extreme sexual deviant.

The big story as far as Gothic cinema in the 1990s was concerned was

Bram Stoker's Dracula, directed by Francis Ford Coppola and released in 1992. If the Hitchcock *Lodger* was prefigured by *Nosferatu*, the 1935 *Lodger* echoed the Lugosi *Dracula* and the Hammer *Dracula* foreshadowed the 1959 *Jack the Ripper*, then Coppola's *Dracula* did the same for *From Hell* (2001). Certainly both films suffered from some of the same criticisms from genre fans.

Whilst Ford Coppola emphasised his fidelity to his source novel to the point of putting the novelist's name in the title, *From Hell* was adapted from Alan Moore's acclaimed graphic novel. Asked in advance by *Rue Morgue* how faithful he thought the adaptation would be, Moore was philosophical: "I have to say that the sets are supernaturally accurate . . . I'm quite an habitué of Whitechapel and the surrounding area, and there's some streets that I know very well; Fountier Street between Christchurch, Spitalfields and the Ten Bells pub, which is just across the road. And I saw a picture of that set; intellectually I knew that this was an enormous façade built over six blocks of Prague, but down to the last cobble I could have sworn that that it looked exactly like the street that I myself had stood on . . . My distance from the film is purely self-created . . . I recognise that, however good the film is, the chances of it having an awful lot to do with my book are probably slim."

Inevitably, perhaps, fans of the graphic novel were unimpressed with the film's fidelity to Moore's original story, while ripperologists could find inaccuracies aplenty. Denis Meikle finds fault in the film's positioning of Mary Kelly's bed. "A minor point, perhaps," he admits, 'but if room layout can be abandoned in the cause of dramatic expedience, what price the novel's supposedly supportive footnotes?" Yet Moore had never meant *From Hell* as a factual work, but rather "an unusual type of fiction in that all of the story elements were culled from true or allegedly true sources". In the transition from Moore's documentary sources, onto the page and then onto the screen, elements of the original case are inevitably lost, distorted even fabricated. This merely reflects the reality of any attempt to transform historical events into a work of art; as such, the film of *From Hell* remains both faithful and exploitative.

Its star Johnny Depp, who is seldom less than compelling to watch, gives us an intriguing if improbable version of Detective Inspector Abberline, the West Country man now an effete, absinthe-drinking cockney and opium fiend tormented by psychic visions. It's one of the few occult elements in the film, though Depp's Abberline has as little in common with Moore's as with the historical original. Inevitably for Hollywood, a fanciful romance – barely hinted at in the graphic novel, intrudes – with Depp's character courting Heather Graham's Mary Kelly, allowing for a tragically sentimental conclusion. As historical recreation *From Hell* is questionable, but as Gothic horror which imagines Victorian London through the lens of a bad opium trip, it's heady stuff.

Denis Meikle takes issue with *From Hell*'s unremittingly bleak tone, its "studied gloom" unleavened by any of the lighter aspects of East End life, such as the music hall, which commonly feature in the cinematic safaris into Victorian London's slums. By way of contrast, in his Docklands lecture, Clive Bloom challenges the glamour evident in many Jack the Ripper movies, "where much is made of breasts and legs, of hints and tantalising glimpses, and where of course champagne endlessly flows . . . Hence the portrayal of Jack's victims, I would suggest, becomes the greatest betrayal and the greatest divergence from the historical fact. In film, Jack's women are bosomy, beautiful, flirtatious and overwhelmingly sexy . . . must exude an erotic atmosphere that will appeal to contemporary audiences. Hence their portrayal in one era is radically different in another, differs from one country to the next, nothing changes so fast as eroticism. So the actresses playing the part of nineteenth-century whores are always up-to-date in their makeup and hairstyles.

"Think of Louise Brooks, for instance, or indeed Barbara Windsor, each dressed in a vague costume of the 1880s," he adds – "it soon duplicates the Naughty Nineties with its aristocratic glamour, fun-filled sex-houses, opium dens and the revue of the can-can. Most of all, these actresses have to replace the brutal casual sexual encounters of their real-life counterparts with the allure of dalliance with a beautiful courtesan. Films must teeter on the brink of pornography without becoming pornographic. Onscreen, the mark of these women is the erotic come-on driven by the seduction of the pure, while in the narrative this come-on is met with the phallic eroticism of Jack's knife in the final *Liebestod*."

As much as the hair or the costumes, when actresses in Jack the Ripper films scream, perfect dental work give the game away, observes Bloom – "it's a giveaway as soon as they open their mouth and you know it's a modern film."

For all that, it's difficult to imagine the Victorian victims of the Ripper taking exception to a makeover courtesy of Hollywood dentists and stylists. "By being portrayed as erotic, oddly, these actresses reinstate the humanity their victims were denied in historical reality," concedes Bloom. Paradoxically, sometimes film needs to distort in its struggle to depict reality – indeed, this is a large part of what art does in all media. The filmic *From Hell* takes a historical ambiguity to allow the Ripper's last canonical victim to escape her fate. A less rosy 're-imagining' of Mary Kelly's role takes place in *Bad Karma*, which does at least relieve her of her victim status, though its alternative take scarcely seems any more respectful.

Bad Karma was one of a couple of Ripper movies released in 2001 which fell under *From Hell*'s formidable shadow. *Bad Karma* was retitled *Hell's Gate* and held back for a year, whilst the 2001 *Ripper* felt it prudent to de-emphasise its subtitle *Letters from Hell*. In the former, Patsy Kensit plays a psychopath who believes herself the reincarnation of Mary Kelly, who was actually Jack's eager accomplice rather than his final victim. It's a passable idea, decorated with the requisite nudity and gore, largely wasted by indifferent execution. *Ripper: Letters from Hell* employs the by now well-worn copycat plot in a film that belongs to the *giallo*-slasher lineage. It has a few post-modern pretensions – the action centres on the study of serial-killer psychology – and isn't without ambition, though too often this manifests in the kind of jump-cut editing beloved of MTV and dreaded by horror aficionados as more likely to induce migraines than tension.

Things almost came full circle when a new version of *The Lodger* hit the screens in 2009. It had set itself up for a fall by taking the title – if not the plot – of an early movie by a revered master like Alfred Hitchcock; its action – relocated to contemporary Los Angeles for yet another riff on the Ripper copycat theme – delivered with competence, if not sparkle. Critics remained stubbornly unimpressed, and the latent anxieties that Marie Belloc Lowndes first exploited in 1911 over harbouring strangers under our roofs seem somehow less relevant today. But if nothing else, it proves that Jack the Ripper is still resonant enough to warrant exploitation.

Ripperologists hoping to find some clue to Jack's identity on the TV or movie screen are obviously doomed to disappointment. But he remains a cipher for our repressed psychosexual urges, the embodiment of our fear of strangers, a political bogeyman against which we can judge society – all of these interpretations and more have been inspired by a quintet of squalid murders over 100 years ago.

The perpetrator of those crimes languishes, long dead, in well-deserved anonymity, but his legacy lives on at the touch of a button. With its insatiable, cannibalistic appetite for saleable source material, cinema has all but swallowed Saucy Jack, leaving little trace of his historical origins. Whilst some Ripperologists may legitimately bemoan the violence Hollywood has done to the facts over the years, there is also some justice in seeing such a vile creature slowly disembowelled by his own myth.

Chapter XII

A Pestilence of Rippers

Although she'd fallen from grace with the Sisters of Mercy, Mary Jane Kelly was the last Ripper victim to be canonised. The crowds that had thronged the streets of Shoreditch looked on her almost as a latter-day saint, Our Lady of Earthly Torments.

The extremity of her demise haunted local people and Scotland Yard alike. In December 1888, according to one press story, there were over 120 officers then assigned to the case. The story was printed in a New York newspaper, indicative of how the Ripper was no longer a London-based story (or even a British story), but world news. And then . . .

And then, it seems, the canon of victimhood was sealed into history, never to be reopened.

***

They perform all the hits of the day at the Cambridge Music Hall: 'Aldgate Pump' and 'Mother Blow My Little Nose'; 'After the Ball' and 'Only a Violet from Mother's Grave'.

Claypipe Alice is sat there with her bloke for the night, little Georgie Discon. George is a blind boy but he's drinking it all in same as Alice. He can't see the singers or the dancers, or view the opulence of their surroundings, but he can pick up the warm human atmosphere, the proximity of nearby bodies and the carousing in the air. It's all innocent between Alice and Little George, but he's her escort for the night, her chaperone if you like.

Alice has promised him a night out and she's been good as her word. Life doesn't offer much for George, short of packing matchboxes at the Bryant & May factory, so it's as well for a girl to give him a little treat here and there. But now the evening's winding down, and the chairman of the music hall leaves his coveted vantage point in front of the stage.

It's still an early hour for the late-night drinkers, but Alice has to get Georgie back to Mr Tenpenny's lodging house at Gun Street, Spitalfields, where they're both staying. She's paid for the evening out of her charring money, but her own kindness needs to be recompensed from the purse of some kind gentleman. There's this one gent that's brought her a few drinks this evening, and it looks as if Alice is on a promise.

But that's business for later. First she has to get her Georgie back to his lodgings . . .

***

"Murder!" It's between the hours of midnight and one when the constable gives out the alarm. "Murder!" The PC's notes will record that, on the early morning of Wednesday 17 July 1889, the body of a big, blousy woman was found lying flat out in Castle Alley, close to the Brick Lane end of Commercial Street. Sprawled close to a lamppost, her head facing the kerb. She must have lost consciousness just shortly before the constable arrived, going by how the thick red blood from two deep gash wounds in her throat keeps gushing into the gutter.

Her killer has left 'Claypipe Alice' McKenzie with little dignity. Nicknamed for the cheap little handcrafted baccy bowls smoked by men and women alike, she was an emigrant from the Midlands who cohabited with a bloke named John McCormack at Tuppenny's. Alice was down on her uppers, but hadn't given up on life. Nor was she without friends – after seeing young George Discon home, she'd gone to a boozer with three local women she was familiar with, before heading off again into the night to meet her fate.

Now she lies indecent and forlorn, her skirt pitched way up around her thighs. Another ghastly fresh wound runs from her bosom down to her bellybutton. It gapes red, whilst other, more superficial cuts and scratches run in the same sequence all the way down to the pudenda.

There is little doubt in the constable's mind what has transpired this evening, as he blows sputum out of his alarm whistle and calls for assistance. It's him. He's been quiet these few months since last autumn, but now he's brought his bloody business back to the East End.

An old farthing found with Alice's pipe beneath her lifeless rump will lead some among the Met to suppose the dirty scoundrel's up to his tricks again. The same coin found near Annie Chapman led some to surmise he'd tricked her into taking a farthing for a sixpence, or even a sovereign. He's not even prepared to pay the full price out on the streets, whilst the girls pay with their lives . . .

There will be no such consensus among the higher-ups of Scotland Yard and the good doctors who advise them. Dr Bagster Phillips is first on the scene, and submits his report to the coroner within a week:

"After careful and long deliberation I cannot satisfy myself on purely Anatomical & professional grounds that the perpetrator of all the 'Wh. Ch' murders is our man. I am on the contrary impelled toward a contrary conclusion in this noting the mode of procedure & the character of mutilations & judging of motive in connection with the latter."

Dr Thomas Bond, who has proffered his early psychological profile of the Whitechapel murderer, begs to differ upon performing a second examination:

"I see in this murder evidence of similar design to the former Whitechapel Murders viz: sudden onslaught on the prostrate woman, the throat skilfully & resolutely cut with subsequent mutilation, each mutilation indicating sexual thoughts & a desire to mutilate the abdomen & sexual organs."

But this time little notice will be taken of Dr Bond. Perhaps unbeknownst to him and his fellow pathologist, assigning the death of Claypipe Alice to the Ripper is going against the official wisdom of the day.

So it is when the hacked and headless torso of another unfortunate woman is found under a railway arch in Pinchin Street, a turning that runs off of the neighbourhood where Cable Street in the East End conjoins with Royal Mint Street in the City. Eternally lost to history, some will speculate that this mutilated lady, her legs severed along with her head, is a streetwalker named Lydia Hart, not seen these last few days – nor will she ever be seen since.

As her mortal remains are found in the earliest stages of decomposition on 10 September 1889, some will also conjecture that the nameless lady was murdered two days prior – on the first anniversary of the death of Dark Annie.

But this is idle speculation that leads nowhere. Whoever took the head and the identity of our faceless lady was attempting to break her down to her component parts, her brass tacks. It echoes the abandonment of a similarly mutilated torso a year earlier, at the Whitehall Embankment – in the bowels of the building that will become New Scotland Yard, several short days after the murders of Long Liz Stride and Katie Eddowes.

The belly of the Pinchin Street victim is torn open and mutilated – though not as extensively as some of the horrors which have been witnessed over the last year. But this, some experts will opine, is a different kind of crime; this is not an act of exhibitionism but utilitarianism. Instead of leaving his victim indecently exposed, the murderer, having committed the fatal act, seeks to remove the identifying features of face and hands, to bloodily saw down and reduce the female body to a convenient shape and size that might be fitted into a trunk or a suitcase for disposal.

And besides which, as those 'in the know' tell each other with a nod and a wink, the Ripper is dead . . .

***

Jack the Ripper has resolutely refused to fade into history. With his soubriquet almost certainly the invention of the kind of resourceful hack that would fuel Fleet Street in the 20th century, his very anonymity has ironically ensured his immortality.

In the decades that preceded the late-1970s coining of the term 'serial killer', the popular press would have many occasions on which to term a miscreant individual a 'ripper' or 'strangler', or perhaps in later years a 'slasher'. As the brutal unfolding of history suggests, in his historical context the Whitechapel murderer was less likely to be an anomalous one-off, or a figure at the centre of some dark conspiracy, as part of a homicidal continuum.

In more than a century since we first recognised the presence of the anonymous Ripper, a veritable plague of his counterparts have preyed upon the most vulnerable segments of Western society. We have already glimpsed the horror of the Yorkshire Ripper case, but there are others whose transgressions have – however briefly – placed them in a line-up with the still-unidentified Whitechapel murderer.

***

The Düsseldorf Ripper
In the Weimar Republic era that ran from the end of World War 1 to the election of Hitler as Reichschancellor, the gradual escalation of crimes by a habitual thief and sexual sadist named Peter Kürten led to a brief infamy rivalling the Ripper in the fatherland.

Born five years before the Whitechapel murders, Kürten claimed to have enjoyed reading about Jack the Ripper as a boy, and when visiting a local Chamber of Horrors, announced proudly, "One day I shall be as famous as they are."

Although introspective and intelligent, Kürten had a lifelong criminal record and built an independent existence away from his abusive father by thieving. Before his arrest for his ultimate crimes, he had already served 17 years in prison under a number of sentences, some of them inordinately lengthy given the nature of the offence. It was here that he learned to fantasise about taking his revenge on society, and to live his life in the type of sadistic daydreams that the Marquis de Sade had indulged in when imprisoned in the Bastille.

"Other prisoners would think of naked women and masturbate," the offender later candidly recounted in his confessions. "This I did very seldom. I got no pleasure from it. I got my climax of enjoyment when I imagined something horrible in my cell in the evenings. For instance, slitting up somebody's stomach, and how the public would be horrified. The thought of wounding was my peculiar lust and it was in that way that I got my ejaculations." The crucial difference is that, unlike Sade, Kürten would turn many of his most extreme fantasies into reality – as did the Ripper, and it's here that we might imagine (though we can never truly know) that the German deviant becomes a mouthpiece for his nameless London forebear.

Prior to his capture, he was variously dubbed by the press as the 'Monster', 'Vampire' or 'Ripper' of Düsseldorf. Finally captured in 1930, the prim little sadist had left a trail of sexual homicide and compulsive brutality in his wake that almost makes the Whitechapel Ripper crimes pale by comparison.

Yet to identify Jack the Ripper books or a Chamber of Horrors as a catalyst, or even a contributory factor, in Kürten's descent into murderous deviance requires a substantial leap of faith. The German's childhood was a textbook case of grim dysfunction, of incestuous assaults upon his sisters, of the sexual torture of animals which provided him with his fetish for bloodshed, of petty crime escalating to drowning two of his boyhood companions. Next to this, a few penny dreadfuls about the Whitechapel murders and a visit to a waxwork museum seem small beer indeed. Like other serial murderers, Kürten was keen to ascribe his actions to a psychological state beyond his control (just as he would later direct blame at his victims in court, for making it 'easy' for him), but, given the pathological mentality already shaped by his environment, his morbid interests just added fuel to an already existing fire. As George Godwin, an English criminologist who studied the case, wrote, "If Kürten was irresistibly attracted to that case, it was for the reason that in 'Jack the Ripper' he saw a murderer in his own image. One may doubt the soundness of Kürten's estimate of the importance of that story in his career of murder; that it was even a contributory factor seems a dubious proposition."

Kürten continually fantasised about an indiscriminate revenge on the public, in payment for all the indignities visited on him in his early years. Essentially these were fantasies about terrorist atrocities, but there can be no doubt that the motivation for his actual crimes was sexual. Apart from the nine murders he would confess to calmly, dispassionately and in great detail, there was also a string of attempted murders, assaults and arsons that came close to producing a similar level of excitement in him. "I committed my acts of arson for the same reason, my sadistic propensity," he told Dr Karl Berg, the psychologist who interviewed him at length in prison. "I got pleasure from the glow of the fire, the cries for help. It gave me so much pleasure that I got sexual satisfaction in these cases."

Kürten's crimes were committed on an appallingly wider scale to the Whitechapel Ripper. His murder victims included young women, one hapless man and several young girl children – in every case the prime motivation was the drawing of blood, intensified by a reflexive sense of the cruelty of his outrages which excited him still further. His first sex murder was that of a 13-year-old girl, whose throat he cut whilst molesting her during a burglary – a mundane crime of theft which may sometimes have a surprisingly sexual origin, dubbed 'fetish burglary'.

Kürten remained violent, but his crimes were contained by the continuing terms of imprisonment he served. The reign of terror that he inflicted on the industrial city of Düsseldorf would not come to pass until the late 1920s. Kürten would later confess to the murder of a pre-teen girl in February 1929, whom he stabbed with scissors in the face and chest; his sadistic pleasure was enhanced by burning her body and imagining the outrage it would cause. It was in August of that year, after many non-fatal attacks by Kürten, that the locals were horrified by the murders of two little girls discovered in a local park. Both had been strangled and had their throats cut. Unlike the closed-off environs of the Whitechapel murders, the Düsseldorf Ripper had many such open green spaces and patches of woodland as his hunting ground.

In the autumn of that year a five-year-old girl was found, strangled and stabbed 36 times, at a factory near her home. It was then that the Düsseldorf Ripper decided to emulate his Whitechapel counterpart and write to the press. Again, this was a form of imaginative stimulus. As he later confessed: "I expected that the influence of these letters and the excitement that they would cause would have a sexual effect upon me, and it was for that I wrote the letters and the reactions came as expected."

Kürten was intoxicated by the Ripper legend and never questioned whether the letters were authentic – he merely wished them to be so. But there's no doubt that the information contained in his own correspondence was genuine – it led the police to the buried body of a woman named Maria Hahn, who the killer had multiply stabbed, later reburied and raped after death in his excitement. As he later confessed, he would often return to the burial site and masturbate upon it; when his letters led to the body's discovery, he camouflaged himself among the public throng and relived the excitement all over again.

Like the Whitechapel murderer, the methods of strangulation and multiple stabbing were utilised to achieve his desired ends; like the Yorkshire Ripper in the 1970s, a variety of weapons, including hammers, were used as a prelude to the frenzied post-mortem slashing that appears to have provided the climax, both figuratively and sexually; unlike the Whitechapel Ripper, the wounds were inflicted on the surface of the body and there was no apparent compulsion to open up the interior.

Investigative psychologist Jon Ogan believes there is one identifiable syndrome that links all three perpetrators. "You look at any kind of diagnostic criteria," he says of the forensic profession's attempt to categorise such crimes. "I really think if you're looking at paraphilias you really want to look at picquerism."

'Paraphilia' is the term that's come to denote any sexual deviation that extends beyond the compulsive lure of a mild fetish – that is, the kind of all-consuming sexual obsession that welds itself fast to the individual's sexuality and can never again be extricated. 'Picquerism' is another piece of forensic jargon that refers to the sexually sadistic pleasure inherent in repeated stabbing. It might almost be called 'Ripper Syndrome'.

"It's just the pleasure gained by a violent guy," Ogan matter-of-factly explains, "there's an orgasm at the end of it, I'm sure, and the reinforcing aspect is in the fantasised behaviour. The sexual interest is just in the stabbing and slashing. Your Freudian would say the knife takes the part of the penis, I guess." As a behavioural researcher, Ogan is loath to attribute motivates which cannot be empirically observed. Nonetheless, it's a foregone conclusion that such compulsive crimes do not exist in a psychological vacuum and are not, as old-fashioned police terminology would insist, 'motiveless'.

In the case of Kürten, although the modus operandi of the crimes varied, multiple stabbing was a chief component of every attack where a victim died – including puncturing head wounds to the temple in every case. With Kürten, the main stimulus was the sound and appearance of flowing blood – a vampiric fetish formed in childhood, when he escaped from the incestuous family atmosphere via the friendship of a sadistic dogcatcher who liked to torment animals. So it was that the 'Vampire of Düsseldorf' made the following confession to Dr Berg: "I used to stroll at night through the Hofgarten very often, and in the spring of 1930 I noticed a swan sleeping at the edge of a lake. I cut its throat. The blood spurted up and I drank from the stump and ejaculated."

'The Vampire' remains a seminal case in the annals of criminology, but its shadow only passed briefly over popular culture. Peter Lorre's portrayal of the child murderer Hans Beckert in Fritz Lang's expressionist cinema classic *M* (1931) is said to be based on Kürten; certainly, the panic inflicted on a German city by his crimes seems to replicate the case, though Lang's research at institutes for the criminally insane brought him into contact with other deviants but not the imprisoned Kürten. French movie star Robert Hossein would take the lead in *Le Vampire de Düsseldorf* (1964) – a rarely-seen obscurity criticised for making Kürten into an antihero whilst all but ignoring the murders. (Such a romantic approach may be the true legacy of the mythologisation of the Ripper.)

It's extraordinary to think that this dapper and articulate little murderer would excite any kind of public sympathy, but nonetheless there was a campaign to commute his death sentence to life. (Perhaps this echoes what Mel Gordon says about the Weimar era's blurred lines between violent crime and sex – see the previous chapter.) But still Kürten calmly walked to the guillotine on 2 July 1931, after a hearty meal of sausage, potatoes and white wine, without concern and without conscience.

"Tell me," he is reputed to have asked Dr Berg, author of *The Sadist*, a criminological monograph on the case, "after my head has been chopped off, will I still be able to hear, at least for a moment, the sound of my own blood gushing from the stump of my neck?"

Answered in the affirmative, the doomed blood fetishist opined, "Then that would be the pleasure to end all pleasures."

***

The Ripper of the Blitz
In Randy Newman's early 1970s song, 'In Germany before the War', the sardonic balladeer sang of a man who watches young girls from the banks of the Rhine. ("In nineteen hundred thirty-four, in Düsseldorf" runs his rhyming artistic licence – Kürten was executed three years earlier.) It was during the war itself that Britain experienced the crimes of the next murderer to earn the soubriquet of 'Ripper'.

When 28-year-old RAF cadet Gordon Cummins was arrested during 1942, he was stationed at St John's Wood in northwest London. Papers had briefly warned of a 'Ripper' who operated during the blackout hours of Germany's nightly bombing raids, who had taken the lives of three married women in early middle age.

The women themselves may have been particularly susceptible to the attentions of the young man, in the loneliness and uncertainty of London's Blitz years. The first of them was found strangled in an air-raid shelter in Marylebone, her handbag and purse stolen (as would be the case with all of them). The mutilative elements came to the fore with the second victim, who was found naked with her throat cut, her lower abdomen and genitalia disfigured by a can opener.

The third and fourth victims suffered similar indignities inflicted with a razorblade. (The intensely misogynistic violence may put *giallo* watchers in mind of Lucio Fulci's *The New York Ripper*.)

Cummins was apprehended after an abortive attack where he abandoned his gasmask, which contained his airman number. A social climber from the lower middle classes with fantasies about being linked to the aristocracy, Cummins exhibited a similar mix of social pretension and sadism to Neville Heath, a fellow RAF man arrested at the end of the war.

Cummins himself was hanged on 25 June 1942, during an air raid. Meanwhile, the sex murderer Christie was becoming active (see Chapter Three), initially using his status as an air raid warden for cover. At least two of Christie's victims died during the Blitz. (Stray pubic hairs collected in a tobacco tin suggest there may have been others.) His name has remained infamous, whilst the 'Ripper of the Blitz' faded into history – probably because the Notting Hill necrophile's name is forever linked with a likely miscarriage of justice.

***

'Jack the Stripper'

More soberly known as the Thames Towpath Murders, the 'Stripper' killings were originally thought to have begun in February 1964 and to have undergone an escalation until suddenly stopping in January of the following year. The first victim, a 30-year-old prostitute, was 'found naked and dead' (as one of the earlier books about the case was titled) in the Thames below Hammersmith Bridge. She had been asphyxiated, with her bra and knickers stuffed into her mouth.

The five subsequent victims were all similarly throttled, but the presence of semen and male pubic hair in their throats suggested they had not merely been choked *during* but *by* the act of fellatio. The killer apparently snuffed out their lives when he was at the very point of orgasm, and the removal of some of the victims' front teeth suggested that he had continued to enjoy oral sex with their bodies post-mortem. To this official tally were later added two earlier murders, one that occurred in the summer of 1959 and one in the November of 1963. The trajectory of the killings followed the west London route of the Thames towpath – from Hammersmith via Chiswick to the nearby suburb of Brentford in Middlesex.

On a more minor scale to its Victorian antecedent and namesake, the Stripper case has elicited several conspiracy theories. This seems to have originated from the fact that the chief investigating officer, Detective Chief Superintendent John du Rose of Scotland Yard, had narrowed his prime suspect list down to three when one of his men in the frame committed suicide, and the crimes ceased.

The fact that the suicide by gunshot of ex-boxer/nightclub owner Freddie Mills occurred in the July of that year has led to one longstanding theory that Mills was implicated in the towpath murders. The former Scotland Yard detective Leonard 'Nipper' Read, who briefly looked at the possibility of murder and a Krays connection to the Mills case, disputed it vociferously. "The investigation closed when, after the discovery of the last body in January 1965, a man committed suicide," Read related to James Morton for his memoir, *Nipper*. "The man, who was never named, had been a boxer. Quite wrongly two and two were put together to make five and the rumour grew that the boxer had been Freddie Mills . . . I was horrified. These rumours were outrageous for there is no justification for any suggestion that Freddie was, in any way, a suspect in the investigation."

"The story of the man who became known as Jack the Stripper is certain to have as prominent a place in the annals of crime as Jack the Ripper," claimed du Rose in his autobiography, *Murder Was My Business*. This seems like gross exaggeration until we consider how long the details of the Whitechapel Murders languished in obscurity, and how what we now know as the various Ripper legends have largely accumulated since the second half of the 20th century.

David Seabrook's recent compellingly exhaustive study, *Jack of Jumps*, may be the catalyst that ignites future interest in the case – though it simultaneously demonstrates the dangers inherent in theorists pursuing a case they had no primary exposure to. Seabrook moves toward identifying his own suspect in the book, who he frustratingly declines to name. Post-punk novelist Stewart Home stepped into the fray with an online review that identified Seabrook's suspect – Andrew Cushway, a septuagenarian ex-policeman sacked from the force – whilst insisting that

Jack of Jumps posited nothing even vaguely conclusive against Cushway. Identifying him merely as a corrupt policeman, sacked after a conviction for burglary in 1962, Seabrook's research materials were tested by Home who pointed out the huge imaginative leap between the crimes Cushway was convicted of and the Stripper crimes. (This does rather overlook how some sex murderers begin as fetish burglars – though nothing in Cushway's record appears suggestive of this psychosexual element and, as Home points out, why should a bent copper who was easily apprehended for burglary remain at large for so long as a serial killer?)

Maintaining his adversarial position, Home expresses a preference for the theory advanced by ex-gangster Jimmy Evans in his autobiography, *The Survivor*. Whilst living in Norwood, south London, Evans won a sizeable libel payout from the *South London Advertiser* when they suggested his home (referred to as 'the house of peacocks') was being investigated in connection with the Thames Towpath Murders – which had taken place in a different area of London altogether.

Evans, a friendly acquaintance of this writer, was the basis of the gangster character Chas Devlin in cult movie *Performance* and has identified his own Stripper suspect – Inspector Tommy Butler of the Yard, famous for collaring the Great Train Robbers, and apparently acting here as an assassin to prevent revelations of decadence in high places. It all seems engagingly fanciful, in the vein of crime novels that reinterpret 1960s/70s history (like Jake Arnott's Harry Starks novels or David Peace's *Red Riding Quartet*), until one at least takes into account that Butler – a middle-aged mummy's boy – still lived at home along the west London towpath where the murders took place. Add the fact that the penultimate victim, Frances Brown, found dead between Kensington Gardens and Holland Park, was a witness in the trial of Stephen Ward – society pimp of Profumo scandal girls Christine Keeler and Mandy Rice-Davies – and you have a conspiracy theory which echoes those surrounding Mary Kelly. Or as Stewart Home paranoically suggests, wouldn't the Met (who granted Seabrook full access to their files) rather have a writer focus on a petty criminal who was drummed out of the police force than on someone who was a veritable legend as a thief-taker?

The police have never officially identified their main suspect, except to say that he was a driver and a married father who worked nights and had access to an industrial estate at Acton, close to where final victim Bridie O'Hara was found. Flecks of paint from a workshop he serviced were found on the skin of at least several of the victims – all of whom had died by so idiosyncratic a method that a single killer seemed a foregone conclusion.

According to Sunday tabloid *The People*, "Jack the Stripper was just John, a quiet 'respectable man' in his forties, living in a quiet 'respectable' London suburb. To this day his wife and children do not know the secret of their loving, devoted father. They believe that his suicide was caused by worry and overwork."

The unnamed suspect had apparently complained of buckling under great pressure at a time when du Rose claimed the police were closing in. As we have seen with the Whitechapel murders, of such mysteries are great conspiracy theories made.

***

The Rostov Ripper

In terms of modern criminological jargon, the most prolific known serial killer of the former Soviet Union is the classic 'picquerist'. Possibly the most hideous series of crimes ever to be committed outside of wartime began at Christmas 1978. (The holiday only held unofficial status in the professedly atheistic state.) The victim was a nine-year-old girl outside the Russian mining village of Shakhty; apart from being sexually assaulted and strangled, in an appalling echo of the Whitechapel crimes the child had been disembowelled in a multiple stabbing. This was the first in a seemingly endless series of crimes in and around the provincial city of Rostov, in which most of the victims were children or teenagers of either sex – although the murderer's voracious appetites also extended to grown adults.

The basic details are hellish. Virtually all the victims were disfigured by stab wounds around the eyes, as if the killer was trying to gouge their eyeballs out with his blade. In this he may have echoed his Western contemporary, Sutcliffe, the Yorkshire Ripper, who once plunged his weapon through the eye of a dead victim because he felt she was giving him reproachful looks – or perhaps it may have been redolent of the superstitions of some contemporary Whitechapel theorists, who believed that the image of the Ripper would have remained in the dead victim's pupil.

Disembowelment was also a common feature. As if that were not extreme enough, the killer often bit off his victims' tongues and nipples and cut loose their genitalia, sometimes eating a part of the organs. Suggestions that he had also devoured two excised uteruses from female victims led later, incredibly enough, to a debate among forensic psychologists as to whether the offender's actions actually constituted cannibalism. (It may actually offer an anecdotal clue as to what happened to the gynaecological sections of Annie Chapman's and Katie Eddowes' bodies, in 1888 Whitechapel.)

By the time of the last murder, in October 1990, witnesses from around the woodland where the predator last struck led to the arrest of middle-aged, bald-headed Andrei Romanovich Chikatilo. As with Sutcliffe in England, who had been interviewed nine times prior to arrest, Chikatilo had fallen through the gaps in the criminal investigation when an earlier arrest suggested he was the wrong blood type for the killer. More up-to-date scientific analysis would reveal this was not the case. (By 1990, DNA profiling was already in use in the West; in 1987 it had made history by trapping an English sex killer. But its use does not seem to have been introduced by then into the decaying Soviet bureaucracy.)

Chikatilo would be tried behind a bulletproof screen in 1992, as post-Soviet society was in its first stages of flux. Unrepentantly articulate, he put on a villainous performance which, via photographic record, suggests the sinister English character actor Donald Pleasance, though his histrionics went far further. (At one point he stripped naked and waved his flaccid penis around, seemingly intent on feigning insanity.) He was ultimately convicted on a colossal count of 52 sexual murders and mutilations – although he confessed to a total of 55.

Much more is known about Chikatilo's traumatised upbringing than can ever be gleaned about the Whitechapel Ripper, his less prolific counterpart. Born in Ukraine in 1936, young Andrei's family and their rural neighbours all fell victim to Stalin's dogmatic policy of collectivising all farms. The net result was mass starvation, and by the time that the region was suffering under Hitler's Operation Barbarossa (the invasion of the USSR) during World War 2, the boy had already witnessed many harrowing scenes close up. Compounding all this was his mother's insistence that his elder brother Stepan, who had been missing for the last seven years, had been killed and cannibalised by starving neighbours. (Readers may recognise the scenario as the fictionalised origin of Thomas Harris's antihero's pathology in the last of his Lecter novels, *Hannibal Rising*.)

It's rather too pat to attribute such a monkey-see-monkey-do explanation to Chikatilo's cannibalism. But, as we will continue to witness, traumatised children often fetishise their formative experiences as a way to overcome or assimilate them. Perhaps more pertinent to the murderer's sexual compulsions is his lifelong impotence. Taking a girlfriend after National Service in the Red Army, Chikatilo had endured her mockery after failing to sexually perform. "I was very angry with that girl," he would later recall in a series of confessions that match those of Kürten for candour. "I dreamed of catching her and tearing her to pieces as a revenge for my disaster." No omnipotent Hannibal but an impotent sadist, the Rostov Ripper would find apparent sexual release in the fulfilment of his depraved revenge fantasies – though they were projected onto other victims. (Sutcliffe similarly began his crimes by battering a prostitute with a brick in a sock, after a local whore had mocked him after a bout of impotence.) His case is probably the hideous exemplar of the old-fashioned Freudian metaphor of the knife as displaced penis, and the consistent extremity of the crimes testifies as to how hatred meshed with sexual excitement. There is little doubt that orgasm was often achieved in this way, in a manner that was far more satisfactory to Chikatilo than his attempts at conventional sex.

No less pertinent to the Rostov Ripper's remaining at liberty for so long, perhaps, is the fact that Chikatilo desperately wanted to be a good citizen of the communist society that had sent his soldier father to the gulags as a 'traitor' at the end of the war. Though falling socially from a position as a schoolteacher to various stock-clerk jobs, the murderous deviant remained a card-carrying member of the Communist Party for most of his adult life; in the case study *The Killer Department* by Robert Cullen (filmed as *Citizen X*), it's made clear that the investigation squad sent from Moscow were hampered by the refusal of local political leaders to warn the public that a serial killer was at large. This, according to Soviet propaganda, was the sole province of the decadent West, manifest in the Dickensian Whitechapel slums that gave rise to the original Ripper.

It had become apparent at Chikatilo's trial that a suspect had been charged and convicted of the very first crime, the murder of nine-year-old Lena Zakotnova. Aleksandr Kravchenko, a known sex offender, had apparently been targeted purely on the basis of his prior behaviour; denied appeal after conviction, the Soviet justice system had dispatched him by the same method faced by Chikatilo in 1994, after the fall of communism: a bullet in the back of the neck.

***

The Plumstead Ripper

At the time of Chikatilo's trial in the former Soviet Union, the most infamous 'Ripper' killing in the nation that gave the world that generic name was the murder of Rachel Nickell on Wimbledon Common. It was all the more horrifying for being committed on open public land, on the sunny mid-morning of 15 July 1992.

Rachel, an attractive 23-year-old mother of one and former model, was out for her morning constitutional with her two-year-old son, Alex, and their little mongrel dog. At around 10:20 a.m. Rachel was suddenly attacked by an assailant who made a shallow stab wound in her back and walked her off of the main path into heavy foliage. Her toddler son was viciously grabbed, dragged off of the gravel path and thrown into the brambles. Then Rachel had her throat cut, the first of 46 such frenzied knife wounds made in the space of a couple of minutes. When her punctured body was found, her traumatised little boy was pleading with her, "Get up, Mummy!" Many of the wounds carried the imprint of a knife's hilt, indicating how hard it was rammed into her flesh. One such wound was to the anus, suggestive of an implicit sexual motive.

The nation was outraged. Not merely by the callous horror of the crime, but by its timing and location. Sections of the tabloid press suggested it was indicative of a lawless society and, by inference, the product of liberal permissiveness. A more rational judgement might have suggested a psychotic perpetrator, to whom the social ethos was little but an irrelevance, but cool-headedness was not to prevail. This was the most distressingly visible of crimes, and the news media demanded on behalf of the public that police should put the collar on their man soon.

So it was that the prime suspect would be named, the following year, as one Colin Stagg – a local unemployed man from the nearby Roehampton Estate. The unfortunate Stagg was put in the frame by a number of circumstances, including one ID sketch on BBC1's *Crimewatch* which bore an apparent resemblance. As Stagg has insisted to this writer, however, the determining factor was the suspicions of some of his neighbours on his estate, who regarded him as the 'local weirdo'. Rather awkwardly, perhaps, for the newspapers that would persecute him for over a decade (the *Daily Mail* was a particularly vehement Stagg hunter), his only criminal record was for carrying a set of Bruce Lee-styled rice flails as a teenager. (This was before an admission of nude sunbathing on the common led to a charge of indecent exposure – to pull Stagg into the criminal justice system.)

As some of the 'regular blokes' on the estate were violent binge-drinkers or drug dealers, as Stagg points out, he was demonised in part *because* he had no criminal tendencies.

This wasn't how the police investigation saw it. Initially sceptical of the 'magical' new science of offender profiling, as propagated in the various Lecter novels and films, investigating officers were seduced by the impressive track record of their psychological consultant, Paul Britton. As the head of Forensic Psychological Services in Leicestershire, Britton had advised on cases of sexual murder previously, and his insights had resulted in successful outcomes. However, as Professor Laurence Alison and Marie Eyre have demonstrated in their book, *Killer in the Shadows*, Britton's profile of the offender in the Nickell case was predicated on the personal hunches he had come to trust, rather than on any empirically observable evidence.

So it was that, for example, Stagg's possession of the rice flails was dovetailed into an interest in martial arts – an apparent feature of the offender's profile, for reasons difficult to discern. It was on Britton's advice that the police embarked on an ill-advised experiment aimed at eliciting a confession from the lonely, sexually-inexperienced Stagg – by putting an attractive young policewoman into the persona of a sadistic occultist, turned on by the prospect of Stagg as the Wimbledon Common killer.

For all this manipulation, Colin Stagg resolutely refused to admit to any involvement. This did not prevent his arrest, charge, imprisonment on remand and trial for murder – albeit the trial was halted by the judge on the first day, who described the operation as "deceptive conduct of the grossest kind". For this, Mr Justice Ognall would have to endure his own demonisation by the press as the 'liberal' judge who let a killer free on a technicality.

In the prelude to the trial, Laurence Alison had been called by the defence – along with his colleague, Prof. David Canter – to refute the essence of Britton's profile of Stagg as the offender. When the 1994 trial was aborted his services were no longer required, but for years he maintained an interest in a convicted offender who was apparently ruled out of the Nickell investigation due to geographical factors.

Robert Napper, an institutionalised paranoid schizophrenic, had been a lifelong resident of the Royal Borough of Greenwich in southeast London. His particular neighbourhood, the suburban town of Plumstead, was a full 12 miles from Wimbledon in southwest London; as seems reasonable in such circumstances, Napper – who did not drive – was therefore not considered a primary suspect.

In the years that followed, however, a definite connection would be belatedly shown: Napper – who had a good working knowledge of south London's rail networks – was in fact receiving out-patient psychiatric treatment at a clinic not far from Wimbledon Common, in the weeks and months prior to the murder. Alison was also interested in Napper's prior criminal record – particularly the very definite links with a string of offences known as the 'Green Chain Rapes', on his home patch.

From 1989 through the early 1990s, a seemingly connected series of violent rapes took place along the parks and open green spaces of the Borough of Greenwich. In 1995, Napper would be convicted of two such rapes and one attempted rape, all linked to his local area, but the tally of such crimes is believed to reach as high as 70. (How many involved Napper is impossible to say. There may of course have been other offenders at large.) The crimes would escalate from the morning invasion of a young mother's home (on the edge of a common) to outside attacks where the victim's breasts or vagina were threatened by the use of a knife – apparently a penis substitute for the attacker, who had difficulty in maintaining an erection.

To Laurence Alison, this escalation held great significance. "First of all, a lot of sexual offenders *do not* enjoy the aggressive acts involved in the offences," he insists. "In other words a huge number of rapists use aggression simply to get sex, they don't enjoy it for its own sake. Sadism is quite a rare psychological phenomenon where someone actually gets aroused by the victim's suffering. Rapists will, after committing several rapes, get conditioned to finding the aggressive act pleasurable in and of itself, but that's not on the first few attempts. The sadistic angle is the second bit.

"The third bit is specificity of victim. A lot of those are just murder victims of opportunity, irrespective of whether male or female, young or old, et cetera. The offender might have marginal preferences, but I think both Jack the Ripper and the 'Plumstead Ripper' – Robert Napper – were quite specific. Also, a lot of murderers will have different weapons but a lot of those weapons are instrumental, rather than psychologically significant, and I think with both the Ripper and Napper they were very specific weapons of choice from a psychological angle, significantly using the knife as a kind of penis substitute. The mutilation is quite similar as well, as is the escalation – the famous pattern of increasing aggression and mental deterioration."

Napper was almost quaintly labelled the 'Plumstead Ripper' by his local press, after his apprehension for a shocking double murder in that quarter of the southeast London suburbs. It trailed the Nickell murder by 16 months, by which time Colin Stagg was on remand awaiting trial. On 3 November 1993, Napper broke into the Plumstead flat occupied by a single mother, 27-year-old Samantha Bisset, and her four-year-old daughter, Jazmine. He had earlier spied on Samantha and her boyfriend making love through their basement flat window.

Samantha's death was brutal but perhaps mercifully quick. She received eight rapid stab wounds, one of which severed her spinal cord. Napper then adjourned to the child's bedroom, where he sexually assaulted the little girl and then smothered her with her duvet. But it was back in the living room where Napper enjoyed the luxury of unrestricted time with his victim's corpse, just as the Ripper had with Mary Kelly. The infernal scene is described by Alison and Eyre in their *Killer in the Shadows*:

"He inflicted a further sixty knife wounds on her body; sawed her open from the neck to the pubic bone; opened her ribcage to display her internal organs; tried, but failed, to dismember her legs; took a part of her lower abdomen away with him as a trophy; propped her hips up on a cushion (just as he'd seen her positioned through the window, with her boyfriend) to show her mutilated genital area prominently, and, finally, covered her with a robe and other items he had taken from her linen cupboard." Robert Napper's 'exploratory' abuse of Sam Bisset's body evokes the obliteration of Mary Jane Kelly. It also echoes the age-old question of whether the Ripper really needed medical training to perform such mutilations.

The scene was so shocking that the female police photographer had to take long-term sick leave. When Napper was apprehended for the murders and several of the Green Chain rapes – due to forensic and DNA evidence – Samantha's mother insisted that the same man who murdered her daughter had also killed Rachel Nickell. But Stagg was already in prison for that offence (Paul Britton notoriously claims no connection between the Nickell and Bisset cases in his memoir, *The Jigsaw Man*), and it would be a further 15 years before enhanced DNA techniques convicted Napper of Rachel's murder at the Old Bailey. Samantha's mother would die of a heart attack in 1995, on the eve of leaving Scotland to come to London for the trial of her daughter's killer.

Napper would ultimately be found guilty of manslaughter due to diminished responsibility, and confined indefinitely to Broadmoor high-security psychiatric hospital. So how does Professor Alison reconcile his knowledge of Napper with the Ripper, a man of whom all we know is guesswork?

"I think the Ripper would be very similar to Napper both in terms of his background, his upbringing, the evolution of his offending, everything," posits Alison. "I think the psychology is very similar. It is speculation, even around Napper, but the kind of internal thoughts and cognition that I *think* would have gone through Napper's mind I *think* were similar to what would have been going on in the mind of Jack the Ripper. I think the planning and preparation, the feelings of godlike potency, were similar as well. I'd be amazed if Jack the Ripper didn't commit some kind of prior offence – not necessarily that he was convicted for – of attacks on other women."

So the model of the Whitechapel murderer, as posited by one of the UK's foremost forensic psychologists, is no criminal genius or sinister conspirator but a man who would fit the clinical definition of mental illness. He is also a sex offender, whose behaviour escalates rapidly from violent rape to murder. But, going by Alison's own criteria, how can we *know* this, when there is no conclusive proof that the original Ripper crimes were in fact sex murders?

"In my area of homicide there are a few behaviours that occur in the sexual region that are not necessarily to the offender's sexual gratification, but are sexually demeaning to the victim," elaborates Alison's colleague Jon Ogan. "No obvious sexual activity – no masturbation at the crime scene, no object penetration, no vaginal or anal penetration with the penis, but there's a sexual display. Jack the Ripper obviously left the vagina a couple of times legs-apart, exposing Tabram and Nichols. (I think PC Barrett, who found Tabram, made her a bit more decent by pulling her skirts down.) It's difficult to explain, because thankfully most people don't have to deal with these activities on a theoretical or practical basis like the police do.

"Most people think that sex is sex – the penis entering the vagina, or another orifice, and the guy ejaculating," continues Ogan. "But it's not necessarily the case in these kinds of murders. I wish I could remember the guy's name, but there was a judge who orgasmed when he gave the death sentence." The investigative psychologist concurs that this may be the apocryphal case in De Sade's *120 Days of Sodom*. "And maybe Jack the Ripper orgasmed in his own way when he did the cutting. If you're that type of person – loner, dissociated – sex is probably just going to be you and what you're fixated upon; maybe the organs."

It is this visceral fixation which eludes those who think of sex as the conventional response to ideals of feminine or masculine attractiveness. Or, as one of the co-authors put it to the other, "Just what is *sexual* about removing a kidney?"

If the answer lies anywhere at all, it may be with the origins of Robert Napper's own peculiar madness. When he was 11 or 12 years old, the south London schoolboy became increasingly withdrawn as he lost his faith in the adult world around him. His father had abandoned Robert and his siblings for a new life abroad, and the young boy had suffered the ordeal of rape by a formerly trusted male friend of the family. (The case would be tried in court.)

It was in this time that young Robert suffered a visible panic attack in school, as his teacher read aloud to the class from Edgar Allan Poe's classic short story 'The Tell-Tale Heart':

"First of all I dismembered the corpse. I cut off the head and the arms and the legs . . . There was nothing to wash out – no stain of any kind – no blood-spot whatever. I had been too wary for that. A tub had caught all – ha! ha!" In Poe's vignette of perversity and monomania, the narrator has killed the old man he lives with out of an irrational obsession with his 'vulture eye'.

As the police arrive, alerted to screams in the night, the narrator believes he can hear the old man's heart still beating in his resting place beneath the floorboards. "I found that the noise was *not* within my ears," he claims, denying that it's his own agitated central engine he hears beating within him. "It was *a low, dull, quick sound – much such a sound as a watch makes when enveloped in cotton.*" It's at this point that young Robert Napper appears increasingly uncomfortable to his classmates – pale and agitated, taking nauseous gulps of air. "I admit the deed! – tear up the planks! here, here! – it is the beating of his hideous heart!"

This is not to proffer a short story as an ultimate explanation. But it remains a fact that, when at his most vulnerable and experiencing the first stage of slippage into what would become full-blown schizophrenia, a young man who would later commit unspeakable crimes had an acutely sensitive overreaction to a literary description of one such crime. We also know that the development of fetishes is often a means of reconciling oneself with extreme experiences or traumas in childhood and that, to Napper, who was raped during this same period, human biology + pain = sex. And he is not unique.

If a sexually 'normal' man were to cut a woman's genitalia open, he wouldn't find much that was pretty about the exposed clitoris either – though it's one of the major sex organs. Consider also that most sexually normal men are aroused by parts of the body other than the genitalia – face, legs, breasts. In fact it's normally only the most unsophisticated, pornographically-minded or misogynistic who are interested in nothing but a woman's genitalia.

But there is a small piece of common ground between the law-abiding Lothario – who just wants to bed the maximum number of women before losing interest in each one – and the sexual sadist who wants to inflict harm. It's the element of challenge, of social or moral prohibition: "You can't go *there*," insists the social or moral conscience. "Oh yes I fucking *can*!" answers the untamed libido.

And hence the escalation of Napper's crimes – and, so Laurence Alison suggests, of the Ripper's: any organ is a sex organ to the sadist, when to touch it is absolutely forbidden. There couldn't be a greater charge to anyone who truly equates sex with violence: any opening is a vagina, and a vagina is just a bloody opening.

***

The Camden Ripper

At the very end of 2002, as the Christmas season passed into New Year, a homeless man was foraging for food in the inner northwest London neighbourhood of Camden. This was not the Camden Town of Walter Sickert. Though the area has long retained a reputation for upper-middle-class cosmopolitans and bohemians – who live a few hundred yards but a veritable universe away from the area's established working class or the transient poor – the murders of this era were not committed in genteel boarding houses and discussed over sherry, but took place among a particularly vulnerable underclass.

The transient man's find eclipsed his expectations and exceeded his nightmares. Inside the black plastic bin liner were parts of the hacked legs of a murdered woman. He alerted the police, who also discovered a full dismembered female torso, sans head and hands, in a wheelie bin several feet away. They quickly made the connection to local man Anthony Hardy, who lived on a council estate in nearby Royal College Street. Suggestions have been made that they were literally led to his door by bloodstains.

Tony Hardy – as he was to any locals who knew him – was an eccentric former mechanical engineer who'd migrated from his native Midlands to inner London via way of Australia. Formerly a married father, he'd left stability behind, along with his well-paid job, when he spiralled into bipolar depression in the 1980s and became violent towards his wife, once trying to drown her. Drifting through the fringes of London life in the 1990s, he embraced the culture of heavy drinking and crack-cocaine abuse.

(As in fact do many mentally-ill people. It should perhaps be born in mind that apparent links between any given substance and acute mental health problems are sometimes inflated by the fact that mental patients tend to self-medicate. The psychosis often precedes the drug, which may exacerbate it.)

The bearded boozer's flat was decorated by a strange mixture of black crucifixes and anatomical photographs. Hacksaws and power tools suggested that bloodstains in the bath were the result of dismemberment having taken place there. A mask crudely representing the Devil was found nearby a note which read, 'Sally White RIP' – the name of a prostitute who had died in Hardy's flat a year previously, whose death had been attributed to natural causes. Most damningly, another hacked female torso was found, apparently in preparation for its disposal.

Hardy went on the run for a short period, but was easily traced when he went to obtain a prescription for diabetes at a north London hospital. His psychiatric evaluation a year previously – after the body of Sally was found at his flat – had suggested he was a danger to the public, but had been lent little weight by his local health authority. But mental health workers periodically sent to assess his situation were too scared to enter his flat, and would arrange to meet him at local cafés.

During the search for Hardy, his headless victims were also identified: the remains were those of Elizabeth Valad, 29, and Brigitte McLennan, 34. Both were crack-addicted prostitutes, though in appearance Elizabeth in particular was far removed from the prematurely-aged Whitechapel victims of 1888 – of Persian extraction and distinctly glamorous, she had drifted aimlessly into hard-drug addiction and whoring when a sugar-daddy figure stopped supporting her. She would also prove particularly difficult to identify, her name eventually located by the serial numbers on her breast implants.

At trial, Hardy was disarmingly candid about the death of Sally White, belatedly admitting that he'd choked her to death too and was preparing her body for participation in his private rituals when the police came calling. In this sense Hardy can be termed an 'occult' murderer, as the ritual element seemed to involve the religious symbols and devil mask found in his home. But he was playing to a purely personal, internal agenda. Photos were also found of Elizabeth Valad's dead body adorned with the mask, along with many other more sexually-explicit pictures. (In this sense, Hardy is one more example of the 'trophy-takers' discussed in Chapter Five. Given the opaqueness of his motives, living out these fantasies may be his main reason for killing.)

Sentenced to three terms of life imprisonment in late 2003, Hardy has had little to say about two other dismembered female torsos found earlier in different parts of London's waterways. In late 2000 and early 2001, two other young prostitutes had been dismembered and dumped. Zoe Parker, from the Middlesex/west London suburbs of Feltham and Hounslow, had been bisected, her upper body found in the Thames near Battersea Bridge; much closer to Hardy's home, the incomplete disarticulated remains of Paula Fields, resident of Highbury, were recovered from the Regent's Canal at Camden.

Given the slight deviation in method of disposal, it's possible that only one – or perhaps neither – is attributable to Hardy, as this method is recognisable from the Pinchin Street murder and the various 'trunk murders' that became common in Britain in the late 19th and early 20th centuries.

What binds all the identified victims and the 'Camden Ripper' himself together is the use of crack cocaine. Its violent cycle of briefly ecstatic euphoria followed by vicious depression seems to have been one spur to Hardy's darkening mentality; its use as a lure for addicted women made it an essential tool for the killer.

***

The Ipswich Ripper
"They lived such poor lives their only escape was to get sloshed, and dream whatever dreams to get away from that awful life they had," says Jon Ogan of the 1888 Whitechapel victims. "I can't blame 'em for that. It's still as true today, as we see from the documentary about the Suffolk stranglings [Channel 4's *Killer in a Small Town*], where all of them were hooked – maybe for different reasons."

They first called him the 'Ipswich Ripper' in December 2006, when it became clear that several murders and a couple of disappearances of prostitutes from the East Anglian town were possibly linked to the same man. The excitement of a newly recognised British serial killer appearing out of the ether led the press to dust off their traditional 'Ripper' soubriquet, and a new series of headlines were born.

Except that, as the stories made clear, the killer was murdering by asphyxiation and there was no actual 'ripping' taking place. In later stories he would become the 'Suffolk Strangler', but in one sense the melodramatic title was not entirely a misnomer. As in the Whitechapel murders of 1888, the killings in the Suffolk town of Ipswich were subject to a breathless escalation and ever-diminishing periods between the perpetrator's 'cooling off' and his next crime.

In fact, the homicidal timeframe encapsulates an even shorter period than that of 31 August-9 November 1888:

30 October 2006 saw the last living sighting of Tania Nicol, 19, after leaving her family home to find punters for the night. She would not be seen again until 4 December, when she was found floating, naked and dead, in a pond at a nearby Suffolk village.

Prior to the discovery of Tania's body, a second victim had already been found. Gemma Adams, a 25-year-old friend of Tania, had not been seen since 15 November. When she failed to return home that night, her boyfriend duly notified the police. Unlike her estranged family, he was aware that she was prostituting herself to maintain her heroin habit. Gemma was found naked in a stream at the village of Hintlesham on 2 December; the stream runs directly into the pond where Tania was found two days later.

On 5 December, 29-year-old Annette Nichols went missing; on 10 December the naked body of 24-year-old Anneli Alderton was found in the village of Nacton. She had been three months pregnant and was the first victim confirmed as having died from asphyxiation. Within the next few days the Suffolk police would confirm that Annette's body had also been found in Nacton, along with that of 24-year-old Paula Clennell, who had vanished from Ipswich on 10 December and was confirmed as having died from "compression of the throat". Annette's and Anneli's bodies were both supposedly found in cruciform, briefly leading to a search for the meaning of this in the press and at trial. (The possibility that this was how they fell before rigor mortis set in seems to have been a latter consideration.)

All were prostitutes. None showed signs of sexual assault. All were heroin addicts.

"I don't know whether it was due to the lifestyles or not," says Ogan. "It's difficult to determine whether it was the drug abuse that ruined their 'decent lives', I'm not making any assumptions about commercial sex workers. But in terms of Jack the Ripper, you'd look at who you'd prefer to assault. Would you prefer to assault someone who's smashed out of her head, or someone who's relatively streetwise, able to fight back and shout, 'Help!'?"

The case restarted the traditional conservative vs. liberal dogfight in the press on the subject of drugs, between abstemious moralists who enjoy prescribing punishments for other people's vices and those who have faith in the state licensing and controlling those same vices. In truth, with Britain as the most drug-saturated society in Europe, the most realistic attitude was probably espoused by the prison warder quoted in *The Observer*, who opined that society either had to decide to kill all drug dealers or else legitimise all drug use via legalisation. All else is merely tampering at the edges, and whilst the more extreme methods are diametrically opposed, they would eventually arrive at different kinds of equilibrium. Whichever means one prefers is merely a matter of temperament.

(A similar argument for and against tolerated red-light zones for prostitutes tended to flounder against both sides' fudging of the facts that prostitution is not illegal in the UK, whilst soliciting for that purpose very definitely is.)

To the police on the ground, the more direct concern was the individual responsible rather than the social conditions which facilitated the crimes. Their second man in the frame, bankrupted former ship's steward Steven Wright, would be charged on 19 December and stand trial in January 2008. He was found guilty on all charges and sentenced to life imprisonment, with the recommendation that he should never be released.

As of this date, Wright continues to appeal against his sentence. The consensus wisdom seems to be that he is definitely the Suffolk Strangler – after all, supporters of his conviction point out, the crimes ceased immediately on his arrest. (Wider knowledge of such cases does suggest there may be other causes – such as the killer changing location, or even committing suicide, as has been posited for Jack the Ripper.)

Others are less comfortable with his conviction. One acquaintance of the authors, who liaised with the press on publicising the crimes, noted how the prosecution acknowledged how the body of Anneli Alderton showed no sign of having been dragged from the roadside to her dumping ground and may have required the strength of two men, whilst no accomplice has ever been suggested for Wright. The fact that DNA linking Wright – an acknowledged patron of prostitutes and self-professed friend of some of the girls – with the victims was the sole plank of evidence against him was also a cause of disquiet: "The guy's a punter. Why wouldn't his DNA be on them?"

All conjecture about the conviction aside, Jon Ogan has written a chapter about the vulnerability of sex-trade workers for an undergraduate textbook about victimology. As he describes his main points: "They're the perfect victims: you have someone who's into substance abuse and who has to quite willingly go to a dark place with a stranger. What more can you want if you're Jack the Ripper? Saying that, commercial sex workers would take him to places that *they* knew! They were quiet and 'safe' – in other words, safe from being moved on by a copper.

"Jack the Ripper probably didn't need to approach women, the women probably approached him. He wouldn't need to chat them up. Just the flash of a coin and that was it, maybe not even that. As long as he had cash in his pocket they were willing to go with him."

***

The Whitechapel Murderer (2007)

Echoes from the end of the century-before-last were heard in 2007. In early September, 24-year-old crack addict Bonnie Barrett vanished from the streets of Whitechapel. As a working girl, the single mother of a primary school-age child habituated the backstreets and industrial estates of the area once frequented by the 1888 victims. The old alleys and backyards that formed the backdrop to the original crimes had long since gone, but the predatory spirit of homicidal sexuality remained unchanged.

Bonnie was last seen around 8 September – the 119th anniversary of Annie Chapman's murder. If not for her reported disappearance, the police may not have been so quick to investigate that of illegal Chinese immigrant Xiao Mei Guo. 29-year-old mother-of-two Mei Guo was trapped in the typical debt cycle of those smuggled into the UK, and was forced to work for her Chinese paymasters as a seller of pirate DVDs. When the police checked local CCTV footage from the streets of the East End, they were able to conclude in the space of a month what had left their Victorian counterparts at an open-ended loss forever.

Xiao Mei Guo was seen on camera walking into Whitechapel tube station with a burly man later identified as Derek Brown, a truck driver who had come to London from his native Preston, Lancashire. The date was 29 August, which was coincidentally (or otherwise) two days before the anniversary of Polly Nichols' killing. Brown was also identified as being a punter of Bonnie Barrett.

The suspect himself was not a resident of Whitechapel, but the law did not have to go far to collar him. Living at a flat on the other side of Tower Bridge, at Rotherhithe, southeast London, the driver's possessions were found to include a hacksaw and power tools. More damningly, blood traces of the two women were found in the flat and in the apartment block's communal hallway. No further trace of either woman has ever been found since. The suggestion is that their disarticulated body parts would have been dispersed in a suitcase or in bin bags.

When Brown stood trial at the Old Bailey in October 2008, importance was ascribed to his having borrowed a true-crime anthology entitled *Killers: The Most Barbaric Murderers of Our Time* by Nigel Cawthorne. (The same writer is co-author of a book positing an extraordinary new Ripper theory – see our final chapter.) According to the prosecution, the 48-year-old convicted rapist and burglar's boast to a friend that he would be 'famous soon' related to his desire to emulate the nation's most infamous serial killers.

The most obvious contention is that Brown was trying to be the new Jack the Ripper – based on his choice of locale, if nothing else. Whether or not that was part of his motivation, the papers all ran with it when the killer was sentenced to life imprisonment with a minimum tariff of 30 years. It's a strange irony that he doesn't seem to have actually become a 'serial killer' (in as far as these terms have any meaning, the FBI define such an offender as killing on a minimum of three separate occasions). And perhaps more ironic was the showing of a new British TV serial entitled *Whitechapel* in early 2009, in which a homicidal Ripper buff sought to emulate the original crimes of 1888. Its perpetrator turned out to be a seemingly benign, rational figure named Dr Cohen – by the time the TV show was conflating the historical theories of the Ripper as either a medical man or a Jew, the far more prosaic figure of Derek Brown had already faded from memory . . .

Your Own Personal Jack the Ripper

Carrotty Nell's done for.

The peeler finds her gasping for air and lying on her back in an alley beneath a railway viaduct close to the Royal Mint. Close to Pinchin Street, and on the edge of the great City of London. Close to the hub of the most far-reaching empire the world has yet known, where yet another desperate woman dies walking the streets.

Nell is only 26 and a fine-looking woman. Up till now, that is.

The bobby tries to stem the bleeding from her throat, but it's no use. Every desperate wheeze just pumps up more of the red stuff, like a poultry hen drowning on the flow of her own blood. The peeler's torn, not knowing whether to stay with the wounded and dying – like he's been told to – or to chase after the footsteps he hears making off into the darkness. Into anonymity, and speculative legend, as Frances 'Carrotty Nell' Coles gurgles the last of her life away on a police stretcher.

PC Thompson, who diligently declines to give chase in favour of tending a dying woman, will spend the rest of his life regretting that he didn't go after Jack the Ripper. But how is he to know who is and who isn't the Ripper? And how are we? How are we to know whether the ruffian who'll plunge a knife into Ernie Thompson at a coffee stall and kill him stone dead, nine years hence, isn't the Whitechapel murderer still knocking about the area? . . .

***

On this very early morning of 13 February 1891, the murder that precedes St Valentine's Day, some of the Scotland Yard brass reconvene on the edge of the East End for the first time. There's a few of them present: Chief Constable Macnaghten, Assistant Commissioner Anderson, Inspector Reid. All want to be sure that the man that they sought – or perhaps still seek – has not returned to the scene of his previous crimes with a dramatic flourish. Even the Chief

Constable, who's allowed himself to believe that the Ripper is probably dead and gone, wants to be sure.

There are none of the trademark mutilations on Frances Coles, but still, it's better safe than . . . They said the same about Long Liz too, but it seems he didn't do his worst only because he was disturbed in the act. If that proves to be the case here, then it'll be a sorry old to-do for all concerned.

They've got someone who looks good for it now though – or at least for Nell Coles, if not the official 'canon'. Name's Jimmy Sadler, and he seems like a nasty piece of work. Works as a ship's fireman aboard a seagoing vessel, currently docked down at the quays whilst he stays with his wife at lodgings in Thrawl Street.

But it's not to be when they have him up before the coroner at the official inquest. Turns out that – whilst he's been seen with Nell around the docks, and even bought her the new hat she was wearing when she croaked it – when he came back to his lodgings covered in blood, he was telling the truth about being in a punch-up.

Going by the witnesses, Sadler may well have come off worst, and even have been robbed of his wages into the bargain. But he very nearly turned grey in the dock when he realised a committal for the killing of Carrotty Nell might put him up on charges for all the Whitechapel murders that happened not-this-last-year-but-the-one-before-that.

He'll be acquitted of all charges, the defence put up by the Seaman's Union proffering a number of credible witnesses who place him everywhere but with poor Nell at the time she was dying. But the cynics at Scotland Yard are not so sure, noting how Sadler sold his knife for a shilling to a fellow sailor on the morning after her murder.

So if the killer of Frances Coles, to dignify her with her christened name, walked free from court, what does that make him?

Might he perchance be Jack the Ripper? Inspector Reid certainly believes that the Whitechapel murderer got Carrotty Nell too, but the higher-ups exclude her from the holy canon. In the years to follow, Sir Melville Macnaghten's handwritten memoranda will describe Sadler as "a man of ungovernable temper & entirely addicted to drink, & the company of the lowest prostitutes."

But then, as Sir Melville doesn't believe that Carrotty Nell was killed by the Ripper, it follows that he doesn't believe Sadler was their man. So then, who did those in the know at the Yard consider the Ripper to have been? . . .

***

In the absence of much hard evidence, the more reputable Ripper theories tend to rest on one or more of three points: the Ripper had anatomical knowledge; Sir Melville Macnaghten knew his identity, and hinted at it in later life; the officially-recognised murders stopped in early November 1888, hence the killer must have died, left the area, been incarcerated or otherwise incapacitated shortly thereafter. But how confident can we be of any of this?

It is perhaps inevitable that the senior police officers responsible for the Ripper investigation would later claim to have known the killer's identity. It makes for the perfect after-dinner anecdote and does something to erase what must be the biggest black mark on a service record. It also continues to provide irresistible fodder for ripperologists.

"The 1970s was the sort of heyday of publications about Jack the Ripper," acknowledged Sir Christopher Frayling at his 2008 Museum of London lecture. "If you look at the bibliography of the Whitechapel murders, there was an astonishing explosion of books between 1972 and 1979: Michael Harrison insisted it was the Duke of Clarence, 1972; Daniel Farson, 1972 – Druitt; Donald Rumbelow, 1975, which was a kind of survey and which concluded, very sensibly, that on the Day of Judgement, when all things shall be known, and you stand there and say, 'Will the real Jack the Ripper please step forward?', assuming we're all in Hell, everyone will say, 'Who?' I think that's probably about right . . .

" . . . If you look at the suggestions of who might have done it, it's the heir presumptive to the throne; it's an MCC-member barrister, Mr Druitt; it's a decadent toff; it's a mad doctor; or it's either a Jewish agitator or a 'kosher slaughterer' with esoteric views on ritual. And they went so deep into the culture that people were still saying the same things almost a hundred years later . . ."

For our own part, we've asked the UK's forensic psychological experts of today to give us their opinions as to the various suspects, whether notorious or obscure, who have become mainstays of ripperology.

"In broad brushstrokes: the first thing you look at is where the first offence occurred, and you should be looking at individuals with some record of violence – not necessarily sexual, but probably – that live near there," Professor Laurence Alison describes the criteria he would use as an adviser to the National Policing Improvement Agency. "The first issue I'd be looking at would be geographic issues – if he lives near to the crime that would make him first port of call – and then I'd be looking at temporal stuff: what has happened recently that isn't necessarily a murder, it might have been an attack on a woman or an attempted kidnapping. And then I'd be looking for links: for example, if you have a child abduction that's been reported, and if the week before a woman has reported a guy that tried to get her into a car and the week after that you have a six-year-old boy plucked off the street, you're going to link them. Even though the victim is different and the MO is different, simply because those two offences are rare and they're both quite serious.

"So the first thing that should have been considered in the search for the Ripper are the other offences that occurred within a reasonably close timeframe and in a close proximity," elaborates Alison, "and are not necessarily the same kind of victim. Just as the Ripper tended to attack older women, there's a strong chance that Robert Napper [see previous chapter] may have attacked slightly older women also and had a slightly different MO. So it's time and distance that are the links – all these dramatic revelations about anyone that lived a very long way away are myths."

***

Montague John Druitt

"There are two documents which really are significant," notes Christopher Frayling in his groundbreaking 1988 documentary, *Shadow of the Ripper*. "The first was written by Robert Anderson, Assistant Commissioner CID, during that autumn, in which he admits that the Metropolitan Police hadn't the slightest clue of any kind, which meant that they had to listen to any old hoax from the public. The second, which is even more significant, was written by Melville Macnaghten, a senior police officer in 1894 – or after the case had actually been closed. Since Macnaghten wasn't really involved in the case it isn't really a primary document. But Macnaghten, a keen detective, actually names three suspects and this makes it important. The first, Macnaghten's favourite, is Mr M. J. Druitt, a barrister who Macnaghten thought was a doctor. He was found floating in the Thames in December 1888, shortly after the last murder."

In fact, Druitt, then in his early thirties, was a qualified barrister who found clients hard to come by and so decamped to become a schoolteacher in Blackheath – then a Kentish village not far from London, now part of the Borough of Greenwich, in any case a good few miles from Whitechapel. Druitt was a sensational suspect when first identified by TV broadcaster Daniel Farson (see Chapter Seven), who was the first to see Macnaghten's notes on the subject: "From private information I have little doubt but that his own family suspected this man of being the Whitechapel murderer; it was alleged that he was sexually insane . . . [one] rational and workable theory, to my way of thinking, is that the 'ripper's' brain gave way altogether after his awful glut in Millers Court and that he then committed suicide . . ."

Up until the mid-1970s advent of Stephen Knight's royal/Masonic conspiracy theory, Druitt remained the hobbyhorse theory of many ripperologists. But, for all Macnaghten's hints, his *only* qualification as the Ripper seems to be that he conveniently killed himself at the end of 1888. His decomposing body was found in the Thames at Chiswick on New Year's Eve and seems to have been there several weeks; in a final letter sent to his brother, he wrote, "Since Friday I felt that I was going to be like mother, and it would best for all concerned if I were to die." This alludes to the belief that there was hereditary insanity in the family, though his mother may have been suffering from what would now be recognised as a disease of the nervous system. Another contributory factor in his suicide may have been Druitt's recent dismissal from his schoolmaster post, for reasons unknown which may have carried a whiff of scandal.

"You get your list of characteristics, and how many ticks does he have?" remarks a sceptical Jon Ogan of Druitt. "How many times out of ten does that person have those characteristics? In terms of your economy of searching and your economy of investigation he should be nearer the top than the bottom. No way would any offender profile say, 'Yeah, this guy is Montague Druitt' – he's of middle-class background, well-educated, plays cricket! He's alibi-ed."

In fact, Druitt's alibis were set out in full in the 2006 book *Ripper Suspect: The Secret Lives of Montague Druitt* by D. J. Leighton. They hinge on the most British form of exoneration – he was playing county cricket on the dates of most of the murders.

"I'm surprised the police didn't discover that, because they were very, very good at checking people out, they were very diligent," insists Ogan. "It's surprising that they didn't pick up on the cricket. There's been a suggestion that he may have been interested in young boys – maybe that's why he committed suicide, because he was exposed for doing that.

"Where did he live? There were hundreds, perhaps thousands of people living in Whitechapel who would have similar problems to the Ripper – I just don't see it as someone drifting in, drifting out, coming in to kill. It's environmental psychology, which my colleague David Canter specialises in – he'd start off in the Whitechapel or Spitalfields area but go a little bit further away. It'd be further afield, a walking distance away, but another safety area."

***

Aaron Kosminski

"The second is Aaron Kosminski," said Professor Frayling of the Macnaghten suspects, "a Polish Jew resident in Whitechapel, said to have been rendered insane by too many years' indulgence in solitary vices." The third named suspect was one Michael Ostrog, "a Russian doctor or barber-surgeon and ex-convict, about whom nothing else is known."

Quaint Victorian diagnoses of the origins of Kosminski's mental illness aside, Frayling notes of the suspects, "there isn't any police evidence to speak of in support of them. And this is where the mystery of the Whitechapel murders really begins to unravel, but not in words which would appeal to those who seek the identity of Jack the Ripper. For consider those three suspects again: a gentleman barrister, a Jew who engages in secret vices and a foreign doctor. And consider how they overlap with all those toffs and outsiders and doctors who are mentioned by the press in 1888, as part of their campaigns against vice in high places, against the existence of slums and against malpractice among doctors . . . This memorandum was carefully leaked to the public in 1898, and it's been the foundation of numerous works of both fact and fiction ever since. It certainly tells us a great deal more about public attitudes and public feelings than it ever does about the case itself."

All such caveats considered, Kosminski does seem to bear more credibility as a suspect. A Polish Jew in his early-to-mid-twenties, at the time of the murders he'd become almost completely incoherent and unemployable, in the care of his brother Wolf at his home in Sion Square, Whitechapel until 1890, when he passed through a series of workhouse infirmaries before becoming an inmate of Colney Hatch Lunatic Asylum in Middlesex. He died in 1919 at Leavesden Asylum for Imbeciles. (Critics of the Kosminski theory note how long he remained in the neighbourhood apparently without any further Ripper murders occurring – assuming Mary Kelly to be the last in the canon, that is.)

According to the Macnaghten memoranda, this apparent paranoid schizophrenic "had a great hatred of women, specially of the prostitute class, and had strong homicidal tendencies"; Sir Robert Anderson's reference to a local man functioning at "a lower level than that of the brute" may also allude to Kosminski. It is not known whether he held knowledge of the Jewish animal slaughter rituals that would fit the 'shochet' theory about the Ripper.

(Anderson may equally have been referring to Aaron Davis Cohen, a mentally-ill Jew arrested for vagrancy in 1888 and sent to Colney Hatch soon after. Formerly a resident of Leman Street, his biographical similarities to Kosminski have led some researchers to conclude the men were one and the same, though there is substantiated proof of Cohen's existence.)

"I think Kosminski, from what little I know about him, is probably quite a good suspect," opines Laurence Alison. "My understanding is that he lived relatively close to the crime scenes, fairly central. He had his 'home base', so to speak, quite close to the Ripper murders. Geographically he fits, temporally he fits, his behaviour does as well."

The authors' only problem with this is Kosminski's demeanour according to the witness statement at the time he became a certified 'lunatic': "he goes about the streets and picks up bits of bread out of the gutter and eats them, he drinks water from the tap and he refuses food at the hands of others. He took up a knife and threatened the life of his sister. He is very dirty and will not be washed."

He's all too recognisable as the kind of schizophrenic that constitutes some of the homeless population of our modern streets. His psychologically-disorganised state suggests difficulty in functioning on a day-to-day level, rather than the ability to commit crime and evade arrest.

"We don't know exactly how many potential victims were approached," contends Alison, "we're not sure exactly how it happened. It depends how deteriorated he was – the thing about schizophrenia is that it doesn't actually cause violence, so it depends on his approach. If he was very deluded, in a very florid psychotic state, in that day and age I don't know how discriminating prostitutes would be anyway, if they would be aware of exactly how psychotic he was.

"But I think the other thing is that schizophrenics have periods of lucidity. Even very florid and damaged mental patients could fit into a very deprived socioeconomic area. I certainly don't think Jack the Ripper would have been some cerebral, intellectually-developed, relatively-aware, canny type of individual who required some kind of reciprocity. Again, specific to Napper: although the guy's a paranoid schizophrenic he has the wherewithal to be quite specific about when and where he attacks the victims. So I wouldn't rule out someone who's psychotic by any stretch of the imagination."

"Kosminski does it for me," Jon Ogan states quite unequivocally. "I'm not saying Kosminski's your guy, but *someone like* Kosminski. If we look at the 'Machnaghten three', Michael Ostrog, well no, he's just a conman,

Druitt, well, possibly, but Kosminski would be favourite. But I'm not saying *I think* it was Kosminski – that's the problem, we don't know, but it could be that he became extremely disturbed after the Kelly case. The only thing that nags on my mind about Aaron is the Leather Apron and anti-Jewish feeling, because he was a pronounced Jewish guy. But I'm trying to think off the top of my head of anyone who commits those kinds of mutilations and is a sociable, witty kind of person. I can't think of anyone at the moment."

***

George Chapman

Under his given name of Severin Klosowski, 'Chapman' is another latter-day Polish suspect. Qualifying as a junior surgeon in Warsaw, he came to England where he worked as a barber. Records show him living in Whitechapel during 1888, before moving off to the next stage of his peripatetic existence. On return to England in 1891, by macabre coincidence he cohabited with a woman named Annie Chapman, whose name he adopted when he anglicised his own. For years he ran a barbershop in Tottenham High Road, north London, but this was not his only career. For Klosowski would be tried as a 'Bluebeard', and hanged in 1903 for poisoning three women who he'd bigamously married. His connection with the Ripper case is cited via a possibly apocryphal remark said to have been made by Detective Inspector Abberline. The apparent connection between a poisoner and the Ripper crimes may also have been the inspiration for the 1990s emergence of the Maybrick diary (if, indeed, said diary can be said to be a fake).

"Any violence in his background?" Laurence Alison tentatively enquires. This of course depends on whether you regard poisoning as violent.

"Unlikely. Very unlikely," he contends. "If you're the sort of person who can't be directly violent, if instead of, say, hitting your wife over the head with a club you resort to poisoning, then the factor is the nature of the offence. I wouldn't exclude him on the basis of it, because he might have developed a different MO. But unless there was some kind of evidence that with those women he had been physically violent – and he may have been – then that would tend to chuck him down the suspect list rather than elevate him."

"When I first read up on Jack the Ripper," reminisces Ogan, "it was in a book of the world's greatest mysteries aimed at teenagers. They obviously thought that Klosowski/Chapman was the Ripper, and that was a big point in forming my interest in the Ripper. I think Abberline's famous quote [upon Chapman's arrest for the poisonings] – 'I see you've caught the Ripper at last?' – has been exaggerated. An interesting guy – most people dismiss him because he doesn't fit their suspect list, because he was a poisoner.

"I just don't see how he moved from being a mutilative murderer to being a poisoner. I don't see him being a mini-surgeon, as Klosowski was [and as many barbers of the time were, unless they were also dentists]. I don't think the Ripper had any medical knowledge – I think he just pulled them apart."

***

Joseph Barnett

Barnett was the latter-day lover of Mary Kelly (see Chapter Eight). More than a dozen years of research resulted in New York detective Bruce Paley positing him as a suspect in his 1995 book *Jack the Ripper: The Simple Truth*, in which the author claims the four earlier canonical murders were committed to scare Mary off the game.

In his book, Paley attaches great importance to an exercise known as the 'Ripper Project', an experiment in psychological profiling conducted by the FBI's nascent VICAP programme in 1981: "it was determined that the man who called himself Jack the Ripper was a white male, aged 28-36, who lived or worked in the Whitechapel area, and probably worked at the sort of job in which he could vicariously experience his destructive fantasies, such as a butcher. He would have come from a family with a weak, passive or absentee father, and would probably have suffered from some sort of physical disability, such as a speech impediment. He would have displayed a strong dislike of prostitutes, and during the course of the investigation he would have been interviewed by the authorities and consequently overlooked or eliminated as a suspect. His ordinary, neat and orderly appearance would not have fitted the prevailing impression of the Ripper as being an odd or somehow ghoulish-looking man."

The profile seems of a piece with its time, and (as with Paul Britton's profile of the Nickell murderer) but a short step away from stating something as specific as, "the murderer will walk with a limp." But Paley claims that the individual it describes is effectively Joe Barnett – who was abandoned by his father, suffered from the repetitive speech syndrome echolalia and was deeply contemptuous of prostitutes, despite cohabiting with one. (It should be emphasised that Barnett was not a butcher but a fish porter.)

The suggestion of domestic violence and revulsion at Mary prostituting herself, whilst marking him down as a strong suspect in the Kelly murder, has never quite explained to this writer why Barnett would take the other victims – or indeed the extent of the mutilations inflicted on Mary herself. It should be noted, however, that the theory has a strong parallel with that pertaining to James Kelly (see Chapter Eight), for which John Morrison was much disparaged. (Kelly was another wife murderer, committed to Broadmoor in 1883, and Barnett's apparent rival in love. According to Scotland Yard records, he was also – unlike most latter-day suspects – a genuine suspect of the time.)

"Unfortunately, women have always had a rather tough lot, until relatively recently," acknowledges Ogan, "probably in our lifetimes, the last twenty-five years. Domestic abuse wasn't recognised by the police, it was, 'What goes on behind closed doors.' But I can't see Jack the Ripper just straightforwardly getting away with murder of the domestic kind."

"The fact of the matter is that a lot of serial killers do have domestic violence in their background," demurs Alison. "*A hell of a lot of them.* So the fact is that his 'CV', with a relationship with a known victim of the series, would put him very definitely in the frame. But the thing that would be curious about it is if he killed a bunch of other women before he killed her, in terms of the sequence and the escalation of it. I suppose one would be struggling to explain why he killed the woman that he had a relationship with at the end of the sequence, which seems implausible. But in terms of A) knowing a victim and B) having some kind of domestic violence in the background, I would put him firmly in the frame. It would be more predictable and more likely if he'd killed her first before continuing with the sequence, so it seems unlikely just because of the sequencing."

"I could see Jack the Ripper murdering his spouse in a bout of anger," concedes Ogan, "but not necessarily butchering and mutilating her like that. James Kelly at least was in Whitechapel at the time – he held the record for escape from Broadmoor, it was about twenty-seven years before he handed himself back in.

"Most murders are committed by somebody who knows the victim," Ogan continues. "Okay, Kelly knew Barnett, but she obviously knew a lot of other people. I think it's an extension of someone saying Kelly was the last one, ruling out Coles and McKenzie, and building it around that.

"Domestic murder would tend towards obliteration," he further concedes. "A lot of violence towards the face, a lot of it's manual, spontaneous. But I would say that the reason Jack the Ripper did what he did toward Mary Kelly was because he wasn't disturbed, he wasn't in the street, she was the only one who had a room of her own. Apart from the hair, that body was like the illustrations you see when you go to a physiotherapist, those kind of diagrammatic muscle and artery models.

"Again, it doesn't necessarily tell us anything about a sexual relationship – just that the guy had a lot of time on his hands. He could have been angry because she was on the game or she'd thrown him, but I've never actually heard of anybody taken apart like that. He might stab her, or it'd be bang-bang-bang or punch-punch-punch to the head. But I don't think he'd mutilate her. You might say, 'He did it to cover it up,' but I don't think there's any evidence to suggest a bang-bang-bang to the head in the others before Kelly."

***

Dr Francis Tumblety

The most intriguing suspect of recent years was, it seems, also a suspect at the time. Tumblety was an Irish-American quack doctor and confidence trickster arrested in London for a series of indecent (i.e. homosexual) assaults with firearms in 1888, one of them occurring on the same night Polly Nichols was murdered. Pursued by Scotland Yard detectives to New York, he vacated his lodgings and embarked on his travels again. By the late 1990s, a fascinating documentary in Channel 4's *Secret Lives* series pointed to a series of sex murders in Nicaragua in 1889, when Tumblety was believed to be in the country; a collection of preserved female uteruses also suggested the Ripper's mutilations may have been for the benefit of some form of research. All of this may overlook – to varying degrees – how sex murder is a geographically universal phenomenon, how only Annie Chapman and Katie Eddowes had their wombs stolen (Mary Kelly was subjected to ad hoc hysterectomy but her uterus stayed in the room) and how sex killers prey upon those they find attractive.

"I think he's interesting in the sense of the perversion of the guy," remarks Laurence Alison. "All kinds of categories fit Tumblety really. You get individuals who are kind of 'general criminals', and then of course there's his extreme range of perversions, particularly collecting wombs. I think his bizarre deviant character, his fascination and yet at the same time revulsion with female genitalia, would make him psychologically a suspect for the Ripper. But on the other hand I think he's a bit too socially gregarious and outgoing really. I think you would be looking for somebody more socially isolated."

But wouldn't his sexual orientation rule him out in terms of targeting women?

"Some offenders have a very specific sexuality, others are more deviant," elaborates Alison. "They may be homosexual, they may be bisexual, they may be all kinds of variations. I wouldn't rule him out on the basis of his sexuality; but the profile of him as a social being doesn't match up."

"The important thing about Ripper suspects is: 'Was he a suspect at the time?'" stresses Jon Ogan. "And of course Tumblety was. There was a time when he was arrested and actively sought – not necessarily as Jack the Ripper, but they were looking for him. The non-English press were able to say that he was suspected of being Jack the Ripper, the Whitechapel murderer, even just after the murders."

***

William Bury

Bury was a wife murderer, hanged in Dundee in 1889; on the door to his flat and the walls of the basement were graffiti (presumably written by Bury himself) claiming Jack the Ripper as the occupier. Bury was living in Bow, in the East End, during 1888; although a fair walking distance from the crimes (approximately a mile and a half), ripperologist-author William Beadle points out that he owned a pony and trap for transport, that he inflicted post-mortem mutilations on his wife and that he fits the modern-day psychological profile of the Ripper produced by the FBI.

"Basically I came across William Bury way back in 1992," explains Beadle, "when I first bought *The Jack the Ripper A-Z* by Fido, Begg and Skinner. They said he's a very possible sort of suspect, and I thought, 'Yes, he's exactly the sort of suspect that fits the bill.' Once again you see, he was the sort of suspect that would fit *my* particular bill, the sort of suspect that would fascinate *me*. So I went to Scotland, did a lot of research and published a book in 1995 called *Jack the Ripper: Anatomy of a Myth*, which went down very well. I like to think it was a good book for eleven of the twelve chapters. In the twelfth chapter I introduced Bury as the Ripper and I hadn't really done the research that I should have done, I felt it was a bad final chapter. I also wrote an article for *The Mammoth Book of Jack the Ripper* [edited by Maxim Jakubowski and Nathan Braund, 1999], called 'The Real Jack the Ripper'. But so much research came to light over the next few years – from 1998 to 2002 – that I eventually decided to write a completely new book which was basically a biography of William Bury as the Ripper [*Jack the Ripper Unmasked*, 2009]."

In terms of what he sees as the compelling factors of his hypothesis, Beadle cites, "Psychological profile; the [physical] description; the murder of his wife, and how totally it relates to the murders of the Whitechapel victims. I've said in the book, 'If this murder had taken place between Polly Nichols and Annie Chapman in Whitechapel, then nobody would have had any doubts that this was a Ripper murder.'

"Serial killers are often very brutal towards their partners, and often do kill their partners. The general belief is that Ellen was threatening to expose Bury as Jack the Ripper, and there are also other factors which would add to the belief in him as the Ripper – the fact that he fled London and lied about where they were going a few weeks after the last murder. He's about the only suspect I've ever come across who you can't sit down and say, 'No, he isn't because of such-and-such a thing,' there is nothing which would eliminate Bury. And in fact when he murdered his wife the only motive you can think of was that she was threatening to expose him – in which case he would have taken care *not* to mutilate her. The fact that he mutilated her only brought attention to him. He did it because he had to do it. This was the Ripper."

Jon Ogan, Beadle's friend and colleague in the Whitechapel Society, begs to differ: "There's nothing in the official records of his trial for the murder of his wife to suggest that he did it for anything other than monetary gain."

"I think it's unlikely," says Laurence Alison, "and I think more so there have been a number of things written about people claiming to be Jack the Ripper. I think the idea of the actual murderer himself emblazoning it on a wall isn't gonna happen. The idea of someone writing it on a watch, or in some other quasi-clandestine, cryptic way – it doesn't happen."

Beadle concedes that Bury's former address is "a good run up the road, though I've often walked it from Bury's place in Bow to the heart of the East End. He had his horse-drawn van, he could have been there in a matter of minutes. The fact is that [Chief Inspector] Walter Dew said that the police were stopping anybody travelling on foot – but they weren't stopping anybody travelling via a conveyance."

"It's possible," concedes Alison, though he shares the authors' doubts about how Bury could make a rapid escape from narrow alleyways and backstreets in a pony and trap. "The maximum average distance most rapists travel is about a mile and a half. In a broad sense, with the geography of these types of offences you get what I call 'commuters' and 'marauders'. A marauder will be someone who has a central base and goes around in concentric circles for the offences, and a commuter is someone who goes into a designated area to find victims. You can discriminate between the two types of offender geographically based on how specific the victims are – there have been cases before where a series of victims have been attacked in a specific car park. So that's more likely to be a commuter, in other words someone who travels to a specific location. I suppose there's a reasonable chance that, whoever Jack the Ripper was, he could well have been a marauder, someone from that specific area. A mile and a half by foot seems a little bit unlikely."

***

James Maybrick

The controversy of the Maybrick diary erupted in 1992, after it was presented to the media by agents acting on behalf of a Merseyside scrap-metal dealer named Mike Barrett and his family. The text purportedly reveals that Liverpool cotton broker Maybrick committed the murders on his trips to London, prior to a death by poisoning for which his wife was convicted but which may have resulted from his own arsenic habit. The context was true: Florence Maybrick was certainly convicted of her husband's 1889 murder by poisoning, a classic Victorian crime for which she was eventually reprieved after fifteen years. But James Maybrick himself had been not so much as mentioned previously in any account or analysis of the Whitechapel murders, and so the new hypothesis was a bolt from the blue.

The 63 handwritten pages of text (apparently in a different hand to that which wrote Maybrick's will) was published as *The Diary of Jack the Ripper* in 1993, with annotations by investigative journalist Shirley Harrison. Its disputed authenticity remains controversial to this day, the original diary being the subject of scientific tests to date the paper and ink, which have both reinforced and undermined the case for its authenticity. Among the diary's initial detractors were the *Sunday Times*, which, having previously snapped up the forged 'Hitler diaries', had backed out of a serialisation deal on the Maybrick diary and gone on the attack instead.

During the several years of argument and counterargument that followed, Mike Barrett, a purported alcoholic, would claim that he had forged the whole thing from start to finish, only to retract his claim when his ex-wife presented a credible case for the diary as an obscure family keepsake.

The schisms it caused between Ripper researchers ran deep. "I'm not a fan of the Maybrick diary," confirms Bill Beadle, "although, having said that, it's an important strand in ripperology. A number of people in the Whitechapel Society do think that there's something to be said for the diary."

Most surprisingly, perhaps, Colin Wilson, one of the original ripperologists, was among the few prepared to raise their head above the ramparts and speak out in its favour. Having listened with interest to various theories down the years without committing to any of them, he now felt able to claim, "Maybrick is far and away the most likely Ripper candidate so far." As perverse as this seemed to many (particularly as Wilson always seemed to adhere to the thesis that the Ripper was most likely a troubled working-class man living in Whitechapel or Spitalfields), his belief did at least have its roots in Maybrick's perceived pathology: having confirmed that small, non-lethal doses of arsenic can have a similar stimulant effect to cocaine, Wilson had formulated a theory that this was what turned Jack the Ripper into Spring-Heeled Jack on the night of the double event.

Many of his peers among the ripperology community were not so ready to be convinced. At his own 2008 lecture at the Museum of London in Docklands to coincide with the Ripper exhibition, esteemed author and researcher Donald Rumbelow, author of *The Complete Jack the Ripper*, made the following introduction:

"The origins of the diary – assuming it is a fake, which I believe it to be – have been described by various sources apart from Mike Barrett and others, such as Mrs Belloc-Lowndes' *The Lodger*, Peter Underwood's *100 Years of Learning*, and even an episode of *The Avengers* called 'Fog' with a villain called, in the original, Jack the Ripper, but in the television version the 'Gaslight Ghoul'. By chance I had a copy of the original script to this particular episode before the script changes were made. I think it's interesting, as the Liverpool connection had been made even then. The following exchange of dialogue takes place between the incongruously named spy chief called Mother and our hero, the bowler-twirling John Steed:"

Mother: "Jack the Ripper Club? A society of harmless eccentrics."
Steed: "Harmless?"
Mother: "Is it viable to something?"
Steed: "Possibly."
Mother: "Thinking of joining?"
Steed: "Yes."
Mother: "Restricted membership, won't be easy."
Steed: "My great aunt Florence will smooth the way. She kept a diary."
Mother: "Did she now?"
(Steed produces the diary.)
Steed: "No, I made it up. Pretended eyewitness account of the Jack the Ripper murders, hitherto undiscovered. You know the sort of thing: 'It was the very witching hour of midnight . . .'"

"So that's one of the earliest references I've ever seen to the diary, or to *a* diary. When you look at the script, there's a thought that this might be a reference to one or two of Maybrick's alleged Manchester murders. That episode, by the way, was transmitted in 1969."

Rumbelow is fond of citing the case of William Henry Ireland in comparison with the Ripper diary. In the late 18th century, Ireland had tried to impress his bibliophile father by forging an entire cache of Shakespearean documents, each new forgery designed to bolster the apparent authenticity of the last.

"I commented more than once that if somebody produces some artefacts, like William Henry Ireland, then we would know the diary was a fake. That moment came for me with the production of the watch. Shirley Harrison says her heart sank when it did surface, and I can sympathise with her."

The so-called Maybrick watch, which genuinely dates back to 1846, was produced by its purchaser, one Albert Johnson, in June 1993. Scratched on its inner case were the signature of 'J. Maybrick', the legend, 'I am Jack', and the initials 'MN', 'AC', 'ES', 'CE' and 'MK' – in other words, the initials of the accepted five canonical victims.

Rumbelow also claims that his research revealed the timepiece to be a 19th-century lady's dress watch, something which a self-professed "gentleman born" like Maybrick would never dare to carry. He also quoted an apparently damning statement made by watch repairer Timothy Dundas on 3 July 1996. Dundas signed a statement to the effect that he had made his repairs to the watch in 1992, before it sold to Johnson:

"Marks on this watch relating to Jack the Ripper have been made on the watch since I examined and repaired it in 1992. The whole suggestion that this watch belonged to Jack the Ripper is completely false. To make it more specific when I say 'completely false', I mean that the marks scratched on the watch relevant to Jack the Ripper are *completely* false, having been made *after* my work was done on the watch."

But it's not the endless claims and counterclaims about the original diary and the watch that concern us here, so much as the suggestion that the text itself is a contrivance which panders to pre-existing knowledge about the crimes. Rumbelow is in no doubt:

"With the so-called diary, which is not a diary at all, we have no dates or even years, most of which have to be guessed at or interpreted in the light of the reader's own knowledge about the Maybrick and Ripper crimes. Now that's the clever thing about the diary: the reader has to do all the work. The reader has to improvise a chronology. If the interpretation is wrong, that's because of the reader's faulty information or lack of knowledge. If it's right, then it's a possible confirmation that the diary is genuine. Sometimes the slightest suggestion will send your reader chasing after interpretations which may or may not have been meant by the writer. In my own case, it was the writer's reference in page 215, quote: 'I will trip the first whore I encounter, and show her what hell is really like. I think I will ram the cane into the whoring bitch's mouth and leave it there for them to see how much she could take.' End of quote. Later on, on page 247, we have some verse we shall quote: 'Sir Jim came. / Am I insane? / Came Sir Jim with his fancy cane / Will soon strike again.' End of quote.

"My instant reaction was that perhaps these were oblique references to the murder of Emma Smith who'd been attacked and, after she'd been raped by several men, had had a stick thrust deeply up inside her, causing such injuries that she died of peritonitis. Now, was this something that the writer intended us to deduce? Had the killing actually been a Jack the Ripper killing? Certainly, one contemporary, Walter Dew, who was to become famous as the man who caught Crippen, always believed that Emma Smith was his first victim, and for whatever reasons he chose to conceal the true facts that the murder had been committed not by several persons but just by one man.

"This is exactly what I mean by doing the diary's work for him or her," expounds Rumbelow. "As David Canter said, some of us are searching for confirmation of our beliefs."

The authors put it to Professor Canter's colleague, Jon Ogan, that the diary seems to play to pre-existing knowledge without delivering anything too obscure or personal for the reader to comprehend, which one would expect to find in a stranger's diary.

"It did seem contrived to say, 'I'm Jack the Ripper, because these are the victims,'" agrees Ogan. "In looking at your Maybrick as the Ripper, I don't think he possessed the qualities that your Ripper would. I don't think the Ripper is a sophisticate – Maybrick was the director of a company, came down to London from Liverpool. There's no proof whatsoever that he had his little hidey-hole in Brick Lane – we know now because forensics have been looking at the scene of the crime. I think the Jack the Ripper type is a 20-to-30 kind of person, very unskilled worker, likes his alcohol, bit of a quiet loner-type chap, bit of a criminal record (not necessarily a criminal mastermind) and obviously doesn't like women – can't communicate with women as people. Maybrick seems to go from one extreme to the other, from his wife who he idolised to the commercial sex workers who were just fodder for him. No," Ogan insists emphatically, "not the kind of guy."

As for the suggestion that Maybrick commuted down from Merseyside to the East End, Ogan, based at the University of Liverpool himself, seems positively amused: "I always think logically that the guy had some local knowledge, because in the culture of the day he wouldn't commute, he wouldn't come from Liverpool for goodness' sake! *Commuting* to commit murder!"

***

Walter Sickert

The most highly-touted recent 'revelation' about the Ripper came from best-selling crime-fiction author Patricia Cornwell. In line with Jon Ogan's statement that Ripper authors are now turning to individual strands of the former royals/Masons/Gull/Sickert scenario, according to Cornwell's first work of non-fiction, *Portrait of a Killer: Jack the Ripper – Case Closed* (2002), the Ripper was Impressionist artist Walter Sickert. In fact, although Sickert was first fingered as the perpetrator of the crimes in Jean Overton Fuller's 1990 book, *Sickert and the Ripper Murders* (which Cornwell conspicuously fails to credit), her Ripper book is a sincere portrait of obsession – though seemingly her own, rather than Sickert's.

In fact, just as Bill Beadle cites Knight's *Jack the Ripper: The Final Solution* as the best-written work of ripperology, this writer finds

Cornwell's work similarly compelling in its breathless subjectivity – though its conclusions are no less questionable. The millionaire novelist's research was testament to both her financial and emotional investment; having spent $2m on several original Sickert paintings, she destroyed one of them by cutting it to pieces, in search of the concealed images she believed would prove her hypothesis. In its own way it seemed like a crime in itself.

As a crime novelist, Ms Cornwell created the popular character of forensic pathologist Dr Kay Scarpetta; her influence is felt across the Western media every time someone watches one of the innumerable *CSI: Crime Scene Investigation* spin-off shows. But, in her earlier days as a writer, as a former assistant pathologist she opined that she could know the forensic detail but could not penetrate a killer's state of mind.

In her recent work, Cornwell has taken a turn away from forensic detail and into the inner psychological workings of her characters. *Portrait of a Killer* may have heralded a sea change in this sense, though it offers a glimpse at the personal bugbears of a superstar novelist rather than a revelatory glimpse of the 'real' Whitechapel murderer.

Viewers of the BBC arts show *Arena* witnessed Ms Cornwell passionately branding Sickert an "evil old man"; in her text, the Sapphic novelist berates the artist for sharing some of the unenlightened gender views of his day, making a conceptual leap that suggests (without any evidence) that he may have been in favour of the horror of clitoridectomy.

In fact her only real pieces of evidence are the paintings: *The Camden Town Murder* sequence (1908) is naturally Exhibit A, though it was painted a full two decades after the Ripper murders and relates to the 1907 killing of Emily Dimmock (allegedly by local man Robert Wood, though he was acquitted); the broad impressionistic brushstrokes that paint a seated woman's features in *Putana a Casa* supposedly represent the dead Catherine Eddowes' missing nose; a sketch of an ascendant male beating a weaker prone figure, entitled *He Killed His Father in a Fight*, allegedly represents the evisceration of Mary Kelly.

"I don't know much about Sickert's paintings," Laurence Alison tells the authors when they ask about Patricia Cornwell's theory, "but I'd be interested to know if he had any convictions for anything else." The answer is apparently not. "Many artists are obsessed with horrific things, but it's just the subject of fantasy. But again, if you are a relatively well-to-do artist/painter/whatever, the chances of you being involved [in sexual murder] are remote." As with Colin Wilson, Alison sees the focused effort and fulfilment of the creative life as the polar opposite of the unrestrained violent impulse.

Most tellingly to this writer, as an American Ms Cornwell does not take into account the parochial nature of London as a series of interlinking urban villages. She seemingly does not question at any point her assumption that a resident of Camden, before the advent of motor transport, would somehow regard Whitechapel as part of his extended neighbourhood.

Patricia Cornwell has been revising and updating her extraordinary work of ripperology; in the interim, she claims, there is no information anyone has put forward that has refuted her hypothesis. But that's the wonderful thing about ripperology – it's as nigh-on impossible to refute a theory as it is to prove it.

**

Carl Feigenbaum

Former Met detective Trevor Marriott's theory of the Ripper as a merchant seaman is posited in his 2005 *Jack the Ripper: The 21st Century Investigation*. Prosaic and workmanlike in its approach, it couldn't be more unlike the literarily polished arguments of Patricia Cornwell. Yet this writer feels it's by far the most credible new theory in years.

Marriott, who has a feel for how the Victorian East Enders were forced to live their lives, has long believed that the Ripper was likely to have been a merchant seaman. He has traced the movements of his suspect, the German Feigenbaum, to reveal that the seaman was not only present in the East End in 1888 but also apparently in regions of the USA and Germany when a number of women (including prostitutes) were murdered over the years 1890-94. Feigenbaum would end in Sing Sing's electric chair in April 1896 for the last of these crimes, the killing of his landlady, Juliana Hoffman. It's a purely circumstantial set of evidence yet very difficult to refute; if it ultimately has credence then the Ripper may have resembled his later namesake, Jack Unterweger – the Austrian sex-killer-turned-writer who exported his crimes across the Atlantic.

"Again, if he was in the location at that time, and it can be proved he lived here, then yes, he's a suspect," Laurence Alison reiterates his nuts-and-bolts criteria. "You have to look as well at the other murders: was there a different MO, or were they murdered with a knife? But I would look at what he was doing here and where he was living at the time."

In fact all the overseas victims seem to have been murdered with blades too, though the extent of their injuries and debasements varies – as it did in Whitechapel. Marriott has an intriguing theory as to why the East End victims may have been surgically mutilated – but not by the killer, his own suspect having no medical knowledge. According to him, the urethras and kidneys of Annie Chapman and Kate Eddowes were only found to be missing during the post-mortem procedure, and therefore suspicion falls on mortuary attendants bribed by anatomists to gain access to human organs. It's a purely speculative theory – made redundant, some claim, by the legal granting of permission for surgeons to dissect cadavers – and it takes us back into the earlier world of Burke and Hare. It has also naturally excited controversy in the world of ripperology.

"Marriott is a good man," acclaims the Whitechapel Society's Frogg Moody. "He's taken one hell of a lot of flak for *21st Century Investigation*. He came to our society and he faced all his critics and tied them all up in knots. The Whitechapel Society organised a conference at the Docklands exhibition [*Jack the Ripper and the East End*]. It was the most well-attended out of all the series. The great thing about it was that Trevor Marriott produced a whole series of slides from an actual autopsy that showed just how difficult it was to get inside the body and get to the kidneys. Whereas other experts have said, 'You can just cut a woman down the middle, reach in and grab them and wrench it out,' no you can't! Marriott showed everybody who went to that presentation that it isn't easy. There's so much fatty tissue that you have to cut through first, you can't just reach in and cut something and pull it out! He knew what he was looking for. It was very gory, all the slides were in full colour and it was on a big screen, and it was absolutely fascinating."

"The good thing about him being a merchant seaman is that there are documents that could link him," says Jon Ogan of the theory, recalling how there was a contemporary belief at the time that Portuguese sailors may have been responsible. "Again, we need to look at his mental state: Did he kill the other women in a similar manner? There were quite a few knife murders in those days; people needed knives for their work so stabbings weren't uncommon. Mutilations and the picqueristic nature is what's unique about the Ripper."

***

'Walter'

And so the Ripper industry continues. 2009 will see the publication of *Jack the Ripper's Secret Confession* by television producer David Monaghan and prolific author Nigel Cawthorne. It posits Monaghan's entertaining hypothesis that the Ripper was in fact the pseudonymous 'Walter', author of *My Secret Life*, a multi-volume series of Victorian sexual confessions best described as 'true porn'. Truly a man in a state of satyriasis, the narrator tells in full Rabelaisian detail of his many (mostly female) sexual conquests – from the older domestic servants of his middle-class family when he was a boy to child prostitutes during his days as a London businessman.

Monaghan and Cawthorne are aided in their narrative by the full posting online of every volume of *My Secret Life*, a copious catalogue of Victorian sex that only saw underground publication in its day to escape the various vice and decency laws. In effect they're going for the 'double-whammy' of identifying both the anonymous Walter and the Ripper himself; going by the minimum of background information obtained by this writer (who once worked with Monaghan on the documentary series *Fred and Rose: The West Murders*), the prostitute murders may have been Walter's revenge for the venereal disease wracking his mind and body.

But there's also a more socially-conscious angle to their hypothesis. After the publication of W. T. Stead's *The Maiden Tribute of Babylon* in 1885, the age of sexual consent was raised from 12 to its present-day 16, to combat child exploitation. As Christopher Frayling put it in his documentary, "the image of the decadent aristocrat, the toff who gets his kicks by going east and finding either a child prostitute or other form of prostitute, was very much in the news in autumn 1888."

In *My Secret Life*, it's saddening to experience at secondhand Walter's erotic fervour as he deflowers a child: "The demon of desire said, 'It's fresh, it's virgin, bore it, bung it, plug it; stretch it, split it, spunk in it,' and I laid hold of her . . ." This, according to Monaghan and Cawthorne, is the origin of the Ripper crimes: since the passing of the law had made child sex taboo, 'Walter' was galvanised into protecting himself by killing off the prostitutes who had previously acted as his paedophile procuresses. It's a hugely interesting conspiracy theory, redolent of its times and almost a lowlife inversion of the more grandiose conspiracy popularised by Stephen Knight. It may also be undermined by the fact that the man the authors claim was Walter was a 67-year-old syphilitic in 1888.

So how do ripperologists feel about it?

"Makes you wonder what he would find so interesting in the Ripper murders if he was so successful sexually," reflects a sceptical Jon Ogan. "Syphilis might affect his mental state, and he might have found the victims when they were drunk, but he would need *major* strength really. One of the suspects who was identified with Chapman was about forty – 67 is pushing it a bit though. If he was having sex with young children then young children might have been the Ripper victims, not necessarily older women."

Bill Beadle is less dismissive. "I have a book which I'm intending to review for the Whitechapel Society, called *Celebrity Ripper Suspects*, and I think he's mentioned in there," he says of 'Walter'. "It sounds fascinating." As to whether a kernel of belief in the theory is required, that really isn't the point: "It's all part of what you might call the 'Ripper family', basically." Given the extreme unlikelihood of the Ripper ever being definitively identified, many ripperologists are happy for others to come to the table with their own personal Jack the Rippers, weaving an elaborate alternative historical tapestry.

***

The concept of 'your own personal Jack the Ripper' is perhaps brought into the present by a personal theory of co-author Paul Woods. In recent years, two reinvestigations have been launched into the Ripper-esque 1975 murder of bunny girl Eve Stratford, in the east London borough in which he lives. The original 1970s investigation had descended into a bewildering mire of conspiracy theories about Arab playboys and private harems – though Eve was no longer working at Mayfair's Playboy Club when she died, but was murdered at home in her flat. Woods has long believed that a local tradesman – who produced a press cutting of Eve and boasted of knowing her in the year after she died – was probably her killer, being located less than a mile from her door. The deaths of other local women in Ripper-like attacks over the ensuing years only serve to compound this.

"I was acquainted with this guy; he came into our home; for a long while he pestered my mother, who had a strong resemblance to one of the victims," describes Woods. "Over the years I've accumulated more and more background on him and the case; he's dead now – he died shortly after a very strange encounter with me in the street. The police now know what I've been doing, and they've admitted I may be onto something. Whether or not I can ever prove it, he remains my own personal Jack the Ripper – and we're talking about the east London suburbs in the 1970s/80s, not 1888 Whitechapel."

Meanwhile, interviewees who grew up with Eve Stratford at military bases in the Far East speak of her as murdered by an assailant from "where knives are more a part of the culture" – redolent of the Ripper theory about the 'Hindoo cultist'.

But to sum up our obsession with the Whitechapel murderer, lifelong ripperologist and investigative psychologist Jon Ogan sounds a note of realism. "I don't think he was the very first of his kind. I think he was a very incipient serial killer, sex fiend or picquerist. People bandy round words like 'psychopath'. But picquerism really sums up what he did. He wasn't a sadist insomuch as his victims appear to be killed very quickly. Jack the Ripper's interests, his motives and signature would be sexual mutilation, sexual organs.

"I'm a behaviourist, and in terms of the murders now I would say there's a behavioural aspect of just the 'achieving' of the murders, the committing of the murders, that announces the self-importance of the guy. If he's a quiet, lonely little chap then he'd be pretty happy with himself. And what are you going to do? You like that buzz? When it begins to wane after a few days, let's do it again! Kill somebody else. We can look at in the behaviourist sense of behaviour and consequences, the consequences being higher self-esteem. The factors that led to the murders – whether it was his poor upbringing, bad anger-management skills, you've probably got alcohol in there as well, the guy probably wasn't sloshed but was probably onto alcohol as a disinhibitor. I'm sure the guy was into a bit of drinking – the murders occurred either at weekends or at a Bank Holiday with Tabram, if she was another victim. And he probably had a drink after the murders as well. I think the guy killed at the times associated with after-payday.

"A lot of people use profiles to try to find Jack the Ripper. I'm afraid the closest they'll get is the kind of person who *might have been* Jack the Ripper. That's as good as it gets, I'm afraid. It's 'confirmation bias' – people will believe what they want to believe. But if we could go back just a few decades, to get every police docket that's gone missing, there'd be a whole lot more suspects in there – even if they were just interviewing people on a casual door-to-door basis. Maybe he killed someone after the interview."

The real truth behind the Ripper crimes is not so much that we'll never know as that it doesn't matter. Royalty or ragged beggar; midwife or mason; sorcerer or surgeon – it is difficult to imagine a suspect who, if conclusively proven, would make much difference to the world beyond the realms of macabre memorabilia and books such as this. It seems implausible that it would tell us anything new about violent crime, and the dramatis personae and their immediate relatives are too long dead to care.

So with this in mind, and in the tradition of Ripper books, the authors will now reveal their pet suspect in the final chapter:

It was the geezer up the road whodunit. It nearly always is. Unfortunately we don't have his name, but we hope that's not too much of a disappointment. The principle still remains the same.

As Alexandra Warwick posited in her astute lecture on the cultural aspects of ripperology, "We can say that the Whitechapel murderer and Jack the Ripper are two distinct entities: the Whitechapel murderer is simply the person who committed the crimes, whereas Jack the Ripper is the title of a far more complicated being, the discursive construct or imagined figure arising from those killings."

One aspect of the almost certainly fraudulent letters that gave us the name 'Jack the Ripper' is seldom commented upon: their jocular, even jovial tone. On the surface this may seem deeply offensive and disturbing. But it might also suggest the role that the Ripper – the quasi-mythical monster, as opposed to the unknowable historical killer – plays in our lives and which allows him to survive. For Jack the Ripper puts a face on death – particularly violent death – which gives us a way of dealing with the inevitable. It becomes a melodrama where the rictus grin is the most appropriate response – perhaps the only rational response to the absurd horror of it all.

SELECT BIBLIOGRAPHY

Ackroyd, Peter – *Dan Leno & the Limehouse Golem* (Minerva 1995)

Alison, Laurence and Eyre, Marie – *Killer in the Shadows: The Monstrous Crimes of Robert Napper* (Pennant Books 2009)

Anglo, Michael – *Penny Dreadfuls and Other Victorian Horrors* (Jupiter Books 1977)

Barnes, Peter – *The Ruling Class: A Baroque Comedy* (Random House 1969)

Beadle, William – *Jack the Ripper Unmasked* (John Blake 2009)

Begg, Paul – *Jack the Ripper* (Pearson, Harlow 2004)

Begg, Paul, Fido, Martin and Skinner, Keith – *The Jack the Ripper A-Z* (Headline 1996)

Bloch, Robert – *Night of the Ripper* (Harper Collins 1986)

Bondeson, Jan – *The London Monster* (Free Association Books 2000)

Boyd, Andrew – *Blasphemous Rumours* (Fount 1991)

Cahill, Tim, based upon the investigative reporting of Ewing, Russ – *Buried Dreams: Inside the Mind of a Serial Killer* (Bantam 1987)

Canter, David – *Criminal Shadows* (Harper Collins 1994)

Cavendish, Richard – *The Black Arts* (Pan 1969).

Cawthorne, Nigel – *Satanic Murder* (True Crime 1995)

Chapman, Pauline – *Madame Tussaud's Chamber of Horrors* (Constable 1984)

Cornwell, Patricia – *Portrait of a Killer: Jack the Ripper – Case Closed* (Time Warner 2003)

Crowley, Aleister, with Kenneth Grant and John Symonds (eds.) *The Confessions of Aleister Crowley* (Arkana 1989)

Cullen, Robert – *Citizen X: Killer Department* (Ivy Books 1993)

du Rose, John – *Murder Was My Business* (Mayflower 1973)

Dawidziak, Mark – *Night Stalking* (Image 1991)

Evans, Jimmy and Short, Martin – *The Survivor* (Mainstream Publishing 2001)

Fishman, William J. – *East End 1888* (Duckworth 1988)

Gilbert, R. A. – *The Golden Dawn Companion* (Aquarian Press 1986)

Gordon, Mel – *Voluptuous Panic* (Feral House 2000)

Graysmith, Robert – *Zodiac* (Mondo 1992)

Harris, Melvin – *The True Face of Jack the Ripper* (Brockhampton Press 1999)

Harris, Thomas – *Red Dragon* (Corgi 1983)

Harrison, Shirley – *The Diary of Jack the Ripper* (updated edition, Smith Gryphon 1994)

Hickey, Eric W. – *Serial Murderers and Their Victims* (Second Edition, Wadsworth 1997)

Jakubowski, Maxim and Braund, Nathan (editors) – *The Mammoth Book of Jack the Ripper* (revised edition, Robinson 2008)

Kendrick, Walter, *The Thrill of Fear* (Grove Press 1991)

Jay, Mike, *Emperors of Dreams* (Dedalus 2000)

Killer in a Small Town (Channel 4 TV 2009)

King, Francis – *The Magical World of Aleister Crowley* (Arrow 1987)
Knight, Stephen – *Jack the Ripper: The Final Solution* (Grafton 1977)
von Krafft-Ebing, Richard – *Psychopathia Sexualis* (Creation Books 1997)
Lachman, Gary – *The Dedalus Book of the Occult: A Dark Muse* (Dedalus 2003)
Leighton, D. J. – *Ripper Suspect: The Secret Lives of Montague Druitt* (Sutton 2009)
Lessing, Theodor / Berg, Karl – *Monsters of Weimar: The Stories of Fritz Haarmann / Peter Kürten* (Nemesis 1993)
Lewis, James R. – *Satanism Today* (ABC-Clio 2001)
Marriott, Trevor – *Jack the Ripper: The 21st Century Investigation* (John Blake 2005)
McIntosh, Christopher – *Eliphas Levi and the French Occult Revival* (Rider 1972)
Meikle, Denis – *Jack the Ripper the Murders and the Movies* (Reynolds and Hearn 2002)
Monaghan, David and Cawthorne, Nigel – *Jack the Ripper: A Secret Life* (Robinson 2009)
Moore, Alan and Campbell, Eddie – *From Hell* (Knockabout 2000)
Morland, Nigel – *An Outline of Sexual Criminology* (Tallis Press 1966)
Newton, Michael – *Serial Slaughter* (Loopmanics 1992)
Ogan, Jon – 'Martha Tabram – The Forgotten Ripper Victim?', *Ripperologist* #5 (March 1996)
Paley, Bruce – *Jack the Ripper: The Simple Truth* (Headline 1996)
Pearsall, Ronald – *Night's Black Angels* (Hodder & Stoughton 1974)
Pearsall, Ronald – *The Worm in the Bud* (Pimlico 1993)
Poe, Edgar Allan – *Tales of Mystery and Imagination* (J. M. Dent & Sons Ltd 1908)
Read, Leonard with Morton, James – *Nipper* (Warner Books 1991)
Ressler, Robert K. and Shachtman, Tom – *Whoever Fights Monsters* (Simon & Schuster 1992)
Rigby, Jonathan – *American Gothic* (Reynolds and Hearn 2007)
Rigby, Jonathan – *English Gothic: A Century of Horror Cinema* (revised edition, Reynolds & Hearn 2004)
Rumbelow, Donald – *The Complete Jack the Ripper* (Fully Revised and Updated, Penguin 2004)
Seabrook, David – *Jack of Jumps* (Granta 2006)
Sinclair, Iain – *White Chappell, Scarlet Tracings* (Paladin 1988)
Stevenson, Robert Louis – *Dr Jekyll and Mr Hyde* (Bancroft Classics 1967)
Symonds, John – *King of the Shadow Realm* (Duckworth 1989)
Tatar, Maria – *Lustmord* (Princeton University Press, Princeton 1995)
Timewatch – 'Shadow of the Ripper' (BBC2 TV 1988)
'Walter' – *My Secret Life* (Volumes One-Five, Wordsworth Editions Limited 1996)
Wilson, Colin – *A Casebook of Murder* (Leslie Frewin 1969)
Wilson, Colin – *A Criminal History of Mankind* (Grafton 1984)
Wilson, Colin – *Ritual in the Dark* (Victor Gollancz 1960)
Wilson, Colin and Damon – *A Plague of Murder* (Robinson 1995)
Wilson, Colin, Damon and Rowan – *World Famous Gaslight Murder* (Magpie 1992)
Wilson, Colin and Pitman, Patricia – *Encyclopaedia of Murder* (Pan 1964)
Wilson, Colin and Seaman, Donald – *Encyclopaedia of Modern Murder* (revised edition, Pan 1989)

INDEX